eBay the Smart Way

Selling, Buying, and Profiting on the Web's #1 Auction Site

Second Edition

Joseph T. Sinclair

American Management Association
New York • Atlanta • Boston • Chicago • Kansas City • San Francisco • Washington, D.C.
Brussels • Mexico City • Tokyo • Toronto

Special discounts on bulk quantities of AMACOM books are available to corporations, professional associations, and other organizations. For details, contact Special Sales Department, AMACOM, a division of American Management Association, 1601 Broadway, New York, NY 10019.
Tel.: 212-903-8316. Fax: 212-903-8083.
Web Site: www.amacombooks.org

This publication is designed to provide accurate and authoritative information in regard to the subject matter covered. It is sold with the understanding that the publisher is not engaged in rendering legal, accounting, or other professional service. If legal advice or other expert assistance is required, the services of a competent professional person should be sought.

Library of Congress Cataloging-in-Publication Data

Sinclair, Joseph T.
    eBay the smart way : selling, buying, and profiting on the Web's #1 auction site / Joseph T. Sinclair—2nd ed.
        p. cm.
    Includes index.
    ISBN 0-8144-7118-8
    1. Internet auctions. 2. Auctions—Computer network resources. I. Title
    HF5478.S482001
    381'.17'02854678—dc21   2001016125
                                                              CIP

Printing number
10   9   8   7   6   5   4   3   2   1

Contents

Acknowledgments

Many thanks to Don Spillane, who introduced me to eBay, and who is the quintessential retailer on eBay. Thanks to my agent, Carole McClendon at Waterside Productions, who always does a fine job, and to Jacqueline Flynn and the folks at AMACOM, including Lydia Lewis and Mike Sivilli, who contributed to the book. I certainly can't overlook the clever people at eBay, who have done a great job of creating a new marketplace—a huge and dynamic new marketplace. And they continue to improve it. Good work! And finally thanks to my wife Lani, daughter Brook, and the new member of our family my son Tommy, who endured without complaint the period of intense effort it takes to write a book. Well, almost without complaint. Thanks.

This book is dedicated to my grandfather, Joseph Treble Sinclair, who was a master of commerce in Detroit in the first half of the twentieth century. And to my father-in-law, Ollie Jack Wallin, who was a master of retail in Oklahoma City during the second half of the twentieth century.

I

Introducing eBay

1

Online Auctions and eBay

It's true that eBay is an auction. It's also true that eBay is online. But put the two together and you have a dynamic new international marketplace that operates 24 hours a day, 7 days a week. It's not like anything that has existed before. It's very exciting and offers you significant opportunities whether you're a buyer, seller, or retailer.

How exciting? Quite exciting! In January 2001, eBay had over 5 million items for sale in over 4,000 categories (up from 2.4 million items and 1,600 catagories in July 1999—figures used in the first edition of this book). Not bad considering that the longest auction was ten days, with many auctions lasting only three, five, or seven days. eBay also had almost 16 million registered users and held nearly 90 percent (measured by sales) of the online auction market. (Figures from *San Francisco Examiner*, p. C-6, August 20, 2000.) Early in 2000, the eBay website was receiving 50 million hits per day. (eBay no longer publishes its hit statistics.)

When you read this chapter, look at the eBay home page (*http:// www.ebay.com*) to get the latest published figure on the number of items being auctioned (see eBay home page Figure 1.1).

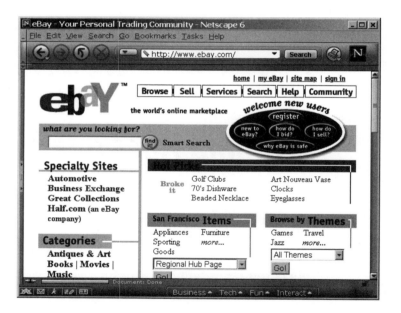

Figure 1.1   The eBay home page.

If you check prices on eBay, you will find that prices are often a bargain for buyers. Yet, sellers can get more money for their used products and closeout products on eBay than perhaps anywhere else. How can this be?

Markets

It's actually easy to explain. Local markets are not very efficient; they are not large enough. Typically a seller takes a used product to a local dealer to sell. For instance, a seller might take a used Nikon camera to a camera dealer. Because the local market is not huge, it will not include many buyers for the camera. The dealer takes a substantial risk that the camera will not sell in a timely manner. Consequently, the dealer will not pay much for the camera. The seller sells at a low price.

On the other hand, the dealer has to charge a lot for the camera. He or she must seek a profit that covers the risk of the camera's staying on the shelf a long time. The profit must also cover the cost of doing business, which includes paying rent and employing sales clerks (overhead). The buyer buys at a high price.

Thus, a low sales price along with a high purchase price is the rule in a local market, particularly when most of the transactions take place through a local dealer.

Sometimes a periodic local show (or flea market) offers an exchange (or swap) that brings together buyers and sellers more efficiently, and prices grow a little higher for sellers and a little lower for buyers, particularly for transactions where no dealer is involved. For instance, at a camera show with a camera exchange, a seller can get a higher price for the Nikon camera, and a buyer can buy at a lower price than in a transaction through a dealer. Nonetheless, even in a large city, for most products except the most popular, an exchange is not the ultimate market. It simply never has a large enough population of buyers and sellers.

eBay is an international marketplace with no peers except a few of the stock and commodity exchanges. The sale and purchase of used goods are rationalized—best deal for both buyers and sellers—as much as it will ever be anytime soon (until more people join eBay). That is, there are always the maximum numbers of buyers and sellers. The auction feature of the eBay marketplace provides a mechanism that dynamically establishes market values quickly and efficiently. The transactions are not necessarily through a dealer. Consequently, a seller can usually sell for a higher price than in a local market, and a buyer can usually buy for a lower price than in a local market. You can say that the eBay marketplace promotes disintermediation. This fancy word means that the dealer (the intermediary) has been eliminated. Again, referring to the camera example, the seller should be able to sell the Nikon camera for more on the eBay market than to a local dealer, and the buyer should be able to buy the Nikon camera for less on the eBay market than from a local dealer.

The Dealer

A dealer can still fit nicely into the eBay environment. If a dealer can count on turning over used goods quickly, the economics of his or her business practices will adapt. Consequently, a dealer who sells on eBay can afford to pay more for used goods and sell such goods for less than in a bricks-and-mortar location where overhead is higher and the market smaller.

The more buyers and sellers there are for any particular product, the more the price will be rationalized. Thus, popular items (used), such as popular brands, will exchange hands at a price closer to the price the items sold new. Less popular items (used), such as less popular brands, will sell at a price well below their price new.

Law of Supply and Demand

Does the law of supply and demand work on eBay? Sure. When many sellers of a particular product want to sell to a few buyers on eBay, the price will go down. When many buyers want to buy a particular product from a few sellers on eBay, the price will go up. In a huge market like eBay, however, there are a maximum number of buyers and sellers compared to other markets. Due to the large number of buyers and sellers, the market will tend to be more balanced (more rational) than a smaller market.

Keep in mind used goods are not the only goods sold on eBay. New goods comprise a substantial percentage of the goods sold. However, eBay is not a place to sell new goods at full price or even at a discount price. More often it is a place to sell new goods at a deep discount. Consequently, buyers can expect to get a pretty good deal. But what about sellers? Can they get a good deal too?

The answer is yes. A seller can sell a product new that he or she has not used or has decided not to use. These mistaken purchases happen to all of us sooner or later. What about that fishing reel you unwrapped at Christmas but never took out of the box? What about that food dehydrator you bought for making beef jerky but never got around to using? It's often difficult to return such merchandise for a refund, particularly after it sits in the garage for six months (or six years). But it's new, and if you sell it, you are undoubtedly receptive to selling it at a deep discount from the full retail price. eBay provides you the opportunity to sell it at the highest price you can expect to get.

New goods also come from sources other than wholesale, such as distress sales and closeout sales by manufacturers and retailers. These are usually bulk sales. For instance, if you can buy 1,000 high-quality baseball caps for $1,000 at a closeout sale and sell them on eBay for $3 each, that price is substantially below the normal $8–$16 price in the retail stores. Both you and the buyer can consummate a satisfying transaction. The buyer buys cheap, and you make a reasonable profit.

Moreover, if you are a dealer who has no retail store and no expensive website operation, you can afford to sell new goods on the eBay market in the regular course of business at even lower prices than a discount store, assuming you buy in comparable quantities. This provides a good deal for buyers and a profitable business for you.

Now, if you'll take a look at what's happening on eBay—if you haven't already—you'll see the transactions described above happening every minute of every day. eBay is a huge market. At any time, there are millions of items for sale and millions of potential buyers looking over the merchandise. If you were to put all of this in a physical setting, there is no building ever built that could house all of this commercial activity. It would take about 100 football fields to accommodate a market of only 1 million people. eBay is, indeed, a huge and rational marketplace.

Other Online Auctions

What about other online auctions? eBay has the lion's share of the online auction business. For any market to be highly rationalized, it must have a huge number of participants. Thus, so long as eBay has a major portion of the market, it is very difficult for competitors (other online auctions) to compete effectively. The competitors will simply find it difficult to grow to a size where both buyers and sellers get the best deal. Size is perhaps the single most important characteristic of an online auction marketplace, and eBay got there first.

Yahoo! and Amazon.com

Yahoo! offers free auctions and may eventually cut into eBay's market dominance, but in over two years it hasn't made much of a dent. Amazon.com started a general auction in the spring of 1999, and it hasn't made a dent either. There are no other general online auctions on the horizon that appear to be able to compete with eBay.

How did eBay get there first? That makes a fascinating story but one which is beyond the scope of this book. Like other Web business success stories, eBay made customer convenience the primary goal for improving the eBay infrastructure. The result is a finely tuned system that works well and is reliable. But transactions require trust as well as procedural mechanisms. eBay has been an innovative leader in creating a system that supports trust. Easy to use and trustworthy. What else do you need for a marketplace?

Specialty Auctions

Because eBay has no strong competition, this book will not waste space covering other online auctions alleged to compete with eBay, even for comparative purposes. You can make the argument that some specialty online auctions will compete with eBay in their specific specialties. However, because market size is so important and because eBay caters to specialty markets, you can expect eBay to dominate even individual submarkets.

Specialized Auctions

Some auctions that exist offline, such as Sotheby's and certain real estate auctions, will be successful in extending their offline auctioning online. But this is an idea different from a general online auction, and such auctions will be strictly limited to

their respective specialized markets. In fact, eBay bought Butterfield & Butterfield, an old offline auctioning establishment
similar to Sotheby's, to establish specialized auctioning online.
See eBay Premier in Chapter 25.

Will eBay continue to dominate? The eBay people are bright and
innovative. They have well-financed potential competitors such as
Yahoo! and Amazon.com breathing down their neck, which are
likely to keep them running at full speed. eBay has the momen-
tum and the market. eBay made a successful public stock offering
in September 1998. Its stock went up 3,900 percent in value by the
end of June 1999. This provided the capital to remain successful,
and eBay has been profitable. All signs indicate that eBay will continue to dominate the Web auction scene for the foreseeable
future.

The *San Francisco Examiner* calls eBay the largest online auction
with 90 percent of the market. If this figure is accurate—and all
estimates I've read indicate a similar market share—eBay domi-
nates the market in spite of the efforts of Yahoo! and Amazon.com.

Auction Games

A few retailers doing business on eBay have reported that bidders
don't take auctions seriously at some other online auctions. The
retailers have tried auctioning things, but the high bidders don't
pay. Because eBay is firm in driving deadbeat bidders away, it leads
one to believe that eBay is an auction almost everyone takes seriously, but that mischievous bidders treat some of the other online
auctions as games. I haven't done a study to determine whether
that is true, and I encourage you to try other online auctions. But
you might keep that point of view in mind when you experiment
with selling on other online auctions.

What's Up?

What do you make of all this? eBay is a new marketplace like none ever known before. It is currently without a strong competitor. It features an efficient market for the exchange of used goods, good news for both buyers and sellers. It also brings with it new opportunities for those who want to wheel and deal in goods on a broader scale, even new goods. In the true capitalistic spirit, it brings with it new opportunities to make money, lots of money.

Let Me Know

This book is not the final word on eBay. It's not even close. eBay is still being invented. It's being invented by the clever people at eBay headquarters in San Jose, California. It's being invented by buyers and sellers. And it's being invented by those who create new businesses using eBay. Join me in keeping up to date on this new marketplace. If you have a new idea about eBay or a new slant on eBay from personal observation—or an idea you've dreamed up—and you want to share it, email me at *jt@sinclair.com*. If you're the first to mention it and I use it in another edition of this book, I'll give you credit. Thanks.

Check the BookCenter website (*http://www.bookcenter.com*) for additional information about using eBay and for information on my other book *Web Pages the Smart Way* (AMACOM, 2001), which shows how to make Web pages easily with freeware Web authoring programs.

As in every marketplace, it is the knowledgeable who reap the profits. Although eBay is simple and straightforward, it provides the infrastructure for complex business strategies and activities. And although eBay is simple to use, there is a lot to know to put it to profitable use. Whether you are a buyer or seller of one item, a bulk buyer or seller, or a buyer or seller of used or new goods, this book provides the information you need to operate intelligently on eBay. This isn't a book for dummies. This is an easy book to read but one for those who want to learn how to operate on eBay the smart way.

2

Opportunities for Buyers

The primary opportunity for buyers is to buy at the lowest possible price. The questions are: Which buyers, what products? Those are tough questions to answer, because eBay evolves every day. Can an individual buy goods on eBay? Certainly. That's how eBay got its start. Can a business buy goods on eBay? Today the potential for business purchases may be limited. Tomorrow, perhaps unlimited. See Chapter 24 for more information on business purchases; this chapter covers individual buyers.

Individuals

Individual buyers (bidders) are attracted to eBay because they can buy merchandise at a good price, sometimes at a spectacular savings. This is a deal that's hard to beat. After all, this is the age of high-quality mass-produced consumer products. A Hoover vacuum cleaner works the same whether you buy it at full price from a retailer, at a discount price from a discount store, or at a deep discount price on eBay. Fortunately for buyers, there are plenty of sellers. eBay is a huge market consisting of millions of people. Among those millions are many sellers. With a good balance between buyers and sellers, the market works well for buyers.

The bottom line is that you can often buy things less expensively on eBay than you can elsewhere. This is a general statement that may not prove true in some particular cases. For instance, I usually price computer equipment on eBay and also at my local monthly computer show (*http://www.marketpro.com*). Sometimes eBay offers lower prices. Sometimes the show offers lower prices. They both offer prices significantly lower than elsewhere. At the least, eBay provides a good reference for price comparisons, and if I couldn't make it to the computer show, I would have no reservations about buying computer equipment exclusively on eBay.

eBay offers a wide variety of merchandise. Although eBay commerce seems to be top-heavy in things like collectibles, this hides the fact that there are millions of products for sale on eBay that have nothing to do with collectibles. Likewise, if you don't like used (pre-owned) merchandise, a significant portion of the merchandise being auctioned is new.

eBay's Role

eBay is just a marketplace to buy and sell, nothing more. eBay is not involved in the transaction. The seller pays a small fee to eBay—analogous to renting a booth at a flea market. As a buyer, you make your own arrangement with the seller for payment and shipping. The eBay auction process sets the price.

The Time Factor

The transaction time is not favorable to buyers. If you want something right now, you can't buy on impulse. You have to wait until the auction is over, and you have to be high bidder too. In addition, you have to tend your auction; that is, you have to have a bidding strategy and follow it through. Once you win the bidding, you must arrange payment and shipping with the seller. Often the seller will wait until your check clears before making the shipment. Thus, the total time of a transaction tends to be measured in days or even weeks.

All of the above assumes that the item you seek to buy is available on eBay. It may not be. When looking to buy microphones over a two-month period (January–February 1999), I found that the number of microphones being auctioned at any particular time varied between 110 and 215. When I looked for a copy of FrameMaker (specialized, expensive software) over the same two-month period, sometimes there were six copies being auctioned and sometimes there were none. Consequently, you may have to wait to buy what you want to buy. It may not be continuously available on eBay. But eBay is so huge that sooner or later it will show up.

Interestingly, you do not have to wait for some products. Some retailers running auctions have a link in their auction ad to their websites where you can order the merchandise immediately at a price comparable to the auction price. Don't overlook this opportunity if you're in a hurry.

The Market

The market for buyers is a smorgasbord. You can find almost everything you want. The eBay market is huge and sets eBay apart from its would-be competitors. In a real sense, eBay is your personal asset. You can always turn to it to buy merchandise at good prices, merchandise that you otherwise might not be able to afford. And it's a long-term asset. There's no reason it won't work just as well for you five years from now as it does today. Probably better.

Risk

Is it risky to buy merchandise on eBay? If it was, eBay wouldn't be so successful. Nonetheless, you need to keep your eyes open and always be cautious. Never pay more for something than you can afford to lose, because there's always the risk that you will lose your money to a commerce criminal (i.e., someone who doesn't deliver the goods).

If you can't afford to lose more than $500, you should take proper precautions for all transactions over $500. Fortunately, there are online escrow companies that you can use (for a fee) to make sure you're protected in a transaction. The escrow company doesn't pay your money to the seller until the specified goods are delivered in reasonable condition.

eBay has its own free insurance program that covers goods up to $250. It covers fraud but not shipping damage or loss.

There are ways to be conned by criminals other than the non-delivery of goods, and there will always be con artists working eBay. But there are always con artists working your local community too. They are a risk you take just by opening your front door. There might even be less fraud on eBay because eBay fraud is often easy to trace online to the criminals responsible.

The good news is that eBay has a superb system for establishing reputations. In many cases, you will have full confidence that the seller will deliver the goods. The reputation (feedback) system is the heart and soul of the eBay system—truly a work of genius—that you need to learn how to use when evaluating sellers. See Chapter 7 for details. The eBay feedback system makes eBay a great opportunity for buyers because it decreases the risk of fraud significantly.

Transaction Overhead

Buying things on eBay entails some routine expenses. Although most of the items are incidental, they add up. What you thought you bought on eBay so inexpensively might start looking like a purchase from a store in your neighborhood before you're done.

Shipping and Handling

The shipping and handling charges are a fact of life on eBay just as they are for mail-order purchases. Don't forget to estimate them in your price calculations. Often a seller will charge a flat fee, so you don't have to estimate.

Insurance

What happens if an item you paid for is not delivered? At best it causes a mess. Insurance is the best defense against this awkward situation. Unfortunately, insurance probably isn't cost-effective for inexpensive items. For expensive items, request insurance. Or, if insurance is offered, take it (even though you may have to pay for it).

Sales Tax

As with mail-order purchases, one of the attractions of buying on eBay is that the seller is likely to be out of state and you don't have to pay sales tax. Nonetheless, the shipping and handling costs often negate this savings; taken together, the shipping (cost) and sales tax (savings) are often a wash, particularly for items between $30 and $100.

Don't forget, however, when you make a purchase in your state (i.e., buyer and seller are in the same state), you have to pay sales tax (assuming your state collects a sales tax).

Escrow Fees

If a large amount of money is at stake, you should go to the effort to put the transaction in escrow. The fees seem expensive, but the process protects you from nondelivery of the merchandise. The escrow agent doesn't send payment to the seller until the buyer is satisfied that he or she received what was represented by the seller.

Payment by credit card may relieve you of the need for escrow because you can charge back (get your money back) the purchase within 90 days, if you have good cause to be dissatisfied.

Payment

If you need to send a money order or cashier's check, you will have to pay a nominal fee for it. It's better to request to use a credit card. You can always ask for a charge-back to recoup your money if the seller doesn't deliver the merchandise as represented.

Rent or Buy at Auction?

Need expensive equipment for a project? Buy it used (in excellent condition) on eBay. Use it. Keep it in excellent condition. When you're through with the project, sell the equipment on eBay (in excellent condition). You'll probably sell it for about what you bought it for if you kept it in excellent condition. That's the same as an inexpensive rental.

Summary

eBay provides solid opportunities for buyers to buy new and used goods, and even services, at low prices. eBay's system for establishing reputation takes much of the risk out of the auction transactions. In some cases buying, using, and reselling an item even simulates renting such an item at low cost for a special project. eBay provides you with a new low-cost alternative for acquiring the goods and services that you need.

What About Businesses?

This chapter discusses individuals. To get some ideas about how businesses can buy on eBay, read Chapter 24 about eBay's new Business Exchange.

3

Opportunities for Sellers

The primary opportunity for sellers is to sell at the highest price.
After all, isn't that what auctions are for? eBay provides an excellent means of potentially getting the highest price because there
are so many potential buyers in the eBay marketplace. On eBay,
individuals can successfully sell to individuals, and retailers can
successfully sell to individuals. This chapter covers such auction
opportunities. For more information on business-to-business
sales, read Chapter 24 about the eBay Business Exchange.

Individuals

Suppose you have a five-year-old Sony TCM5000EV portable professional audio cassette recorder in excellent condition you want to sell. This is the type of recorder that a radio station news reporter uses in the field to do interviews. Sony has made the same model for many years. This is a fine piece of electronic equipment with a very limited local market. If you sell this to a dealer, chances are you will not get a good price. If you sell it through classified ads, you may not get many calls for it. But if you auction it on eBay, there are probably a few among the millions of eBay buyers who will appreciate the quality of the equipment, need it, and bid on it. Because of the size of the eBay market, you can find numerous people interested in what you have to offer. The more people interested, the more likely you can sell it for a higher price than elsewhere.

It doesn't have to be a specialized piece of equipment like the Sony TCM5000EV. There are even more buyers for a popular Sony consumer audio cassette tape recorder like the Walkman WM-GX552, and with the maximum number of buyers, you are more likely to get a maximum price.

With a quick trip to your garage, you can probably make $1,000 in the next week ridding yourself of things you haven't used in years by selling them on eBay. Maybe $5,000.

Advertising

How do you promote your auction on eBay? You advertise it. eBay provides you with an advertising section at your auction (a portion of the auction Web page). You use this section to present whatever you want using Hypertext Markup Language (HTML), the simple markup language of the Web. Although this might sound like a chore if you don't know HTML, it's just the opposite. It's a substantial opportunity.

You can put anything you want to in your HTML ad. There's no limitation. Naturally, you will want to describe the item you're offering for auction. But you can also advertise your business, include a picture of the item for sale, and even include a hyperlink to your own website. Chapter 13 will show you how to use HTML templates for attractive ads without having to learn HTML.

The Time Factor

eBay is not a quick fix. You can take your Sony TCM5000EV, put it in the car, drive to a dealer, and perhaps get a check today, albeit a small check. eBay is a longer process. The shortest auction is three days, and you might want to use a longer auction just to make sure you get the maximum number of bidders.

Nonetheless, creating an auction on eBay does not take long, and there is nothing for you to do during the auction period except perhaps answer a few questions via email from prospective bidders. Once the auction is over, you simply arrange with the winning bidder for payment and shipment, and the deal is done. Presumably the auction has taken the negotiation out of the deal, and you will not have to waste time with offers and counteroffers.

Although not immediate, eBay does provide for a reasonably short sales period without a great deal of effort on your part.

The Market

The market is at least a national one and at best an international one. This means that you will send the item being auctioned via normal shipping channels, or in the case of a foreign sale, you will have to ship the item overseas. In other words, the buyer is not going to appear at your front door to hand you a check and pick up the item. Thus, it's an additional time commitment on your part to sell this way. You have to pack the item in a box and go to the post office or wherever to ship the item. On the other hand, you will not have strangers knocking on your door either (as you might with classified ads), perhaps a greater benefit.

You can assume that the market is full of serious buyers. There will be occasional buyers who do not complete the transactions for which they were the high bidders. Fortunately, eBay provides a system that discourages such behavior, and you shouldn't have to repeat an auction often.

The best news is that the market is vast. There are millions of buyers, and eBay keeps growing. This is a market where you will always find a significant number of potential buyers for common goods and where it is likely that you will find buyers even for uncommon goods. This huge eBay market, always waiting for you, provides a convenient way to sell merchandise that's no longer useful to you.

Retailers

Retailers are businesses that have merchandise to sell to consumers. Most retailers prefer to sell inventory in their stores at full price or even in store sales at a discounted price. But there are always the times when retailers have excess or outdated inventory that will never bring a full retail price. For such inventory, eBay provides a potentially profitable new outlet. Indeed, many retailers are doing quite well auctioning on eBay. eBay provides a golden opportunity for excess-inventory sales and closeout sales. In addition, it provides a golden opportunity for retailers to buy at distress sales or closeout sales offline and turn around and profitably sell the inventory at retail but for deep discounts on eBay.

For retailers used to fulfilling mail orders, selling on eBay is a natural fit. Retailers who have not sold via mail will need to get organized to conduct multiple auctions and fulfill eBay sales, not a huge task but nonetheless one that needs to be taken seriously.

Online Retailers

Retailers that exist only online will find eBay to be a natural extension of their online sales. Undoubtedly, they are well set up to handle online commerce, and eBay becomes a welcome additional outlet. They can use their existing infrastructure to handle and fulfill orders easily and quickly.

eBay Retailers

A new breed of retailers has materialized who sell only on eBay. They don't necessarily even have the expense of a commerce website and certainly not the expense of a store or warehouse. These people seek inventory at distress, closeout, or otherwise low prices and then sell it on eBay at deep discounts. In some cases, their overhead is so low that they can afford to sell at deep discounts even while purchasing their inventory through normal wholesale channels. These sales efforts are not necessarily fly-by-night retail operations. They are serious businesses making profits in this new kind of market.

Off Welfare

In the spring of 2000, President Clinton at a televised press conference claimed that by becoming eBay retailers, 20,000 people got off the welfare rolls. I wouldn't have believed it if I hadn't watched it myself. Where the president got his figures or whether they're accurate, I don't know. But there are definitely tens of thousands of people retailing on eBay, that is, auctioning merchandise routinely on eBay, whether part-time or full-time, as a source of steady income.

Special Retail Sales Projects

What is a fly-by-night retail operation? Is it one where a one-person retailer purchases a huge inventory of a closeout item for a low price, spends two months selling it on eBay, goes on vacation for a month in Bermuda, and then returns to start the cycle over again? If so, I want to be a fly-by-night retailer. Indeed, such special retail sales projects are possible on eBay. There is no requirement that you have to have a store, warehouse, commerce website, or permanent address to be a reputable and honest retailer on eBay. You simply must be diligent in finding the inventory, running the eBay auctions, fulfilling the orders, and keeping after your travel agent to make the appropriate hotel reservations in Bermuda.

Offline Auctioneers

Some auctioneers, such as estate sale auctioneers, look to eBay to extend their auction activities. Why not? For certain types of merchandise, they can get more on eBay than they can in a normal auction offline. They make more money for their clients and more money for themselves in higher auctioneering fees. With a larger pool of buyers, they can sell for higher prices with potentially lower overhead.

Buyers Become Sellers

It's no secret that many people routinely buy things for very deep discounts at local estate sales and garage sales and turn around and sell the merchandise on eBay for a profit. There are many other local sources where someone with an entre-

preneurial inclination can buy at low prices and sell on eBay.
For more auction ideas, read Chapter 19.

Offline auctioneers who cannot take advantage of eBay tend to be
ones that handle real estate or goods that require a lot of paperwork. For instance, state statutes may prevent real estate from
being auctioned effectively on eBay. In addition, real estate
requires a lot of paperwork just to get ready for auction. Another
example is the Sotheby's type of auction. The items (works of art
and the like) to be auctioned are so valuable that they require that
written bills of sale, receipts, certificates of authentication, and
other documents be provided for review by prospective bidders
before the auctions take place. These kinds of auctioneers can
extend their operations to the Web but perhaps will do best via
their own websites, not via eBay. However, eBay now provides a
separate auction just for these type of auctioneers. See Chapter 25,
which covers eBay Premier.

Service Providers

There's no rule that says you can't sell your services on eBay.
However, this is a tough sell. Suppose you're an accountant seeking to pick up new tax clients. What do you sell? On one hand, if
you sell your services at a 30 percent savings from your usual fee of
$120 per hour, you might find that you won't get much interest.
On the other hand, a workable strategy might be to offer a package
of services at a reasonable price. For instance, you might offer to
do a complete tax return for a $450 fee. For someone with a com-
plex tax situation, that might look like a bargain. That's the kind
of a client you want to have for the long term. You might work
inexpensively this year, but next year you can charge your regular
fee. However, if that fee looks too expensive to someone, probably

they don't need your services and will always be happy having their tax return prepared by H&R Block at a lower cost.

Marketing your services requires imagination and experimentation to find a magic formula that works on eBay. In the meanwhile, if you're not successful in selling your specific packages of services, you may be successful in picking up clients just by the act of auctioning your packages (i.e., advertising—see Chapter 17).

Risk

As a seller, risk does not have to be a concern. So long as you collect payment before you ship, you will protect yourself as well as you can. If you choose to ship before collecting payment, you will incur much more risk.

Keep in mind, however, that in purchasing via credit card a buyer can always ask the credit card company for a charge-back on an item with which he or she is dissatisfied. That creates the risk that you'll end up refunding the purchase price.

Perhaps the biggest risk you run is having a dissatisfied customer. A dissatisfied customer can make considerably more trouble than he or she is worth. It's better to make a refund or to do whatever it takes to keep a customer from fuming. Your eBay reputation is at stake. With this consideration in mind, the threat of a credit card charge-back becomes almost meaningless.

Transaction Overhead

eBay auctions are not without their overhead costs. Some you can pass on to the buyer.

eBay Fees

Although modest, eBay auction fees paid by the seller are still a significant expense, particularly for items of low value (see fee schedules, Tables 6.1 and 6.2, Chapter 6).

Merchant Credit Card Charges

Like at most retail outlets, eBay buyers like to pay by credit card, and credit cards cost sellers money. It isn't absolutely necessary to take credit cards on eBay, but serious sellers will want to offer credit card buying. Retailers need credit card merchant accounts to receive credit card payments. Occasional sellers can use credit card programs such as PayPal and Billpoint explained in Chapter 16.

Shipping and Handling

Rather than a business chore, shipping and handling seems to be a business opportunity for some sellers. You will see a lot of items selling for $8 on eBay with shipping and handling charged at another $6. Depending on the merchandise, there may be some profit in the shipping and handling.

Normally shipping and handling charges are a wash. The buyer pays them, and it costs that much to package and ship the item, often more. Sometimes sellers take a loss on shipping.

Sales Tax

Don't neglect to charge sales tax to customers in your state. You will need a sales tax license too. If all you do is an occasional sale, your state sales tax laws may exempt you from collecting sales tax on incidental items but probably not on expensive items. The buyer pays the sales tax, and the seller collects it and pays it to the state sales tax agency.

Customer Service

As a retailer, selling via eBay is no different than selling offline. The same laws apply. The same ethical guidelines apply. You have to be ready to take care of your eBay customers just as you would have to take care of your customers offline. Failure to do so may adversely affect your reputation on eBay (covered in Chapter 7). It doesn't matter whether you're selling one item or dozens of items. Customer service is the name of the game. See Chapter 11.

Responsibility

There is an aura of finality to an auction where the buyer buys something used or something new at a low price. If the buyer responds with a complaint immediately after receiving the merchandise, the seller will have to respond diligently. If the buyer complains two months later, unlike Target or other national retailers, the seller will not necessarily be expected to take care of the problem unless a guarantee was provided or implied. Thus, sellers may not be expected to provide quite as much customer service on eBay as in a bricks-and-mortar retail store.

An Individual

If you are an occasional seller, a buyer will not expect much in the way of customer support. A customer will expect the item bought to be as it was represented to be and to be operational (unless represented otherwise). But if a buyer receives something that won't work after you represented that it was in working order, regardless of the legal relationship, you are stuck with making it right. Otherwise your reputation on eBay may

> suffer. People have high customer service expectations when purchasing on the Web.

The point to be made here is that along with the opportunities on eBay come responsibilities. Providing reasonable customer service is one of the prime responsibilities of all retailers and even occasional sellers. Even though customer service responsibilities may be less on eBay than in other markets, this does not mean there are no customer expectations that you must meet. There are, and failure to meet them can affect your reputation.

Opportunity

The most productive point of view is to look upon customer service as an opportunity rather than a responsibility. As in any other market, if you offer great customer service on eBay, you will get plenty of repeat business and plenty of referrals. Never make the mistake of thinking of eBay as a one-shot deal or as a temporary retail selling effort. You may be selling on eBay for years to come. Perhaps decades.

Cost

Customer service is part of your overhead. You have to expend the time and energy to provide it, or your employees do. It's not free.

Summary

eBay provides solid opportunities for sellers, whether individuals or businesses, to sell used goods for higher prices than the same goods might bring elsewhere. In the case of services, auctioning can even mean inexpensive advertising. But the real story about eBay is *retailing*. Retail selling on eBay provides huge opportunities to anyone who wants to provide good customer service and experiment with online auctions as a new type of retail outlet. Capital requirements and overhead are low. The results can be spectacular. This is truly a prime opportunity for many people, and much of this book is devoted to it.

What About Non-Retail Businesses?

Can non-retail businesses sell on eBay? Chapter 24 considers that question. Non-retail businesses certainly have the need to sell used equipment, overstocked supplies, and the like.

II

Learning to Use eBay

4

How eBay Works

An online auction can be operated hundreds of different ways. eBay was not the first auction online. Perhaps not even in the first hundred. But eBay has been able to construct a digital mechanism that accommodates both the potential of the new Web medium and the psychology of human commerce. It is this subtle mechanism—the heart and soul of eBay—which makes eBay successful; it's not merely the translation of the auction to an online format. To understand eBay, you have to start with eBay values.

Community Values

eBay wisely sets what it calls *community values* that it expects to guide the behavior of everyone participating in eBay:

We believe people are basically good.

We believe everyone has something to contribute.

We believe that an honest, open environment can bring out the best in people.

We recognize and respect everyone as a unique individual.

We encourage you to treat others the way you want to be treated.

These statements of values set the tone for the conduct of auctions and the transactions that follow. Should you have trouble dealing with other people on eBay, it might be wise for you to review these guideline values. They might give you some ideas on how to resolve your conflicts.

Values alone are not enough, however, and eBay requires you to sign its User Agreement, which sets forth the rules of the road for eBay members.

User Agreement

The following is not a reprint of the eBay User Agreement dated September 27, 1999 (latest available at the time this book went to press). Rather it's my impression of the high points. Your impression of what the high points are may be different than mine, and I urge you to take the time to read the Agreement in its entirety. It is always available on the eBay website in the SafeHarbor section.

1. The information you provide for registration, bidding, or

listing must be accurate and must not infringe on another's copyright or trademark.

2. eBay is only a venue. This means that eBay is only a place for people to conduct their transactions. It does not take part in the transactions.

3. You release eBay from liability for any claims arising out of the transactions in which you take part on eBay. You indemnify eBay from any claims by third parties arising out of your breach of the Agreement.

4. High bidders have an obligation to buy.

5. Sellers have an obligation to sell once a bid above the minimum (or the reserve) has been made.

6. Bid manipulation or interference is prohibited for both buyers and sellers.

7. You may not auction identical items in more than ten individual auctions (including Dutch auctions) at one time. (You can auction multiple identical items in a single Dutch auction.)

8. You may not use any software that will adversely affect eBay's website.

Additionally, the following documents are incorporated by reference into the User Agreement:

Privacy Policy

Outage Policy

Board Usage Policy

Nonbinding Bid Policy

Listing Policy

SafeHarbor Policy

Prohibited, Questionable & Infringing Item Policy

Nonpaying Bidder Policy

See Appendix V for more information, but keep in mind that Appendix V is not complete. Read the entire User Agreement and its incorporated documents yourself to get a full and complete understanding of what is expected of you.

Trust

If you're new to eBay, you should now understand after reading the preceding two sections that trust lies at the heart of the eBay system. You may be dealing with someone a couple of thousand miles away. To make a deal, you have to trust them. And without trust, eBay would not be possible. Chapter 7 covers the feedback system, which builds the foundation for trust on eBay. Chapter 8 covers recourse against those who don't deserve your trust.

"Ebay, the largest online auction site, says only one of every 40,000 listings results in a confirmed case of fraud, in which an insurance claim is paid," states *USA Today* (August 29, 2000). This indicates that fradulent transactions comprise about 3/1,000 of 1 percent, hardly a commerce-threatening amount. Thus, one must conclude that trust does work when reinforced with the proper rules and regulations. The remainder of this chapter covers the general website mechanism that makes eBay bidding work. But don't lose sight of the fact that the most important ingredient of the eBay magic digital formula for success in buying, selling, and Web commerce is trust.

Navigation

The words at the top of the eBay home page are links that take you to various parts of the eBay website (see Figure 4.1).

Figure 4.1   Page-top links.

Site Map

Perhaps the most important link is *site map*, situated above the navigation bar, which takes you to the eBay Site Map, a longer list of links. This map shows you everywhere you want to go on eBay, and you will find it quite handy (see Figure 4.2).

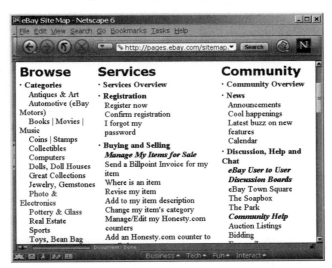

Figure 4.2   Site Map's list of links.

I often use the Site Map rather than the other links on the top of the page to find where I want to go on eBay.

Browse

The Browse link takes you to a few featured auctions. These are auctions for which someone has paid extra money in order to get extra attention. (In most cases, they're not very interesting primarily because they are featured by sellers, not elected by buyers.) A click takes you to additional featured auctions. A much better way to get to the auctions you want to visit is to go below the featured auctions to see a more detailed list of categories than is displayed on the home page—a list that's quite useful. The Browse link (see Figure 4.3) also provides sublinks that you may want to explore.

Figure 4.3   The Browse link and sublinks.

The sublinks enable you to browse auctions via local auctions (*regions*) or even by *themes* (e.g., cooking).

Sell

The Sell link takes you directly to the input form where you enter an auction. See Chapter 6 for information on entering auctions.

Services

In the Services section you can register to be an eBay member, find buying and selling aids, enter your About Me information, or check the status of your activities on eBay in My eBay (see Figure 4.4). You can also access the eBay security sections SafeHarbor and Feedback Forum, which are covered in Chapter 7.

Figure 4.4   The Service link and sublinks.

Note that My eBay also has a link above the navigation bar for a quick check of your eBay activities.

Search

The Search link is handy because it provides you with a new search called Smart Search. This will help you do sophisticated searches without using the helping symbols covered later in the Search Aids section.

Old Search

In addition, you can elect to use the old search method, which is a useful five-way search. Each of the search devices enables you to get a set of useful information. Try each of them to see what you get. They enable you to search by:

- Title of item (words in item's one-line listing)

- Item number

- Seller

- Buyer

- Completed auctions by title

You can search right from the home page, but that search input is limited. The Search link on the navigation bar takes you to a search Web page that is much more complete (see Figure 4.5). You will find it useful from time to time.

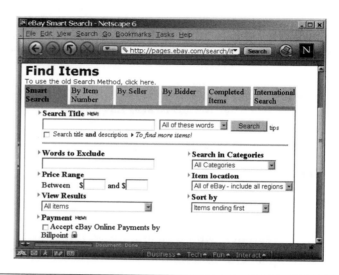

Figure 4.5   eBay Search page.

In addition, the Search link takes take you to the Personal Shopper (see Chapter 5).

Search Aids

You can use certain symbols to help your search. Don't worry about memorizing them, because you can search well without them by using Smart Search. When you get frustrated and can't find what you're looking for, however, you might want to try them.

No symbol Lists all auctions with all the included words in the auction title in any order. Thus, *Shure microphone* will list all auctions with both *Shure* and *microphone* in the auction title.

Asterisk (*) Use as a wild card. For instance, a search on *mic** will list all auctions that include *mic*, *microphone*, or *microphones* in the title. It will undoubtedly list some other unexpected auctions too (e.g., Mickey as in Mickey Mouse).

Quotations (" ") Restricts the search to the words in the exact order quoted. For instance, a search on *"Shure microphone"* will list only the auctions where *Shure* and *microphone* are contiguous and in the same order. Thus, such a search would miss *Shure dynamic microphone* or *microphone Shure*.

Minus Sign (–) Does not include titles with the word after the minus. For example, *microphone –Shure* would include all auctions with *microphone* in the title except the ones that also had *Shure* in the title.

Parentheses ( ) Searches for both words in the parentheses. Hence, *(microphone,mic)* lists all auction titles with either *microphone* or *mic* in the title. You can use with a word outside the parentheses. For example, *microphone (Shure,Sony)* will list all auctions with *microphone* and *Shure* or *Sony* in the title.

Comma (,) Searches for either of the items separated by the comma (uses no spaces between words, only commas). You need this to use parentheses.

Keep in mind that the searches are not case-sensitive; that is, it doesn't matter whether you use upper- or lower-case letters in your words. Don't use the words *the*, *and*, *an*, *or*, and the like. The search engine ignores these words unless inside quotations. To keep your searches narrow and fast, search inside eBay categories, not in all of eBay.

Help

The Help section has information for rookies and old hands alike; try the Basics (see Figure 4.6).

Figure 4.6   The Help link and sublinks.

Perhaps most helpful is the information it has for buyers and sellers. The Buyer Guide link takes you to a substantial amount of information about bidding auctions on eBay. If you are primarily interested in being an eBay buyer, this is an excellent place to start learning about eBay. It's also a reference that you can use anytime you have any questions. Go *Help*, *buyer guide* for buyer's information (see Figure 4.7).

The Seller Guide link takes you to plenty of information on auctioning items on eBay. Use it to get started, and then use it as a reference. Go *Help*, *seller guide* for seller's information (see Figure 4.8).

Community

The Community section provides access to news sources and bulletin boards. You can read about the newest devices and procedures on eBay. You can get support, even live support. The eBay community is alive and dynamic.

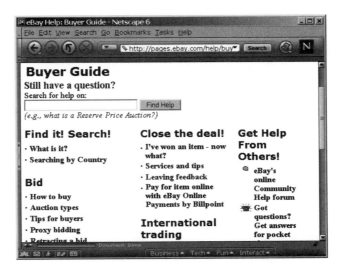

Figure 4.7   Buyer guide.

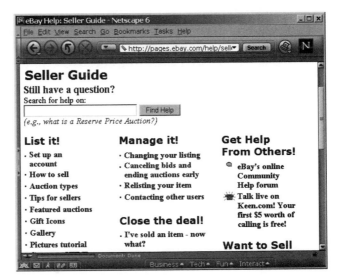

Figure 4.8   Seller guide.

Under *Chat* there are general eBay bulletin boards, which cover using eBay. And there are bulletin boards for a variety of eBay categories (e.g., jewelry). The Community even includes a Library and the eBay Store (see Figure 4.9).

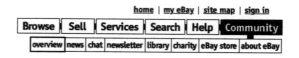

Figure 4.9   The Community link and sublinks.

Preparation

Starting with registration (discussed in the next section), you will be required to fill in forms on the eBay website for one thing or another. This section is a short tutorial to assist you.

Before filling out any eBay form, you can visit the form and save it. You can read it and even fill it in casually offline. In addition, with a few tricks, you can more effectively fill it in online.

Save As

Go *File, Save As* to save any Web page. This comes in handy for reading eBay information casually offline. After you save a Web page, remember where you saved it and what the file name is. Then access the Web page on your hard disk with your browser. With this technique, however, you can't fill in the forms and submit them.

Frozen Browser

After accessing an eBay form with your browser, simply go offline without closing the browser. The Web page will remain in the browser. You can fill in the forms at your leisure. Then get back online and submit the form. This usually works, but not always.

Paste In

You can write text almost anywhere (e.g., in a word processor), highlight it, copy it to the clipboard, and paste it into a form in a Web page. This technique enables you to read, offline, an eBay Web page you have saved that includes forms. You can draft the input for the forms in a word processor offline. You can then get online, go to the forms, and copy and paste the text from the word processor into the eBay forms.

Registration

Registering to be a member of eBay is easy, fast, and free. Just fill in the registration form. You will get an alias (your eBay name, which is a log-in name) and a password.

Welcome New Users

On the eBay home page you will notice a blue oval (see Figure 4.10). It's for new users and includes the following buttons: new to eBay?, how do I bid?, how do I sell?, why eBay is safe, and register. If you're new to eBay, this gives you quick access to appropriate information that will get you started.

Figure 4.10   The blue welcome oval.

The register button will take you directly to the registration form where you can register immediately.

Before You Register

eBay is a lifelong asset. Before you register, take the time to understand how it works. More importantly, take the time to understand what it means. If you register immediately, thinking that eBay is some sort of a game, that attitude may lead you to activities that are unacceptable to eBay and the eBay community. The result is that you may have your eBay rights terminated indefinitely. The loss of rights for perhaps the most dynamic and powerful commerce market of the new century will undoubtedly be a loss that you will regret sooner or later. Read Chapters 7 and 8 to be sure that you know what you're getting into and what the consequences will be if you abuse the system.

Registering

To register, you simply fill out the eBay online registration form. You'll know all the information requested except for your alias and password. You will have to dream those up.

Although you can navigate around the eBay website and even visit all the auctions, you cannot buy (bid) or sell (auction) anything unless you are a registered member.

Alias (Log-In Name)

Pick an alias. Some people pick "cool" names such as *soaringeagle*. Others pick straightforward names like mine: *sinc* for Sinclair. Some use their email address so that people can always contact them. Had I decided not to use an alias, eBay would have automatically assigned to me the alias *jt@sinclair.com*, my email address (default alias).

Password

Don't take your passwords lightly anywhere, especially on eBay. If someone can find out your password, they can cause you much damage on eBay, financial and otherwise. Never use the same password for more than one website or service, and don't use short passwords. If you follow these two suggestions, it will be practically impossible for anyone else to use your account at eBay.

But it's a large burden to remember a lot of passwords, particularly for websites and services that you don't use often. I use Password Keeper (*http://www.gregorybraun.com*), a shareware program, to keep all my passwords. When I forget a password, I can always look it up in Password Keeper. If you protect yourself well by choosing long passwords, you'll need to look them up often, particularly when you haven't used them for a while.

Registration Form

The registration at *Services, registration* is straightforward (see Figure 4.11). Choose your alias and password before you register so that you don't have to make a hurried decision. The registration will ask you for the usual name, address, and phone number as well as some personal questions (optional).

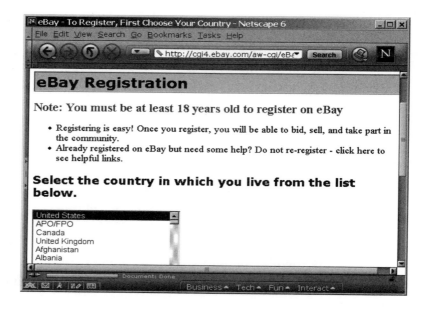

Figure 4.11   Registration form.

Confirmation

Click at the bottom of the form to submit your registration. Next
you will have to wait. eBay will send you a confirmation number
at your email address. You then take the confirmation number and
follow the instructions (e.g., enter the confirmation number at the
eBay website). The instructions will explain the remaining steps
to complete your registration (e.g., enter alias and password). After
you finish the registration process, you're legit. You can now buy
and sell.

Auctions

You can use four types of auctions for over 4,000 categories of goods and services.

Categories

The general categories are on the home page. By clicking on a category, you get to lower-level categories as you go deeper and deeper into the category directory. The number of items currently up for auction are in parentheses after each category (see Figure 4.12). Chances are you will find a low-level category that will fit well what you want to buy or sell.

For instance, a click on *Music* takes you to a level of subcategories in which a click on *CD* takes you to another level of subcategories where you can click on *Blues* to get to auctions featuring blues music on CDs.

Categories
Antiques & Art
Books | Movies |
Music
Coins | Stamps
Collectibles
Computers
Dolls, Figures
Jewelry, Gemstones
Photo & Electronics
Pottery & Glass
Real Estate
Sports
Toys, Bean Bag Plush

Everything Else:
Featuring
Clothing & Accessories,
Home & Garden, Tickets,
Travel
all categories...

Figure 4.12   Categories on the eBay home page.

When you finally get to a category you can use, you will see a list of auctions. The listings you see are one-line (eBay calls them titles) from eBay auctions (a limit of 45 characters). This one line, created by the seller who entered the auction, should indicate exactly what is being auctioned.

The One-Line Title

As you read the list of titles looking for what you want, you'll find it helps quite a bit if the list is easily readable. It helps you to skim through the listings quickly. Titles that have poor-quality typesetting (e.g., all caps) create an impediment to reading.

People use poor-quality typesetting out of ignorance. They think that a technique like all caps will draw attention to their listing. Instead, it makes their listing less readable and creates a barrier to easily skimming the list. They think that if they are selling a Ford pickup truck that all caps will, by some magical attraction, draw in buyers who are looking for a Dodge van. Unfortunately, it doesn't work that way. Someone looking for a Dodge van will not buy a Ford pickup truck no matter what the title says and no matter how it is typeset. Instead, the person looking for the Ford pickup truck will have a more difficult time spotting the title because the title is all caps and more difficult to read.

The eye and brain together can easily pick out of a readable list whatever they look for. The more readable the list, the easier it is for you to find what you are looking for. The less readable the list, the more difficult it is to find what you are looking for. The one-line titles enable you to spot the auction of an item you are looking for. Then the specific auction page is just a click away. Remember this when, as a seller, you enter your auction ad.

Individual Auctions

Click on a title, and you will go to that auction. The auction is one Web page featuring one auction item. It has:

1. Standard information at the top

2. An auction ad (*Description*) created by the seller in the middle of the page

3. A place to bid at the bottom

For bidders, Chapter 5 covers the standard information and the bidding section. For sellers, Chapter 13 covers creating eBay auction ads.

Types

The four types of eBay auctions provide you some flexibility for your auctioning activities.

Normal

The normal auction is similar to a silent auction. The seller sets a minimum bid to start things off. Some sellers set the minimum bid low, some set it high. If it's low, it will probably be bid up to market value. If it's high, it will probably be bid up to market value, too. If the minimum is over market value, it's unlikely to get any bids at all. The normal auction is for one item (or package) only.

Reserve

A reserve is like a secret minimum. You can still use a minimum bid just as in a normal auction, but the reserve is the secret minimum. As soon as the reserve has been exceeded by the current high bidder (assuming it is exceeded), eBay publishes the fact that the reserve has been met. It doesn't make sense to use a reserve unless the reserve amount is higher than the minimum bid. The reserve auction is for one item (or package) only. If no bidders bid the reserve amount or higher, the seller does not have to sell the item.

Dutch

The Dutch auction is for multiple identical items. Bidders bid in the normal way, specifying how many of the identical items they are bidding on. The top bidders win the auction but pay only the bid of the lowest successful bidder. For instance, suppose you auction five identical new toasters. The bids follow in Table 4.1.

Table 4.1 Bids on Five New Toasters at a Dutch Auction

Alias	Number of Toasters	Bid ($)
sinklily	1	34
punkypete	1	33
livefive	2	32
laxtrainer	1	31
bynite	2	29
stonerich	1	27
rainmore	4	26

The bids of sinklily, punkypete, livefive, and laxtrainer take all five toasters. All the winning bidders pay only $31 each for the toasters, the lowest bid of a successful bidder (i.e., laxtrainer's bid). The seller sets the minimum bid, but no reserve is allowed in a Dutch auction.

Private

Anyone can bid at a private auction. What makes it private? The auction display keeps the bidders' identities secret. Of course, eBay notifies the seller of the winning bidder's identity, but that's the only bidder that even the seller will know.

Comparison

The four types of auctions are briefly compared in Table 4.2, showing the advantages and disadvantages of each.

Table 4.2 Four Auction Types

Type	Advantages	Disadvantages
Normal	Lets market set price	No minimum guaranteed price (except minimum bid)
Reserve	Minimum guaranteed price (unpublished)	Item may not sell
Dutch	Can sell numerous identical items at once	If minimum price too high, no bids is a possibility
Private	For bidders who want anonymity	Fewer potential bidders

Restricted Access

This is not a separate type of auction. It's a restricted category. The only restricted auction currently is adult erotica. eBay attempts to ensure that anyone accessing this category is 18 or older by requiring a credit card number prior to access.

Duration

Auctions run for three, five, seven, or ten days. They end exactly at the same time of day as they started. For example, a three-day auction that starts at 7:47 PM on Monday night ends at 7:47 PM on Thursday night. A seven-day auction starts and ends on the same day, same time. Consequently, you choose when you want your auction to end by entering it at the requisite time three, five, seven, or ten days earlier.

Prohibited Auctions

eBay has rules prohibiting certain things from being sold on eBay. The rules make sense, and eBay adds to the forbidden items as experience dictates. The list at the time the book went to press included:

- Alcohol
- Advertisements
- Child pornography
- Current catalogs
- Counterfeit items
- Securities (e.g., stocks and bonds)
- Human body parts
- Credit cards
- Controlled substances (i.e., illicit drugs)
- Perscription drugs
- Tobacco
- Forged autographs
- Embargoed goods
- Animals and wildlife products
- Military weapons
- Firearms and fireworks

- Locksmith paraphernalia
- TV descramblers
- Surveillance equipment
- Replicas of government IDs or licenses
- Law-enforcement IDs and badges
- Current license plates
- Stolen things
- Lottery tickets
- Spam lists or software
- Postage meters
- Things that infringe on a copyright or trademark

For the specific details on these prohibitions and for an updated list, go Help, rules & safety, Is my item allowed on eBay?

In addition, eBay treats some items as questionable. They are not prohibited absolutely, but you will have to be careful that you don't break any rules by selling them. The list at the time the book went to press included:

- Used medical equipment
- Contracts
- Tickets
- Weapons and knives
- Autographed things
- Nazi-related items
- Food
- Batteries

- Used clothing

- Offensive and adult items

- Artifacts

- Freon

- Pre-sale listings

- Police-related items

- Hazardous materials

- Non-FCC-compliant electronic equipment

- International transactions

If something on these lists catches your attention, you need to investigate the details.

The prohibition against infringing materials bears some additional comment. They include copyrighted items such as copies of music, movies, television shows, software, written works, games, photographs, artwork, images, and promotional items. But infringement is more complex than just stating a simple list of banned copies, and you will do best to read what eBay has to say about infringement, or potential infringement, if there is any possibility at all that you might be auctioning items for which this might be an issue.

VeRO

If you are an owner of copyrights—manifested in copyrighted materials—and sellers are auctioning infringing copies of your works on eBay, you can join the Verified Rights Owner (VeRO) program. Go Help, rules & safety, Verified Rights Owner Program. This enables you to work together with eBay to curtail the infringing sales.

Finally, eBay treats real estate in a special way. Real estate auctions are allowed but not binding on either party. eBay also has a special fee for real estate auctions.

Gallery

eBay also presents auctions in a way different from just a list of one-line titles. It presents auctions in a photo gallery. Go *site map*, *Browse*, *Gallery*. This applies, of course, only to auctions that include a photograph. If anything, the Gallery points out how important text (which it does not have) is in identifying items that people seek to purchase. Nonetheless, the Gallery is another place for your item to be displayed. But you can't get there without a photograph in your auction ad.

Keep in mind that, for certain items, looking at photographs is the best way to find what you're looking for. For instance, you might find it more convenient to look at Japanese prints in the Gallery than to hunt them down in individual auctions.

To have your auction listing (together with a photograph) included in the Gallery costs a little extra, but if your item justifies such a display, the Gallery may help you sell it.

After the Auction

eBay is not a party to the auctions. It is up to you as either the buyer or seller to contact the other party to consummate the transaction. As a buyer (high bidder), I am often eager to get the merchandise on which I just bid, and I often have an urgent need for the merchandise. Therefore, I usually contact the seller by email immediately to ask about exact payment, mailing address, etc.

However, contacting an eBay retailer can affect their follow-through system. Such retailers are used to contacting their buyers (high bidders) en masse as much as possible and usually do not want to hear from buyers until after they have initiated contact. Some sellers look upon unsolicited communications from buyers as an unnecessary interference with their follow-up systems. Regardless, I still contact sellers when I need an item urgently.

As a seller, you want to send a communication as soon as possible to the high bidder after an auction. This is especially important if you run many auctions. You need an email follow-up system that works so well that you discourage unsolicited email messages from buyers. Individual email from customers is time-consuming to handle, inefficient, and unprofitable, particularly for transactions involving inexpensive items. Naturally, when a problem arises, you are happy to get it sorted out by communicating with your customers. But, otherwise, you don't have the time and energy to exchange email with all of them any more than is necessary.

Escrow Services

eBay provides escrow services through iEscrow. You can sign up on eBay and make all the arrangements. You must establish a user account at iEscrow, which is easy to do. Go *Services, safeharbor, Escrow services*. You must go through a series of steps, which iEscrow spells out, to complete your escrow. The escrow service costs about 5 percent of the selling price, which is quite high, but it goes a long way in ensuring that the transaction does not harm either party.

Wanted Page

Where do buyers without an auction to bid go? If you can't find something you want up for auction, enter a want ad on the Wanted bulletin board for it. This is not a very robust portion of eBay, but it might work for you. Go *Community, Chat, Wanted Board*.

Researching an eBay User

You can research another user's feedback (see Chapter 7 regarding analyzing a user's feedback). Go *Services, feedback forum*.

You can also research another user's history of aliases and email addresses or full contact information (including address and phone). Go *Search, find members*. In this case, eBay notifies the other user. This can provide you with a wealth of information on another eBay user for evaluating a seller or buyer or for making a transaction work.

Researching Market Values

Because market value is so important to success on eBay and because research is so important to determining market value, use the following list of sources to find the market value of items. Keep in mind that obtaining list prices is a good place to start in determining the used value of manufactured items.

Catalogs Look through printed catalogs and catalogs online of offline retailers and manufacturers.

eCommerce Look through the online catalogs of retail businesses that exist only online.

Completed Auctions You can access completed auctions on eBay where they are archived for a few weeks. You will find the winning bid amounts.

Shop Get in your car and go shopping.

Magazines Read specialty magazines. Many collectibles magazines feature compilations of values, and all specialty magazines have retail ads, many of which feature prices.

Manufacturers Go to manufacturers' websites. Often suggested retail prices are posted.

Books The library has reference books that are price guides. They are usually old news but still may be useful.

Appraisers Chat with an appraiser who knows market values well.

Dealers Chat with a dealer who knows the market well.

eBay Resources Go *Community* on the navigation bar and try the following: (1) specialty chat sessions where you can get advice from eBay retail experts; (2) library where you can find Inside Scoop and Front Page articles for various eBay categories.

Web Search Engines Use AltaVista or Google to look up items, and you will get to some of the sources mentioned earlier. It's a quick and efficient way to research.

Research—meaning the determination of market value—is the one most effective technique for success on eBay for both buyers and sellers. How do you know what to do unless you know the market value?

Representing Yourself

As you will read in Chapter 7, your reputation on eBay generates the trust you need to make successful transactions. If your reputation fails—due to your bad behavior—you will have a difficult time getting anyone to do business with you. You always want to be conscious of how you treat other people and be careful that you don't violate any eBay rules.

Feedback System

You can rate other eBay members with positive, neutral, or negative feedback and also make comments. Such ratings, however, are limited to transactions; that is, buyers and sellers rate each other.

There is no requirement that buyers and sellers rate each other for each transaction, but many, if not most, do. So, there are plenty of ratings on each active member (except rookies) to establish a reputation. The feedback system works well. A person can't treat other people unfairly or with abuse without incurring negative feedback.

If One Doesn't Behave

The positive feedback ratings (for each positive rating you get a +1) and negative ratings (for each negative rating you get a –1) are added. If a person gets to a rating of –4, eBay automatically suspends his or her membership.

About Me

The feedback *comments* tend to be valuable when they are negative (assuming they provide the facts) and useless when they are positive (mostly ridiculous praise), although the *ratings* are always valuable. However, eBay gives you a chance to tell people something about yourself. You make an entry in *About Me*, and everyone can read it. If you do make an About Me entry, an About Me icon goes next to your name so that people will know that your information exists to be read. This eBay device gives you a chance to tell your story and increase your credibility.

You can't be sure about trusting someone based on his or her About Me profile, but it's significant information that together with other information (e.g., feedback) you can use to make an informed judgment.

Be Prepared

Before you start your About Me entry, prepare your information ahead of time offline. Look at a dozen or more of other people's About Me presentations and decide how you want yours to read. Write the information. Find a graphic you want to include (e.g., a digital photograph of yourself). Then log on eBay to make the entry in the form at *Services, about me*. You will find a handy form to fill in. Copy and paste information you have prepared into the inputs in the form. Your photograph, if you use one, will have to be available on the Web somewhere (see Chapter 12), and you put the URL of your photograph in the appropriate input in the About Me form.

A Web Page

If you are not satisfied with what you can enter into the form casually, create a Web page about yourself instead. Submit the Web page into the input in the form. Remember to copy only the *<body>* portion of the Web page when you copy and paste. Do this the same way as when you submit the template for advertising as outlined in Chapter 13 or as covered in Chapter 20 in regard to

using a Web authoring program. In other words, cut off the top
and bottom of the Web page.

Submitting a Web Page

Because Chapters 13 and 20 show you the general means of
submitting a Web page for an input in a Web form, this chapter
does not duplicate such information.

Edit

Don't worry about making your About Me perfect the first time.
You can always go back and edit it or completely revise it.

Security

eBay has started a security program—ID Verify—wherein they
check a member's application against the facts in an Equifax
Secure, Inc., database to ascertain that a person is really who he
says he is. It requires that a person submit via secured transmission (Secure Sockets Layer or SSL—built into Web browsers) certain personal information and a $5 introductory fee. *This program
is optional.* It is an excellent program that all honest and forthright
eBay citizens should embrace. It provides an extra measure of protection against fraud and other criminal behavior. Although it's a
voluntary program, eBay citizens can make it a compulsory program, in effect, by refusing to deal with anyone who isn't verified.
This is part of eBay's SafeHarbor program to ensure that eBay is a
safe place to do business.

Not a Credit Check

The eBay Equifax check is not a credit check. It's just a check to verify name, address, and other basic data.

The additional security fostered by the ID Verify program should encourage the growth of the membership and the additional participation of the members in eBay auctions, particularly auctions for more expensive items.

Naturally, people who are properly identified are more likely to behave (i.e., be trustworthy). You would like to deal with people whose identities have been verified, and that works both ways. Buyers would like to know that sellers are who they say they are. After all, buyers are making payment and trusting that sellers will send the merchandise. Sellers would like to know that buyers are who they say they are. Invariably, sellers have problems with bogus bidding by people who hide behind aliases. Accommodate both buyers and sellers. Have your ID verified.

ID Verify

To have your ID verified, go *Services, safeharbor, ID Verify*. The process takes you through a questionnaire that includes questions about your affairs that only you and Equifax would know. You are later notified as to whether you have been approved (verified).

This provides more assurance to other parties that you are unlikely to be a con artist. Most criminals do not want their true identities known. Look for this new verification to become widely used.

eBay requires ID Verify for buyers for transactions over $15,000. This threshold should be lowered considerably ($500?) and applied to sellers as well. eBay has matured into an important national marketplace. eBay is no longer a place for con artists or miscreants who want to play games. ID Verify will go a long way toward reducing the number of both.

Should you be afraid of the ID Verify process? My experience was that I didn't have to give any information that Equifax didn't already know. Giving your Social Security number is optional (and I didn't give mine), but, in any event, Equifax probably already knows it.

If you are a regular eBay user, either buyer or seller, I strongly recommend that you get ID Verify and require it of the other eBay users with whom you deal, particularly on high-dollar auctions. Widespread use of ID Verify will go a long way toward reducing the risk in the eBay marketplace for both buyers and sellers.

Privacy

An objection can be raised that this is an invasion of privacy. Indeed, you do have to trust eBay when you give bits of personal information. In my opinion, eBay has earned that trust, although everyone must remain alert to be sure it doesn't abuse your trust in any way. The risk of abuse compared to the advantage of greater security seems to be a risk worth taking.

Digital Signatures

Clearly, the ID Verify program is a harbinger of future Web commerce. The verification eBay requires is the equivalent of the middle level of verification for a digital signature. This level of verification is not foolproof. A higher level of verification for a digital signature requires birth certificate and photograph identification before a notary public in addition to other personal information. It seems to me that the higher level of verification is the next logical step for eBay, perhaps five years away.

Don't let me confuse you into thinking that eBay is requiring a digital signature. I mention digital signatures simply because a typical certifying authority's midlevel verification for a digital signature is about the same as eBay's current verification for Verified eBay User status. It won't be too long before digital signatures will be required for Web commerce. eBay's verification program is a step in that direction.

Down the road a few years, mid-level verifications bound (a technical term) to digital signatures will probably be acceptable for small consumer transactions (e.g., under $10,000) between strangers. Eventually, for large dollar transactions, higher-level verifications bound to digital signatures will be required. Today, you might think of that higher level as a superverification, but eventually it will probably become standard. One might expect eBay eventually to adopt a a higher-level verification for those who want to do large transactions.

A digital signature is not really necessary on eBay where each registered eBay member is "known," especially if they are verified. But a digital signature might be required for legal reasons eventually even on eBay. Certainly, outside eBay, digital signatures will soon be required for transactions.

The Secured Electronic Transaction (SET) program instituted by MasterCard and VISA requires digital signatures. It has been slow in catching on, however, because the common SSL-secured transmission available in the Web browsers for years has worked out better than most experts had expected. But it's only a matter of time before digital signatures become a routine fact of life in Web commerce. (A national statute passed in 2000 made them acceptable for commerce.) Check *http://www.verisign.com* for more information on digital signatures.

Digital signatures will give everyone a higher level of protection against fraud and other criminal activity in Web commerce. The better the verification, the more protection. eBay should be applauded for its ID Verify program. Although not a digital signature program, it's a turn in the right direction.

Quality of Protection

A verification or digital signature merely helps ascertain that a person is who he says he is. But John Larkspur (a name I made up) can be who he says he is and still be a Web commerce criminal. Therefore, all a verification or a digital signature does is identify a person.

I suppose if you start chasing a Web commerce criminal for recovery of stolen funds, it's best to know who he is. Presumably without the verification, it might be difficult to know the true identity of the person you want to chase. But knowing the true identity of someone is no guarantee that you will catch him or recover stolen funds. In the final analysis, you have to rely on other indices of trust to do business with a person on the Web.

That's why the eBay feedback system is so valuable. It provides you with an eBay member's reputation. That, together with a verification, is perhaps better protection than you get offline for dealing with someone you don't know.

By-Product

A by-product of the eBay verification and feedback system may be the use of eBay as a general commerce reference. In other words, suppose you want to do some business with an appliance dealer (either on or off the Web) that involves a certain degree of trust (e.g., installment sale). The dealer can run a credit check on you.

But perhaps that's not enough. The dealer can also look up your feedback on eBay. If you're verified, perhaps the dealer can even have more confidence that you are who you say you are without checking your driver's license. Will your alias on eBay be requested on credit applications in the future? That's something to think about.

Community

eBay is a community of people who are drawn together to take part in commerce. Many are just occasional community members, but others pursue activities that make it profitable to take part in eBay often. If you are one of those who uses eBay often, you may be interested in one of the communities supported by eBay.

Chat

Visit Chat on the eBay website. You will find a variety of bulletin boards (discussion groups) that discuss various aspects of eBay operations, including special bulletin boards for rookies. If you need help, need to understand a certain process, want to help others, or want to contribute ideas toward improving eBay, you will be welcome. If you want more specific information regarding online activity, eBay also supports bulletin boards on specific commerce topics.

If you deal in certain types of goods, eBay may sponsor a bulletin board (forum, mailing list, discussion group) that has created a community in regard to such goods. For instance, there are bulletin boards on jewelry, toys, and photo equipment, among many others. Check *Community, chat*.

Is a Community for You?

Many of us do not have enough interest in the goods we use to join a community (unless we are professionals or collectors). Nonetheless, communities can be meaningful. As a buyer, you can join a community, albeit temporarily, to seek advice for making a purchase. Have your eye on a 30-year-old Nikon 300mm telephoto lens on auction and want to find out if you can use it on your 15-year-old Nikon camera? Join the Photo Equipment bulletin board and ask the experts. While you're there, have some good conversations, make some new friends, and enjoy the community in addition to getting the information you need.

As a seller, your participation in specialty bulletin boards will put you in touch with prospective customers and increase your credibility. It's a natural for promoting your business so long as you don't practice blatant commercialism. Promote yourself and your business very subtly. Be helpful, be friendly, and give advice (based on your expertise as a retailer or user). People will recognize your contribution and remember you favorably.

User Tutorials

There are new user tutorials. Look for them via *Help*, *basics*. If you haven't used eBay before, it will help you get going. They cover *Registration*, *Finding Stuff*, *Bidding*, *Selling*, and *Adding Images*.

In addition, there are a variety of tutorials (articles) on specific areas of interest such as pottery, dolls, and stamps. To find them, go *Community, library*.

eBay Customer Service

eBay seems a little weak in customer service for eBay users. True, it has a wide range of assistance features well presented. If, however, you have a special problem to solve, it's tough to find a place to get assistance. For instance, I signed up for ID Verify, went through the procedure, and was approved. Nonetheless, nowhere was it indicated that I had ID Verify. It's supposed to be noted with a special icon in your feedback section.

When I checked my feedback, not only was the ID Verify icon missing but I had at least four positive feedbacks that were not mine. (They could have been negative feedback!) When I tried to get the mess straightened out, I spent a considerable amount of time trying to find where to contact eBay about these problems. Finally, I found a place to email eBay buried in the Suggestion Box. In other words, eBay doesn't encourage custom handling of user problems. Unfortunately, sometimes custom handling is the only way to solve problems.

In answer to my email, eBay told me that the ID Verify icon would be added to my eBay persona immediately but that it was my problem to get the erroneously filed feedback straightened out. Since the erroneous feedback is positive, I have no incentive to correct it. Were it negative, I would be incensed over eBay's unwillingness to take any responsibility.

Nonetheless, eBay is a great mechanism for buying and selling, and it does provide a variety of online customer service devices mentioned throughout this book. A very useful one is My eBay. The link *my eBay* is found above the navigation bar on every eBay page.

My eBay

My eBay is a customer service device that features the following:

- Bidding record
- Watch list
- Selling record
- Recent feedback
- Account status
- Favorite categories list
- Sign-in preferences

The records of your bidding and selling show what you've done on eBay. The watch list shows the auctions you've marked to watch.

Watching

In the basic information on each auction page, you will find a link labled watch this item. You can put any auction on your "watch" list. You can see your watch list in My eBay. The list helps you keep track of items in which you're interested but have not yet bid. When an auction starts to look interesting, you can join the bidding.

The recent feedback shows a partial record of your feedback. The account status shows how much, if anything, you have on deposit with eBay to pay your auction fees. It also can show a record of all your fees paid (going back to your first day, if you're willing to wait for the eBay database to crank out archived data). The favorites list gives you quick access to your favorite categories and saves you some navigation time. Try this. If you're a heavy eBay user, it can save a lot of time.

The sign-in preferences enable you to pick eBay devices for which you will not have to input your ID and password after you sign in. *This is especially valuable for automatically entering your ID and password for bidding; it saves time in bidding contests during the final minutes of an auction.*

Thus, My eBay provides you with convenient one-stop service to review your activities on eBay and even set up navigation and bidding shortcuts. Try the *my eBay* link over the navigation bar. You may find it's just what you've been looking for.

Anywhere

If your question is, Where can I access eBay? the answer is, Anywhere! Indeed, eBay even supports portable wireless devices including:

- WAP (wireless application protocol) phones
- Pagers
- PDAs (personal digital assistants)

This gives you the opportunity to keep up with your eBay commerce even when you're away from your home or your job. eBay's support for these technologies is through the normal vendors such as AT&T and Sprint. Go to eBay Anywhere (*http://www.ebay.com/anywhere*) to get specific information (see Figure 4.13).

Support for these devices means, of course, that as a buyer you never have to miss a final-hour bidding competition, nor as a seller will you miss answering questions by potential bidders in a timely manner.

Figure 4.13   eBay Anywhere.

Charity

Yes, eBay even provides you with opportunities for charity. Go
Community, charity. You will find fund-raising auctions sometimes
affiliated with celebrities such as Rosie O'Donnell.

Summary

Trust is the foundation of the eBay system. Once you understand
that and come to have confidence in the eBay system, you will feel
free to sell or bid and then complete eBay auctions. It's not a difficult system to use. But you must still be wary to protect yourself,
and eBay provides some optional devices that you can use to do so.

5

Bidding

Bidding is where the fun is. It's a kick to bid and win, particularly when you have some competition. But the fun is the frosting on the cake for most people. Most people seek to purchase an item because it's at a good price or because they can't find it elsewhere. And no matter how much fun it is, it's also serious business just as any commercial transaction is serious business. Hence, enjoy your bidding, but don't lose sight of the fact that the winning bidder is obligated to buy the item auctioned.

Bidding

There is a string of steps to go through to bid on an auction. The first step is finding something to bid on.

Finding What You're Looking For

You can use the eBay auction categories, which are organized into a tree, starting on the home page. This is perhaps the easiest way to find what you are looking for. The eBay search mechanism can be useful too.

Categories

Follow the categories from the most general on the eBay home page (or Browse page) to the more specific (see Figure 5.1).

When you get as far as you can go, look at the listings. You will find some items that you are looking for. For instance, to get to microphones, start with *Photo & Electronics* on the eBay home page. Then select *Consumer Electronics, Audio.* That will provide you with a listing of audio equipment. In many cases, you may find more items than you want to look through. You can narrow the search even further.

Searches

Once you get to a listing that contains the item you are looking for (e.g., audio equipment), you can plug a keyword into the search input and narrow the listings even more. For instance, while at the *Audio* listing, input *microphone.* Check *Search only in Consumer Electronics: Audio* (see Figure 5.2).

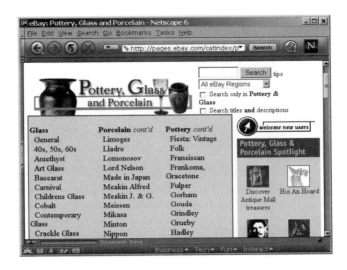

Figure 5.1   The eBay auction category *Pottery, Glass and Porcelain*.

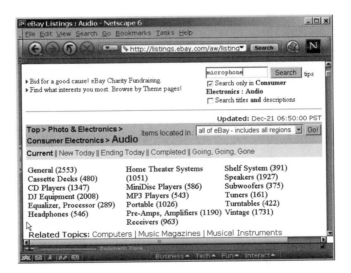

Figure 5.2   Using the search input to narrow the listings.

You will get a new listing of auctions that will be all microphones, or, to be more accurate, all the auctions in the listing will have *microphone* in the title (931 auctions the day I tried this search in December 2000—see Figure 5.3). To further refine the list, add *Shure* (a microphone brand) to the search keywords.

The result is a listing of 61 Shure microphones. You can refine your list with the search function as much as you want to. You don't necessarily have to do it in steps. Simply use several keywords at first (e.g., *microphone Shure*). That will get you to what you're looking for immediately. Try *microphone Shure new* to view only auctions that offer new Shure microphones.

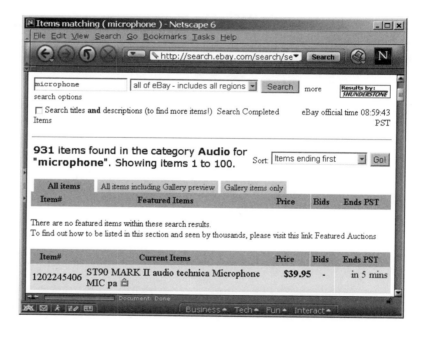

Figure 5.3   Using the search input for further search refinement.

eBay Search Tips

Sometimes the keywords for searches are obvious. Sometimes you have to figure out the not so obvious. And sometimes more than one keyword works. For instance, a microphone is also a *mic*. If you used mic as the keyword in the preceding search, you got 223 mic auctions.

Misspellings

Sellers misspell words. Sometimes if you try some misspellings, you can find items that don't get much traffic specifically due to the misspelling. For instance, if someone were to misspell *mic* as *mike*, few people would find it in a search. Even plural words can leave items out in the cold. For instance, if someone uses *microphones* instead of *microphone*, the items will not get as much traffic (only 34 auctions when searched at the same time as *microphone* and *mic*). If you can find items that are misspelled, you may find an auction with very little bidding competition.

Reading the Listing

Many sellers, surprisingly, can adequately specify what an item is in 45 words. Consequently, when you skim the list of auctions, you will be able to easily spot what you are looking for. Only the poor typesetting and bizarre titles will impede you. Auctions with photographs will have a picture icon beside the title.

New

You can have the listing arranged a variety of ways (e.g., ascending or descending based on closing date). New auctions have a new icon beside them. If you see the new icon at the top of the listing, you will know that the auction is arranged in descending order. However, the default is ascending order (oldest auctions first).

Reading the Auction

When you click on an auction title, the first thing you see is the basic information on the auction (see Figure 5.4). The basic information includes many links, which lead to more information.

The word *Currently* shows the current bid. This is accurate. (The bid amount in the listing for a particular auction title is often inaccurate—a delayed posting.) If you want to know the latest bid, refresh the auction Web page (use refresh button in browser) and look at *Currently*.

Figure 5.4   The basic auction information at the top of the auction Web page for an item.

Reserve

If the auction is a reserve auction, once the reserve has been met or surpassed, the term (reserve met) will appear beside the bid amount. Until that happens, the reserve has not been met and the caption will read (reserve not yet met).

The term *# of bids* shows the number of bids and links to information on the bidding. Try the *(bid history)* link to see a list of the bids in ascending order of amount bid. There will be no bid amounts shown by the bidders, however, until after the auction is over.

The word *Location* indicates where the seller lives or does business. That will determine whether you will have to pay sales tax if you win the auction.

The word *Seller* shows the seller. Click on the seller's alias and you will get a screen that provides the seller's email address, after you log in. Sometimes a seller's name is an email address (default name) in which case a click on the name will bring up your email client. After the seller's name is a link, in parentheses, to the seller's feedback rating. The term *(view comments in seller's Feedback Profile)* is a link to the seller's feedback too.

The term *(view seller's other auctions)* links to a Web page that shows all the current auctions that the seller operates.

Notice that the auction title and the auction number are at the top of the page.

Those are the highlights, but there is other information there too. Look around and check things out. But that's not all. Scroll down the page, and you will get to the auction ad. eBay provides space for an auction—a long one if desired by seller.

Auction Ad

The auction ad is whatever the seller wants it to be. See Chapter
13 for details. This is a seller's chance to provide all the information necessary to help the buyer make a decision to bid. As a bidder, this is your chance to get all the information you need to make
a decision to bid. If you don't get the information you need, you
have three choices. First, you can pass, as will many other potential bidders. Second, you can bid without proper information, a
choice you may regret. Third, you can contact the seller to get
more information. If you have considerable interest in an item,
contacting the seller is sometimes the only way you can get adequate information.

Making a Bid

At the bottom of the auction Web page, you can place a bid (see
Figure 5.5).

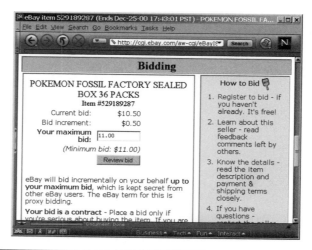

Figure 5.5   Bidding on the auction Web page.

By the input is the current minimum bid. Your bid must equal such an amount or be higher. Click on the *review bid* button when you are ready to submit your bid (see Figure 5.6).

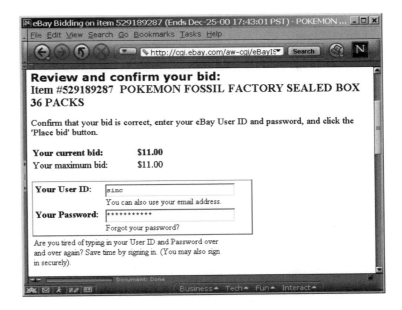

Figure 5.6   The bidding review page.

You need to input your alias and password before you finally submit your bid.

Sign In for Quick Bidding

In the upper right-hand corner of each eBay page, there's a sign-in link you can use to sign in for the duration of your eBay visit. Once you have signed in, you do not have to enter your ID again for the duration of your eBay session. But you will still have to enter your password wherever it's required on eBay unless you take the further step of setting your sign-in preferences. For whichever preferences you check under My eBay

Preferences, you will not have to provide your password during the current session. One preference is bidding, and not having to enter your ID and password for each bid can give you an advantage in the final minutes of a contested auction.

See Chapter 9 for the Double Window technique that saves additional time submitting bids.

Bidding Increments

The bidding increments are automatically enforced by the eBay system. See Table 5.1.

Table 5.1 Bidding Increments

Bid ($)	Increment ($)
to 0.99	0.05
1.00 to 4.99	0.25
5.00 to 24.99	0.50
25.00 to 99.99	1.00
100.00 to 249.99	2.00
250.00 to 499.99	5.00
500.00 to 999.99	10.00
1,000.00 to 2,499.99	25.00
2,500.00 to 4,999.99	50.00
5,000.00 and over	100.00

After All

After all this talk about bidding, sellers can now give you a fixed price too. Look for the "Buy It Now" icon (see Chapter 6).

After Your Bid

Chapter 9 provides much information on bidding, including strategies and tactics. After you bid, you will probably want to keep track of the auction in order to bid again or perhaps just to see the final outcome of the bidding.

Checking Your Email

When you bid, eBay sends you an email acknowledging your bid. This makes a good record. Don't discard it. You can find much information in this email message that you may need later.

Reviewing Your Activity

You get the best information—and the latest high bid—by refreshing the auction Web page. In fact, this is essential to do in the last minutes of competitive bidding for an item in order to keep up with the bidding. This is the only up-to-date source of the latest high bid.

Current Auctions

You can always check the record of the auctions you have bid on (that are still open) should you lose track because you are bidding on several items. Go to the *Search* page and search *Bidder Search* using your alias and password.

My eBay

Another place you can check is the more comprehensive record called My eBay.

Bidding

Go *my eBay* above the navigation bar. It features a record of your bidding. This is a good place to keep track of your bidding where other eBay convenient services are readily available.

Watching

eBay provides a way to make a list of auctions you want to keep track of but have not yet bid on. You put them on the watch list at My eBay. Thus, you can keep track of your bids and auctions you watch in one convenient place.

Being Outbid

As soon as you are outbid, eBay sends you an email message acknowledging you have been outbid. However, this is not a very good way to keep up with the bidding, particularly in the last hours of the bidding.

Winning the Auction

If you win the auction, eBay will send you a message informing you. Thereafter, it's up to you and the seller to get together to consummate the transaction.

Following Up

Traditionally, it's the seller who emails the high bidder to inform him or her of the details regarding payment and shipping. Nonetheless, if you don't hear from the seller in a timely manner, take the initiative to contact the seller. Keep following up until the transaction is completed.

Retracting a Bid

You can retract a bid if you desire, but you open yourself to negative feedback. You better have a pretty good excuse. Don't retract a bid. A little forethought will prevent unnecessary retractions. Go *Services, buying and selling, Buyer Tools, Retract my bid* for instructions on retracting your bid.

Optional eBay Bidding Features

This section mentions some of the eBay devices that are available to help you reduce your risk as a bidder.

Grading and Authentication

Although grading and authentication are not eBay services, they are services you can get from third parties and are well advised to do so in many cases. These processes require third-party experts and usually cost money. They are your best protection against receiving phony merchandise. If a collectible is worth more than you can afford to lose, have it authenticated before you pay for it.

A seller will usually take the position that he or she knows the item is authentic; thus, the buyer must pay for the authentication. Sometimes the seller will offer an authentication that's already been done. This may be acceptable, but be cautious.

Grading

Grading is simply the evaluation of the physical condition of a manufactured item. Unfortunately, grading is different for different items. You have to know the market for a particular item to understand the grading. Grading is subjective (in the eyes of the beholder). And grading is subject to honest mistakes and, yes, even to dishonesty. This all adds up to a situation where a buyer has to be very careful. Investigate carefully the condition of any item being auctioned.

Quality

For some items, grading is a determination of quality, not necessarily physical condition, and should by done by an expert.

Some other books about eBay pretend that there's an agreed grading scale on eBay. Don't believe it. Even if there were, most eBay users would not know exactly how to use it, and it would be unreliable. Always play the detective when it comes to ascertaining the condition of an auction item.

Authentication

Authentication is a process whereby an item is verified to be genuine (and in the condition represented). Is a Beanie Baby really a Ty Beanie Baby? Or, is it a forgery? A third-party expert verifies an item. A verification is an opinion by an expert and subject to being incorrect. Even experts make mistakes. If you are a collector or are buying jewels, for instance, authentication is your best protection against forged or phony items. Go *Help, rules & safety, authentication and grading* for a list of experts who provide authentications. Go to *http://makesureitsreal.com* for authentication of watches, diamonds, and jewelry and to review the website's authentication procedures. At eBay, go *Help, rules & safety, Authentication services.*

Verification

Verification is a means of establishing that an item is authentic in a way that "travels" with the item. For instance, suppose you have a

Ty Beanie Baby authenticated by an expert. How can you make that authentication stick with the Beanie Baby itself? One way is to put the Beanie Baby inside a plastic display case. The third-party authenticator seals the case with his or her unremovable seal attesting to the authenticity of the Beanie Baby.

The Switch?

Unfortunately, the following is a common scenario based on an actual case (not too long ago). A person buys a rare Beanie Baby via eBay for $1,800. She receives it, and it turns out to be a forgery (worth $3). She informs the seller. The seller says it was authentic when he sent it and will not refund the money.

This is a sad case. The seller may not have known that the Beanie Baby was a forgery. Now he has the buyer telling him that it is. How does he know that she didn't switch it with a forgery and is pulling an $1,800 scam? The buyer is stuck for $1,800. She doesn't know whether it was an honest mistake on the part of the seller or a scam. But it doesn't matter. She's the one who is stuck.

Is a prosecutor going to pursue this case? (See Chapter 8 for more discussion on remedies for fraud.) Probably not. The case may be impossible to prove, and the prosecutor will not waste taxpayer resources on such a weak case.

Authentication would have protected the buyer in this case. Authentication is best set up as part of an escrow arrangement. Yet, the buyer could have protected herself in another way. Suppose, instead of opening the package received from the seller, she took the package directly to her local Beanie Baby dealer (expert). There the package was opened by both of them together. The expert examined the Beanie Baby and found it to be a forgery. Now the buyer has a witness. Assuming the dealer has a good rep-utation, he or she will be a credible witness. The witness makes a much stronger case, and the seller may find it prudent to take back the phony Beanie Baby and refund the $1,800.

Appraisal

It's tough to decide whether to put a discussion of appraisal into the buyer's or seller's chapter because it can serve both. An appraisal is an estimation of value that usually includes an authentication. Naturally, the estimate of value has a date. Market prices go up and down. Thus, an appraisal is good for only a limited period of time. Certainly an appraisal can be valuable to a buyer who may need to rely on a third-party expert opinion of value and who needs authentication as well. Then too, a seller can use an appraisal as a selling tool to verify market value for prospective bidders and to provide authentication.

With over 4,000 catgories of items, a short list of appraisers in this book wouldn't make much of a splash. However, the following resources may be helpful:

> **eAppraisals** (*http://eappraisals.com*)
>
> **International Society of Appraisers** (*http://www.isa-appraisers.org*)
>
> **PriceRadar** (*http://priceradar.com*)

Unfortunately, it's sometimes difficult to determine whether an appraiser is qualified. Certainly, membership in specialty professional organizations that certify appraisers provides some credibility, but for many categories of items, there are no professional organizations. Always look into an appraiser's credentials.

Physical?

Generally, if there is no physical inspection of an item, an appraisal is merely an estimate of value, based on information the owner has submitted to the appraiser, and does not include authentication. For authentication, usually the appraiser must physically inspect the item. Keep in mind, in the absence of an inspection, the appraiser relies on the information the owner provides. As a buyer, you will want to know what that information was.

eBay Insurance

Currently eBay does furnish insurance free. The insurance covers up to a $200 loss ($25 deductible). It doesn't cover shipping damages or losses, only the nonperformance of seller after payment (e.g., seller fraud). This is a good program because it covers the inexpensive items where escrow would be relatively inconvenient. For the expensive items, eBay leaves the parties to make their own arrangements (e.g., escrow), which makes more sense for higher-priced items.

The insurance covers the case where the buyer does not get the auction item (after paying) that was described in the auction ad.

iEscrow

eBay—through a third party—provides escrow services. This is your best bet to protect yourself against fraudulent sellers. Don't send a check for an auction item that's more than you can afford to lose. Put the transaction in escrow instead. You then send the check to the escrow agent. The funds are held by the escrow agent until you have received and examined the auction item. If everything is satisfactory (as represented by the seller), you inform the escrow agent, and the funds are released to the seller. If not, then you can return the item to the seller and get your money back.

Is Escrow Enough?

If you review the scenario under the preceding The Switch? subsection, you will find that an escrow by itself could not prevent that situation. However, an escrow together with an authentication is the ultimate assurance that you will enjoy a successful transaction in which you are well protected. In such a case, you make arrangements acceptable to the seller to have an expert authenticate the item.

Personal Shopper

Try the eBay Personal Shopper; go *Search*, *personal shopper*. It will not only find what you're looking for but will also send you an email message informing you of every new auction that offers what you're looking for. This is a great tool for keeping an eye out for items that you want to buy. When you get the email, take a look and make a bid.

Illicit Merchandise

Sooner or later you will be presented with the opportunity to buy illicit merchandise. This is an opportunity you don't want to take. If you knowingly buy what you know to be stolen or pirated goods, you may be guilty of a crime in either your own state or the state in which the goods are offered.

In addition, such participation undermines the integrity of eBay. It's to your advantage to keep eBay a marketplace free of criminal activity. After all, as a buyer, you can get great bargains today and for many years in the future. Why would you contribute to activities that undermine the marketplace that provides you such an advantage? Avoid illicit merchandise, and preserve eBay as a corruption-free, long-term personal asset.

The tougher test comes, however, when you have illicit merchandise sent to you unknowingly. For instance, there are a lot of inexpensive CDs containing expensive software for sale on eBay. Many are legitimate, not pirated. Yet in one transaction, I bought a book via eBay (in a Dutch auction), and in the process of communicating with the seller, I was offered a copy of Adobe PhotoShop, an $800 program, an unspecified version on a CD, for just an additional $15. I had already bought legitimate expensive software (old versions) for very deep discounts on eBay (on CDs) just as I am able to do at local computer shows, so I accepted the offer without thinking much about it. When I received the book, the additional software (up-to-date version of the program) was on a recordable CD, not on a manufacturer's CD (i.e., the additional software was pirated). The seller maintains low visibility by not offering the pirated software on eBay. Rather she offers it via email in the course of arranging the payment and the shipping of the book for a winning bidder.

The hard question is, What do you do? This kind of practice is very troubling and is not healthy for eBay and its legitimate users. In this case eBay accepts reports. So, you can file a report directly with eBay. Look in the SafeHarbor area of the eBay website for information on filing reports. By the time I got around to researching how to report this illicit offer, however, the incident was a few months stale.

Then about a year later I bid on a version of Adobe PhotoShop in a current auction. Afterward I received a deluge of email from people offering to sell me current copies of the program for $15–$50 (undoubtedly pirated). This is called *bid skimming*. I went to eBay SafeHarbor, which provides current guidelines on reporting violations. As per instructions, I forwarded copies of the email solicitations to SafeHarbor. Once you learn what to do, it's easy to do it.

Procedures

eBay checks the skimming email to see if the perpetuators are registered with eBay. I was notified in every case except one (sender warned but not kicked off eBay) that they were not registered.

eBay suggested that I forward copies of the emails addressed to postmaster at the ISPs from which the emails were sent. I didn't think that would generate any result. But I did it anyway (easy and quick to do). It did produce results. I received an email from Yahoo! indicating that it had kicked a sender off the Yahoo! email service. Ironic that Yahoo! kicked off the offender but eBay gave only a warning to another offender.

I also forwarded the illicit email to support at Adobe and received an automated reply, which meant that such was a wasted effort. Then I tried to find an email address at the Adobe website where I might forward the illicit email. That was also a waste of time. Adobe provided only a long form for reporting piracy. It would have taken me an hour to fill out the form for all the incidents of the illicit email. So I declined. Thus, I ended up not getting through to the one organization that might have done something about it. Adobe ought to wake up.

Summary

Find what you're looking for. There are plenty of goods on eBay. Make your bids. The eBay system is easy to use. When you win an auction, follow up by taking some of the extra steps necessary to

reduce your risk. And make your payment promptly. You'll find
eBay to be a reliable source of things you need at reasonable prices.

6

Selling

The life of a seller is easier and more passive than that of a bidder, that is, until the follow-up. The follow-up is where the work is for sellers. This chapter covers the basics up to the follow-up. Chapter 11 also provides a considerable amount of information on follow-up (customer service).

The selling opportunities on eBay are unlimited because the buyers are so numerous and have such varied interests, and the market is continuous 24 hours a day, 7 days a week. But many sellers run auctions, and you will not find a lack of competition.

Prior Chapters

Chapters 4 and 5 include many basics about auctions at eBay. Such basics are not necessarily repeated in this chapter. Consequently, you need to read Chapters 4 and 5, too, to develop a firm understanding of eBay auctions.

Sellers (Auctioneers)

The first step toward becoming a seller is registering to be an eBay member. Only members can auction (sell) or bid (buy). Chapter 4 covers registration, which is the same whether you are a buyer or seller. The next step for sellers is arranging payment to eBay.

Payment Arrangements

eBay makes its revenue by charging sellers two fees. The first is the Initial Listing fee. The second is the Final Value fee based on the winning bid.

You arrange to pay eBay by giving your credit card number to eBay. Then eBay immediately attempts to authorize your card. Assuming your credit card is approved, eBay will bill you via credit card each month for the previous month's fees.

eBay requires a credit card in order to sell to:

- Ensure sellers are a legal age
- Ensure sellers are serious about auctioning
- Protect others from fraudulent or irresponsible sellers

If you do not have a credit card, you can alternatively use ID Verify to establish your identity. See Chapter 16. (eBay users registered prior to October 22, 1999, do not have to meet this requirement.) If you do not establish yourself with a credit card, you must pay in advance by check.

You calculate the Initial Listing fee based on the minimum bid or reserve amount according to Table 6.1.

Table 6.1 Initial Listing Fee

Minimum Bid or Reserve ($)	Listing Fee ($)
to 9.99	0.30
10.00 to 24.99	0.55
25.00 to 49.99	1.10
50.00 to 199.99	2.20
200.00 and up	3.30

The spreadsheet formula for calculating the Initial Listing fee amount is:

```
=IF(E5<10,0.3,IF(E5<25,0.55,IF(E5<50,
1.1,IF(E5<200,2.2,3.3)))))
```

In the spreadsheet, E5 is the cell where you enter the minimum bid or reserve amount.

You calculate the Final Value fee (cumulative) based on the high bid according to Table 6.2.

Table 6.2 Final Value Fee (Cumulative)

High Bid ($)	Fee
to 25.00	5%
25.01 to 1,000.00	2.5%
1,000.01 and over	1.25%

The spreadsheet formula for calculating the Final Value fee
amount is:

```
=IF(E8<=25,E8*0.05,IF(E8<=1000,((E8-
25)*0.025)+1.25,((E8-
1000)*0.0125)+25.625))
```

```
[Attributed to Eric Slone by author
Neil J. Salkind in eBay Online
Auctions.]
```

In the spreadsheet, E8 is the cell where you enter the high bid.
Note that the fee calculation is cumulative; that is, it's 5 percent on
the first $25, 2.5 percent on the next $975, and 1.25 percent on the
excess. For the total auction fees, add the Initial Listing fee and the
Final Value fee (see Figure 6.1).

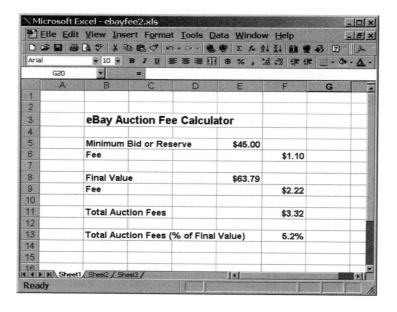

Figure 6.1   Spreadsheet calculates total eBay fees for running an auction.

Of course, you don't have to calculate these fees. eBay does it for you automatically and charges your account. The calculation formulas provided in the preceding paragraphs serve to educate you and provide you with a planning tool should you care to use it.

This is a general view of the eBay auctioning fees. There are additional special fees for special features.

Bold Title in bold. $2.00

Home Page Featured Auction placed in Featured section reached via the Browse button on the navigation bar. $99.95

Featured Plus Auction placed in Featured list at the top of the page in its category. $19.95

Highlight Auction title highlighted with yellow. $5.00

Gallery Auction goes into eBay photo gallery (must have photograph). $0.25

10-Day Auction Longest auction gets a surcharge. $0.10

Reserve Price For reserve price, there's a surcharge; refunded if item sells. $0.50 (under $25) and $1.00 ($25 and up)

For a more complex and complete review, go *Help, seller guide*.

Setting the Minimum

Before you submit your auction, you must determine a minimum bid. If you run a reserve auction, you must determine the reserve. These decisions require knowledge of the market for the item and, in particular, specific knowledge of the eBay market for the item.

One way to get this information is to research eBay auctions and past auctions. A survey of current auctions will tell you a lot. Use the survey of past auctions at the top of an auction listing under *Search Completed Items* to get a selection of completed auctions from which to derive market prices for items identical or similar to the one you will auction.

Additionally, you can research the list prices for consumer items you intend to auction. Many manufacturers have catalogs or price sheets going back many years now posted on the Web. See Chapter 5 for more ideas about research.

Research is a powerful means to get the appropriate information to set the stage for success. A price too high or too low will probably not achieve the purpose of auctioning your item for the highest bid possible. Research can help you set the price at an intelligent value.

Rating the Condition of the Item

It's your job as the seller to accurately evaluate the physical condition of the item being auctioned. Misrepresentation could lead to disputes.

As Is

There are legal ways in many states to sell merchandise as a seller and have no further obligation to the buyer (e.g., the "as is" sale). Those ways may work legally, but they may not work on eBay as a practical matter. (See a detailed explanation of "as is" in Chapter 11.)

You might get the impression from the verbiage in the auction ads on eBay that many sellers are selling merchandise "as is." So long as the merchandise works, there is no problem. But if something doesn't work and there's a resulting dispute, the dispute will be harmful to the seller regardless of the legalities.

The best advice is that if something doesn't work, don't sell it. If you choose to ignore this advice, at least indicate very clearly that the item doesn't work. Statements such as, "I don't know whether it works or not, sold as is," are an invitation to disaster. Statements such as, "Item doesn't work, being sold for parts," may be OK so long as they are promentently displayed.

Know the Market

Each item has a different market. Items within a certain market are often evaluated a certain way using certain terminology. Before you evaluate something, know the terminology. In many cases, you will have to know proper evaluation procedures too.

What's the penalty for ignoring proper evaluation? It might be a misrepresentation that carries liability. If you sell items outside your area of expertise, take a look at some of the auctions for identical or similar items on eBay to determine if there is special terminology or evaluation procedures you need to use.

Common Sense

Absent other terminology, use commonsense terms. Don't stretch the truth.

New This means *unused*, not *used only a little bit*.

Like new or **mint condition** This means *in perfect condition* and *used only a little bit*. If an item has been used more than *only a little bit*, it's not in mint condition unless it's a heavy-duty machine (e.g., auto).

Excellent condition This means *no blemishes and works perfectly*. The assumption is that this item has been used considerably.

Factory refurbished or **factory rebuilt** This means that the item has been unused since being overhauled at the factory into *like new* condition. These items are usually in a factory-sealed box. If the item has been used since coming from the factory, that fact should be disclosed.

Blemishes or malfunctions should be disclosed. A photograph is a good means of disclosing blemishes. If you disclose something, it's unfair for a buyer to complain about the very defect that you disclosed. If you don't disclose blemishes, defects, and malfunctions, you are begging for a disputed sale and negative feedback.

Keep in mind that there are buyers for all items in whatever condition. The potential bidders looking for new goods probably will not buy used goods. The buyers looking for used goods are bargain hunting and probably will not spend extra money for new goods.

Grading

By using commonsense words to describe the condition of an item, you may be inadvertently grading it. See the Grading section later in the chapter. Always provide further detailed explanation for the condition of an item that you auction on eBay, not just commonsense words, grading words, or grading abbreviations. Grading is best left to experts.

Entering an Auction

How do you do an auction? It's simple. You just input the information in the Seller's section on the eBay website. Go *Sell* in the navigation bar. Follow the instructions you find there (see Figure 6.2 for entry of auction information).

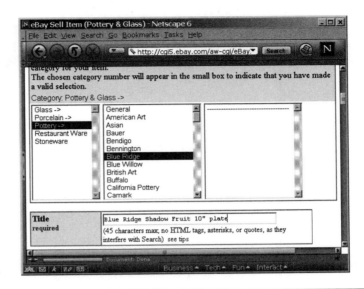

Figure 6.2   Enter an auction and and begin by specifying category.

Types of Auctions

Chapter 4 covers the types of auction (normal, reserve, Dutch, and private) you can run on eBay. You will have to pick one.

Input

You input all the basic information for your auction directly into the *Sell Item* form (see Figure 6.3).

Although the input is not burdensome, it takes time. If you run numerous auctions, the input requirements add up. You will start looking for a more efficient way of entering the auctions. Chapter 15 covers eBay bulk uploads.

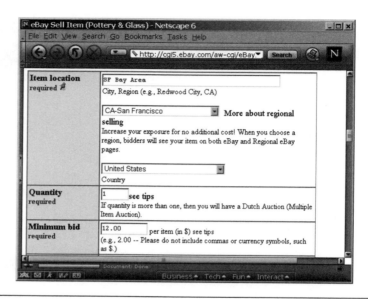

Figure 6.3   Entering auction information.

Length

You control when your auction ends by entering it exactly three, five, seven, or ten days earlier at the same time of day. Those are your choices. It seems to make sense to have your auction end at a busy time on eBay. Perhaps that will get a last-minute bidding frenzy going.

Auction Ad

One of the inputs is for the middle section of the auction Web page. This is the auction ad (*Description*—see Figure 6.4). This is your opportunity to sell your item. You should be well prepared ahead of time to enter the appropriate information here. Chapter 13 shows you how to make an HTML template (Web page template) to make your auction ads look professional. You can enter such a filled-in (completed) template in the Description input window in the form via copy and paste. (You can get free templates at *http://www.bookcenter.com*).

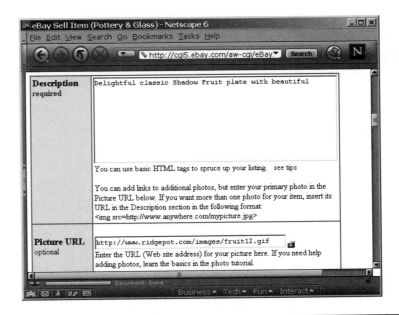

Figure 6.4   Auction ad (Description) input.

Photograph

Photographs sell goods. Chapters 12, 13, and 21 provide you with the skills and knowledge you need to successfully handle digital photographs for your eBay ads.

Bulk Upload

The ultimate time-saver for numerous auction ads is a bulk upload. eBay provides the Master Lister (bulk uploading procedure), and Chapter 15 provides you with a bulk uploading process that enables you to run many auctions with a minimum of effort.

Buy It Now

eBay gives sellers the option to charge a fixed price for their auction items as an additional feature to an auction, not in place of an auction. An icon indicating it's a "Buy It Now" item appears with the auction title, and the fixed price goes to the top of the auction page.

Sellers usually set the Buy It Now selling price higher than the initial bid. So long as no bids have been made, a bidder can elect to take the fixed price.

If the buyer has a credit card on file or has an ID Verify, the auction automatically terminates; the parties proceed to complete the purchase transaction at the fixed price. If not, the buyer is prompted to register a credit card or obtain the ID Verify. Once the buyer completes this procedure successfully, the auction automatically terminates. If a buyer does not or cannot qualify by registering a credit card or obtaining an ID Verify, the buyer cannot buy the item via the fixed-price procedure and will, instead, have to bid on the item.

If bidding has started, the fixed-price alternative is not available. This is a clever way of giving sellers a selling alternative without significantly altering the auction procedure. Combine this feature with the "Instant Purchase" feature enabled by Billpoint (see Chapter 16), and you have a powerful selling machine.

Counter

Many sellers have used counters on their auctions ads (auction Web pages) to determine how much traffic they get. That usually entails going to a counter website and following the procedures for installing a counter. eBay now offers a convenient alternative. You can elect to have an Honesty.com counter installed automatically when you enter your auction information for your auction ad. Go *Sell, Seller Services*. eBay does not charge for this device.

Authentication and Other Protections

Chapter 5 covers authentication and verification. Review that chapter before reading this section. Pay particular attention to the subsection The Switch? which outlines a situation as potentially devastating to the seller as it is to the buyer.

Authentication

Authentication protects sellers as well as buyers. If you have your item properly authenticated as part of an escrow arrangement, the buyer will have a difficult time claiming that you sold counterfeit goods. You can avoid the situation outlined in The Switch? by endorsing authentication for expensive items.

Verification

Use verification wherever possible. Make sure that the verification is accepted within the particular market for the item. For instance, for the Beanie Baby example in Chapter 5, there are a number of verification services on the Web. If someone wants to know about the particular verification that travels with the Beanie Baby, you can point to the verification website.

Grading

It is a mistake to think that there is some agreed grading scale on eBay. Different types of items have traditionally used different words and different grading scales. Never use abbreviations for grading. Many eBay users won't know what you are trying to communicate. Abbreviations are a convenience for you but are terrible customer service. Even words like "mint" and "excellent" do little to communicate properly except in the context of a particular commerce (e.g., antiques, stereo equipment, farm implements). The trouble is that different categories of items use different words or assign special meanings to commonsense grading words.

The better practice is to explain the condition of an item you auction. The explanation is more useful to potential bidders and won't eliminate those who do not understand the jargon or abbreviations for a particular type of item.

If you are determined to use grading, make sure the grader is an expert in regard to the item graded. That might be you or an appraiser you've hired to authenticate the item. Explain that the item is being graded according to traditional custom for such items. *And then also provide an explanation of the grading as well as the grading words or abbreviations.* Thus, every potential bidder is informed.

Appraisal

An appraisal can be a useful selling tool. It indicates market value for potential bidders and lends the authority of a third-party expert. Many appraisals also include authentication. See Chapter 5 for more information.

Shipping Insurance

Insurance that insures shipments against loss or damage is essential for both buyer and seller. If a package disappears or is damaged, who sustains the loss, buyer or seller? Who knows what the answer is to that legal question? It will depend on state law and the circumstances of the particular case. As a practical matter, however, the seller will probably sustain the loss. If not, the seller will surely get negative feedback. Don't try to split hairs here. Get insurance, or be prepared to be self-insured. Don't think the buyer (consumer) will sustain this loss.

On inexpensive items, self-insurance makes sense. For expensive items, buy the insurance. UPS automatically provides $100 insurance (minimum shipping charge is $5), and additional insurance is relatively inexpensive. US Postal Service insurance is relatively expensive. If you state your shipping policy as part of your auction ad, you can charge the entire cost of insurance (or half) to the buyer, although putting the responsibility for insurance on the buyer is probably not wise.

Receipt

Provide a receipt. Make sure it contains all the details of the sale, such as date, price, description of item, buyer's name, and shipping address. The receipt is a summary of the transaction. As such, it protects you as well as the buyer.

eBay Insurance

The insurance offered by eBay is insurance for fraud. Although free, the insurance does not necessarily benefit you. You know you're not fraudulent, and you don't need the insurance. But you have to keep in mind that such insurance is a customer service.

Escrow

An escrow transaction protects the seller as well as the buyer, as the example in The Switch? subsection (Chapter 5) demonstrates. You are asking for trouble if you don't use escrow transactions for expensive items. In contrast to the buyer, however, you have a different interest in the escrow arrangement.

Authentication and Escrow

Escrow without authentication is not important to sellers. It's like fraud insurance, and the seller does not need it. However, an escrow arrangement can provide sellers with protection against credit card charge-backs and fraud. Go *SafeHarbor, Escrow*.

Consequently, you have to ask yourself: Does this item require authentication? If the answer is no, then the escrow arrangement is not a priority for you as a seller.

As illustrated by The Switch? example, a Beanie Baby needs authentication. There are certainly plenty of counterfeit collectibles around. To do a transaction for an expensive collectible without escrow and authentication is asking for trouble. Nonetheless, there are plenty of items that don't really require authentication. For instance, does a factory-refurbished brand-name camcorder need authentication? Probably not. It will come in a factory-sealed box and is unlikely to be a counterfeit. For the buyer to claim it had been used or was a counterfeit would take a blatant act of fraud, which seems unlikely.

What about a used camcorder in excellent condition? Does that require authentication? Suppose the buyer claims it is in average condition and worth less? This is not a disaster as long as you have the serial number on record. Ask the buyer to return the item, and refund the purchase price. It's not like the Beanie Baby where the value goes from $1,800 to $3. Therefore, an escrow and authentication (that the camcorder is in excellent condition) may not be necessary from your point of view as the seller. However, suppose the buyer runs out and misuses the camcorder (out of ignorance) the first day he or she receives it. Now the camcorder is not in excellent condition any longer, and the buyer blames you. In this case, it is possible that the camcorder is permanently inoperable and worth little. To escrow and authenticate, or not? In this case, there's no easy answer, but raising the question at least makes you aware of the risk.

For expensive collectibles or even for expensive used appliances (are they in the condition specified?), an escrow together with an authentication will protect you as the seller as well as protect the buyer. For new or factory-refurbished items in sealed boxes, escrow and authentication may be unnecessary.

After You List the Auction

Once you have entered the input for your auction, you have nothing further to do. The bidding action is up to the bidders. You don't even have to watch. The auction will end three, five, seven, or ten days after you have entered it and at the same time. Only then do you have to follow up. In the meanwhile, you may get email from prospective bidders asking questions. If so, answer them promptly.

Retracting an Auction

You can retract an auction for which there are no bids at any time. Who are you going to irritate? Probably no one. If there are bids, however, you face a different procedure. You must cancel the bids. There is a specific procedure for canceling bids. The cancellation goes on your record and is subject to feedback. Naturally, if you don't have a legitimate reason for canceling, the feedback is likely to be negative. It might be negative in any event. Therefore, be very cautious about retracting auctions. It's probably not worth risking your reputation in most cases.

Auto Auctions

eBay Motors, in my opinion, should be an exception to the rule. A seller should not be allowed to retract an auction. Many potential bidders cannot make serious bids on autos without taking the time to prearrange financing and to develop strategies for making intelligent purchases in faraway cities. After making such preparations, to find an auction retracted is not fair. It wouldn't be so bad if this happened occasionally, but it seems to be the common practice of many used car dealers.

No Bids

When your auction runs its course and receives no bids, you lose the listing fee but do not have to pay the Final Value fee. If you want to run the auction again, you can take advantage of eBay's relisting policy for no additional fee. This policy, in effect, guarantees your success. However, you need to be reasonable in your offering as there is no further fee-free relisting after the second auction failure.

Relisting

When you relist an auction that received no bids, you can get back the listing fee if the auction is completed on the second try. When you're about to relist an auction for which there were no bids the first time, it's a good time to rethink the minimum bid or reserve. You may want to lower it a little.

You can relist any auction automatically without going through the process of entering it again. This is a convenient service when you auction the same goods on an ongoing basis.

Follow-Up

Follow-up is the most important role of the seller. After all, you must contact the buyer and arrange payment. Then you must ship the item.

Accounting

Losing track of your auctions? You'd better get things under control, or you will start to self-destruct. That will invariably result in negative feedback. This subsection covers two devices eBay provides to you to keep track, but you will need an offline system as well. See Chapters 14, 15, and 18 for ideas on how to build an offline system with a desktop database that will keep you efficiently organized.

Seller Search

Input your own alias and password in *Seller Search* (via the *Search* link), and you will get a list of all your current auctions. This can be quite handy.

My eBay

Access My eBay, at *my eBay* over the navigation bar, and you will
get a record of all your selling and bidding activities on eBay. This
is an even more complete record than the Seller Search that you
will find useful. My eBay also includes recent feedback, your eBay
account records, a list of favorite categories, and your sign-in preferences. Thus, it makes a great place to hang out on eBay, a place
where you have a lot of convenience at your fingertips.

Customer Service

Chapter 11 covers customer service thoroughly. The fact that customer service occupies its own chapter instead of a section in this
chapter indicates its importance. Your success as a retailer on eBay
will ride on the quality of your customer service. Even for casual
sellers, the quality of your customer service will directly affect your
eBay reputation. Customer service is not an activity to take lightly.

When an Auction Is Not a Sale

Why would someone want to hold auctions on eBay yet not necessarily want to make a sale? Advertising! eBay makes a viable
advertising medium. If you pay $2 to run an auction for a week
and get 100 hits on your auction ad, those are 100 people presumably interested in what you have to sell. They're hot prospects.
That's pretty cost-effective advertising even if you never sell anything in the auction. (See Chapter 17 for more on using eBay for
advertising.)

Indeed, what many retailers do is to use a hybrid strategy. They
offer one product a week at a serious discount as a draw to their
auction ad. They sell the product at a profit (or perhaps at a loss),
but the effort is not really a selling effort. It's essentially advertis-

ing. As mentioned earlier, a similar strategy can even be effective for advertising services that are difficult to sell via an eBay auction.

Then there are those who want to find out what the market is for a particular class of merchandise. What better way than to sell one item on eBay. In this case, the item is sold, but the act of auctioning is essentially for the purpose of appraisal, not necessarily to make a profit.

Real Estate

Real estate auctions receive special treatment on eBay. First, real estate auctions are not binding. Second, such auctions have a special insertion fee: $50. There is no final value fee.

Summary

Auctioning merchandise is as simple as inputting information into a form at the eBay website and including an auction ad (*Description*). You must arrange payment to eBay also (for the auction). Read Chapter 14 for more details on conducting eBay auctions.

The more laborious task is the follow-up: arranging payment and shipping the goods.

7

Reputation

Reputation is often a subtle thing. A bad reputation doesn't keep you from doing business. Many business transactions are straightforward and essentially risk-free for each party. For instance, in an office supply store, you hand your $235 to the person at the counter, and you get a fax machine. The transaction is direct without much risk on either side.

However, if a transaction requires trust, a bad reputation is a detriment. For instance, suppose you take delivery of the fax machine but pay the $235 for it in installments over a six-month period. The seller has to trust you to make the payments. If you have a bad reputation (a bad credit rating), the seller will not make this arrangement with you.

Or, suppose you pay the $235 to the seller, who promises to order the fax machine and deliver it to you as soon as it comes from the manufacturer next week. You have to trust the seller. If the seller has a bad reputation, you will probably not agree to pay for the fax machine until it is delivered.

eBay transactions require trust. eBay sellers and buyers need good reputations. The idea of an international marketplace with a transaction mechanism that works well is great, but it won't work unless the buyer feels confident that he's going to get the Sony camcorder for which he was the winning bidder when he sends his $675 check to the seller. Why would anyone send a check to another person he or she doesn't know hundreds (or thousands) of miles away? For eBay, the answer is the eBay reputation system, the Feedback Forum. This is the heart and soul of the eBay system. This is the firm foundation on which the whole eBay transaction process rests.

eBay Feedback System

How does eBay establish reputations for its sellers and buyers? Simply, it enables sellers and buyers to rate each other. The ratings are simple: positive, neutral, and negative.

In addition, sellers and buyers can make comments. These comments are often fluffy praise resulting from a successful transaction. When they are not fluff, however, they can provide useful information of interest to the eBay community.

Positive, Neutral, Negative

Some scenarios follow that illustrate how you might enter feedback based on your eBay transaction experiences. These are solely my opinion. Everyone will have their own notions about the feedback that the other party deserves. I think, however, that you have to be reasonable.

For instance, suppose you are on eBay almost every day to pursue your hobby of collecting antique mirrors. You buy a mirror, send a check to the seller, but don't receive the mirror immediately. Understandably, you get frustrated. The seller, however, happens to be a person who works long hours every day at a demanding job and only frequents eBay on the weekend as an occasional buyer or seller. She tends to think of eBay as a weekend activity. She gets your check and subsequently finds out on a Monday that the check has cleared. In all likelihood she is not going to get around to shipping the package until Saturday. Is this unreasonable? Not for her. But if she were a person operating a retail business on eBay instead, it would be an unreasonable delay. Thus, reasonableness must be determined in an overall context.

Positive

Transactions often run into problems and are not always on time. *A positive performance by the other party is one that completes the transaction within a reasonable time (not necessarily on time) and according to the terms of the agreement (as defined by the auction offering).* Often the terms of the agreement may be subject to some additional negotiation based on some reasonable circumstances.

Seller Enters a Positive

A buyer says he sent a check the day after the auction, but when the check gets to the seller, the envelope shows a postmark a week after the auction. Give the buyer a neutral or negative rating? No. Whenever a transaction is consummated, rate the other party positive unless there is a compelling reason not to do so. A check sent a week late is not a compelling reason.

Buyer Enters a Positive

The seller represents that he will charge the winning bidder $20 for shipping and handling. The buyer pays the bid plus $20. When she gets the product, she notices that the package has a UPS charge of $5 on it, not $20. She complains to the seller, but the seller won't budge. Give the seller a negative rating? No. Whenever a transaction is consummated, rate the other party positive unless there is a compelling reason not to. The buyer has a right to complain perhaps, but it doesn't make sense to quibble with a charge that was stated before the auction was closed.

Note that shipping and handling are different from just shipping. Handling does cost money; it's not free. If a seller states in advance a charge for shipping and handling, it's not the basis for neutral or negative feedback that the buyer thinks the shipping and handling charge is too much based on a low shipping charge. The shipping charge is just a portion of the total shipping and handling.

Neutral

Even when the transaction closes, a party may have caused so much distress that he or she does not deserve a positive rating. *A neutral performance by the other party is one that completes the transaction but not without a good deal of seemingly unnecessary frustration-causing behavior.*

Seller Enters a Neutral

Here the story is the same as earlier (see Seller Enters a Positive) except that the buyer takes three weeks (instead of one week) before sending the check. The transaction closes, but the seller doesn't receive the check until almost a month after the auction ends. Give the buyer a neutral or negative rating? It depends. Perhaps a neutral rating. If the buyer had some problems with making the payment but kept the seller informed, a neutral rating is probably not appropriate. If the buyer kept putting off the seller with misrepresentations or no responses, a neutral rating may be justified.

Buyer Enters a Neutral

The seller represents that he will charge the winning bidder a reasonable shipping fee (handling is not mentioned). The transaction closes. The seller charges $20 and ships the product in an old cardboard box stuffed with newspaper. The buyer (high bidder at $45) sees the UPS charge of $5 on the box and complains about the $20 shipping charge. The seller won't budge. Give the seller a neutral or negative rating? Probably not a negative rating. After all, the buyer could have tried to pin down the shipping fee via email before the auction was over, but she did not do so. Nonetheless, it looks as if the seller is attempting to augment his profit by unexpected gouging on the shipping charge. That perhaps deserves a neutral rating.

Negative

Negative ratings should be reserved for situations where the transaction is not consummated or grievous problems remain unresolved indefinitely or for a long period of time. *A negative performance by the other party is one that does not complete the transaction, completes it only after a long delay, completes it only after causing a great deal of aggravation, or completes it according to different terms than defined by the auction offering.*

Seller Enters a Negative

Here the story is the same as earlier (see Seller Enters a Positive) except that after several promises to pay, which extend the transaction for three weeks, the buyer finally admits that he cannot scrape together the money to pay for the product. Give the buyer a negative rating? Whenever a transaction does not close based on the irresponsible behavior of one of the parties, a negative rating is appropriate. The buyer should not have bid without the capacity and willingness to pay the winning bid, and now he deserves a negative rating.

Buyer Enters a Negative

The seller represents that he will charge the winning bidder a reasonable shipping fee but nothing for handling. The seller asks the buyer (high bidder at $45) to pay $20 to ship the product (lightweight and not fragile) via UPS ground. The buyer contacts the seller to complain about the high cost of shipping but never refuses to complete the transaction. The seller immediately reenters the item into eBay for another auction. Give the seller a negative rating? The seller not only is gouging on the shipping but is apparently unwilling to be responsive to or to negotiate the buyer's legitimate complaint. The transaction is not completed due to the seller's unreasonable behavior; he deserves a negative rating.

No Rating

There is no requirement that a seller or buyer must give the other party feedback. Unfortunately, failure to do so sometimes undermines the system. If a transaction does not reflect adversely on either party and no feedback is entered, I suppose the system can survive without the information about that transaction. Indeed, such cases are the norm not the exception, as many parties are too lazy or distracted to enter feedback. When a rating would be adverse to a party, however, and the other party (the offended party) does not enter it, that is an irresponsible act. For instance, suppose a seller operates a bait-and-switch scam. He offers one item of merchandise but substitutes another of inferior quality. A failure on the buyer's part to report such an offense via feedback undermines the system, particularly when it turns out that the seller is routinely unfair to other parties.

Special Cases

There will always be special cases where the transaction did not close because the seller and buyer agreed that it should not close. Suppose the seller auctions a model MX54-A (chain saw). After the auction the seller informs the buyer that he has made a mistake. He has only the model MX54-C, which looks the same but is generally worth 35 percent less. He offers the different model to the buyer for the bid price less 40 percent and offers to ship it for free. The buyer decides not to close the transaction (not to buy the substituted item). Should the buyer provide feedback on the seller?

If the seller has made an honest mistake, there's no reason to rate him or her negatively. After all, in the above case the seller seems to have offered the buyer a favorable deal to atone for his "mistake." In such a case, assuming she believes the seller, the buyer will probably not enter feedback. Probably in most cases where the seller and buyer agree not to complete the transaction, no feedback is reported.

Unfortunately, feedback should be reported in such a case. It can be valuable to fellow eBay patrons, not for its rating value (e.g., neutral) but for its commentary. For instance, in this case, the buyer can rate the seller neutral but also include the following facts:

Proper comment: He mistakenly did not have the item but made a reasonable offer to substitute.

If the mistake was sincere, this rating will not hurt the seller. If the mistake was routine, ratings like this will eventually expose the seller as a careless or shady operator.

Comments

Using positive, neutral, or negative feedback provides little information. Only a straightforward comment will make any sense out of a rating. Just stating the facts will give your comment the maximum impact it deserves.

Negative or Neutral Feedback

Always just state the pertinent facts. Don't make any judgmental, accusatory, or speculative comments. If you do, you may be wrong, and you may lose credibility with other eBay members, presumably just the opposite of what you want to do.

If you make a judgmental, accusatory, or speculative statement, you may be defaming the other party, thus incurring legal liability. It's almost impossible to have all the facts you need to be on legally sound grounds to make such a statement. But you can state the facts as you know them. The truth is always a defense to defamation. If you stick to the facts that you know, you will make it impractical for someone to challenge you legally, and a lawsuit will be unlikely. Fairness also dictates that you cool down and determine what the facts really are before you make comments about someone.

The facts will be more damning in any event. Anytime you make an opinionated negative statement about someone else, people take it with a grain of salt. But facts are facts, and people pay attention to facts.

Improper comment (about seller): He intentionally aggravated me by taking far too much time to ship the vase.

Proper comment: He didn't ship the vase until 25 days after he received my money order.

Improper comment (about bidder): This gal's a deadbeat who needs a psychiatrist to get herself straightened out.

Proper comment: She promised to pay during three weeks after the auction but never did.

Improper comment (about seller): This lowlife tried to triple his profit by gouging me on the shipping.

Proper comment: He asked a huge shipping fee, refused to negotiate, and quickly killed the deal.

eBay provides you with only 80 characters (about 15 words) to make your statement. So, make it concise and factual. Save the expletives for telling the story to your friends.

Positive Feedback

Probably most positive feedback doesn't mean much. Just to give someone a positive rating is enough if the transaction went well. You will see a lot of fluffy praise among the comments for positive ratings. Here again facts speak the loudest. Just state the facts.

Improper comment (about bidder): Winning bidder is the greatest. Will do business again.

Proper comment: Winning bidder paid promptly and was pleasant to deal with.

The improper statement boosts the bidder's ego, which is fine. Nothing wrong with that. And it does convey the message that the bidder did something right. But it doesn't tell us much. The proper statement has more impact because it's factual. Incidentally, the improper statement sounds canned, which it probably is.

Informational Feedback

Occasionally, the use of a comment is primary, and the rating is much less important. In the earlier Special Cases subheading example, the seller made a mistake and didn't have the item auctioned. He made an offer to sell a similar item at a good price and pay the shipping. On one hand, if the seller is sincere, you don't want to give him a negative rating. Even a positive rating might be justified. On the other hand, if he's a con artist pulling the old bait-and-switch trick, you would want to give him a negative rating. You don't know for sure which he is. So, give him a neutral rating. Here the comment you make is more important than the rating, and the comment must be factual to be of use to anyone.

Proper comment: He mistakenly did not have the item but made a reasonable offer to substitute.

When people look at this comment together with all the other comments, they will get a more accurate picture of the seller. If this is an anomaly, people will excuse it. If together with other comments it shows a pattern of undesirable behavior, people will catch on quickly.

Fairness

You can give a neutral or negative rating without making a comment, but fairness requires that you give a good reason to substantiate neutral or adverse feedback. If you cannot give a good reason (state a fact or set of facts), then you should rethink why you are giving a neutral or negative rating.

Communication

Always attempt to work out any differences with the other party. Direct communication works well for resolving problems. Get the other party's phone number and address immediately after an auction is over. Call, write, or email him or her. Get the problems resolved.

Probably most adverse ratings result from a lack of communication or from one party's total failure to communicate. Make sure you aren't such a party. When the other party attempts to contact you, respond in a timely manner. When there's a problem, initiate communication.

Making a neutral or negative rating is not a way of motivating the other party to live up to his or her agreement. It is a way of warning eBay patrons that you couldn't work things out with the other party because he or she was unfair, unreasonable, or fraudulent. Never threaten the other party with an adverse rating as a negotiation ploy (blackmail?). Reasonable people do not threaten others, and if your threat is reported, it will make you look like the bad guy. Reporting negative feedback is not the last resort. Negative feedback is what you report after you've reached the last resort to get the transaction completed and the transaction continues to have problems.

People make mistakes. In a transaction, reasonable people work together to minimize the impact of a mistake on each party. If that can't be done before the transaction takes place, reasonable people walk away and get on with their lives. Getting angry at the other party doesn't serve much purpose. (By definition a mistake is unintentional.) If the mistake happens beyond the point of no return in a transaction, reasonable people understand that life is full of risks and try to work out the best solution to the problem. Assume the other party, in your transaction, is reasonable until specific facts indicate the contrary. If you do so, communication will serve you well when your transactions run into problems.

Few eBay transactions end up with the parties unreconcilable or involve fraud where one party disappears. Yet one must assume that many eBay transactions run into problems. When people communicate, the problems get solved.

Negotiation

The interesting thing about eBay is that the auction process takes all the negotiation out of making a deal. Otherwise, a third of this book would have to be devoted to negotiation. Nonetheless, problems sometimes arise. Solutions must be negotiated. Communication gets the negotiation done. But you have to be careful in your communication when you negotiate. Always keep things open. Never close off communication with unproductive statements like "Take it or leave it." Never stop keeping an open mind; never stop looking for a solution.

Name-Calling

Some people deserve to be called names because they act so badly. Still, you can never let communication degenerate into a name-calling session. The only reason to communicate with someone you don't know who lives far away is to complete the auction transaction. Name-calling will bring an end to the communication and is self-defeating. Reasonable people don't resort to name-calling.

Anger

When a transaction becomes frustrating usually due to the other party's abject stupidity or felonious behavior, you can get pretty mad. Never take any action against the other party in the heat of the moment. You will surely regret it. Cool off first. Then do something rational. If the other party deserves the "worst", you will be better able to administer the "worst" when you are rational. If it turns out that the other party really isn't that bad, you will save yourself some grief or guilt and will certainly save yourself from looking vengeful.

Public Record

The feedback ratings and comments are public record. Anyone using eBay can see them anytime. The ratings are set in concrete. Once made, you cannot change them. You can add information to them later, but you cannot change them. They remain in the public record permanently for all to see. Consequently, a bad reputation on eBay will probably hurt you more in regard to eBay than a bad reputation where you live will hurt you in regard to your locale. Your reputation is always just a click away from anyone who wants to know what it is.

The great genius of this system is that eBay doesn't care about anyone's reputation. eBay is just there to make a permanent public record of it. If you're a big eBay customer, eBay doesn't care. If it's your first time on eBay, eBay doesn't care. eBay is just there to publish the reputations in a public record, and it enables the sellers and buyers to make or break each other's reputations.

eBay Action

If your feedback rating reaches a –4 (positives plus negatives), the eBay system will automatically shut you down as a member. You can have your case reviewed, but you may be out of business on eBay permanently.

On the Positive Side

If you accumulate positive feedback, you earn stars, which go beside your name (see Figure 7.1).

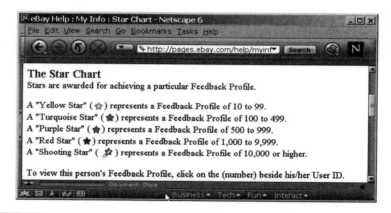

Figure 7.1   eBay Star Chart.

It's Your Reputation

Is your reputation on eBay artificial? Is it more like an attribute in a digital game than the real thing? Can you break your agreements with impunity and walk away without consequences? If you develop a bad reputation on eBay, can you just erase the entire experience? Can you be sure your eBay reputation won't spread beyond eBay? The answer to these questions is no.

Your reputation on eBay is perhaps more real than your offline reputation. After all, it's more accessible to everyone. It's the real thing. But how can a bad reputation on eBay hurt you in the world outside eBay? That's easy to answer. What's to prevent your banker from looking up your reputation on eBay before he or she loans you $23,000 for a new car? Nothing. In fact, a smart banker might do just that. (Will your alias on eBay be a question on future loan applications?) Look at eBay as another credit bureau. Your reputation on eBay is not something to take lightly.

It's Their Reputation

Reputation is not a problem for you because you're a good person who is honest, honors agreements, and treats others fairly. The good news is that the eBay feedback system protects you against all the creeps who deserve bad reputations and get bad reputations on eBay just as they do offline. The system works for you, and you have a vested interest in maintaining the integrity of the system and making it work.

The system relies on you to *tell it like it is*. This means that you must give people a negative or neutral rating when they deserve it just as you are willing to give people a positive rating when they perform as they are obligated to perform. By failing to give negative or neutral ratings when deserved, you undermine the system.

The retailers on eBay who are also retailers offline understand reputation. They know that reputation is everything when it comes to selling online or offline. They have built their businesses on their reputations. Ironically, many are reluctant to give adverse ratings to buyers who abuse them. Their reasoning is that a bad rating given to a buyer who doesn't honor his or her agreement to purchase may result in retaliatory negative feedback. Thus, an aborted transaction can potentially hurt an innocent retailer perhaps more than a guilty buyer who doesn't care about reputation. This is an unfortunate weakness in the system, but the system has survived in spite of it.

This situation is not limited to retailers. Almost anyone of goodwill who cares about his or her reputation will be reluctant to post negative feedback on the other party. This natural propensity warps the entire feedback system.

On one hand, if you see a retailer who has 79 positive ratings and 2 negative ratings, it most likely reflects a normal situation. You can't please everyone no matter how hard you try. It's likely that those 2 negatives represent people who will never be happy.

On the other hand, if you see someone on eBay who has 10 positives and 6 negatives, it seems probable that the warp is present. For each negative rating, there were probably one or more additional parties who should have given a negative rating but didn't. A person who has a substantial number of negative ratings is suspect, particularly when the ratio of negative to positive is high.

Indeed, when a person gets to a feedback rating of −4 (adding together both positive and negative feedback), eBay will terminate his or her membership.

How the System Works

The system invites you to enter ratings on the people with whom you've done business in regard to an eBay auction. To access the reporting section, go *Services, feedback forum* (see Figure 7.2).

Check the appropriate radio button to choose a rating. Then enter a comment in the input below.

Write your comment on a piece of paper offline before entering it as part of the rating. That will allow you plenty of time to avoid making a blunder you might regret. Remember the rating and comment will be there forever, and you cannot change them.

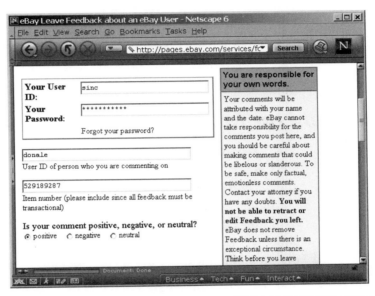

Figure 7.2   Leaving feedback.

Comment on a Rating

Occasionally, you will need to comment on a rating you've already posted. This is permitted by eBay, but it's an addition to the posted rating, not in place of it. Such a comment also becomes part of the permanent public record.

Comment on the Other Party's Rating of You

If someone makes an adverse comment about you, you can answer it. Never answer when you're mad. Cool down and carefully draft an answer. Follow the advice in the next section; just state the facts.

If the adverse comment by the other party is justified, you may be better off not making any comment. If you're guilty as charged but have a reasonable excuse, admit the charge but state why you felt you were justified in doing what you did. This will at least show you to be a reasonable person.

Comment on Your Rating of the Other Party

There will be times when you want to comment on the other party after you've already commented once. Suppose you're the seller and accepted a credit card for payment of the item sold. You rated the buyer positive for paying promptly. Later the buyer asks his bank for a charge-back on the credit card based on a complaint about the item bought. The buyer never contacted you to discuss the problem, if there really was a problem.

This is a situation where the buyer may be attempting to beat you out of payment for the item. If you can't get the matter straightened out with the buyer, you may want to add a comment onto the original rating you made explaining what happened after you thought the transaction had been completed.

A follow-up comment need not always be negative. Suppose you are the buyer in the Buyer Enters a Negative subsection earlier. Your negative rating of the seller catches the seller's attention. The seller tells you that the reason the shipping cost is so high is because a large set of batteries is included with the item and has to be shipped separately, a situation of which you were not aware.

You complete the transaction and receive the batteries as well as the item. At this point, it's reasonable to add a favorable comment to your original negative rating.

Bickering

Is it possible for the parties to bicker back and forth with add-on comments to the original ratings? I suppose it is, but it usually makes both parties look like a couple of loonies. Never attempt to answer the other party's add-on adverse comment. Just let it go if you have nothing new to add. It has to stop somewhere. Sometimes broken transactions get to the point where the best thing to do is just move on. People looking at the public record of your ratings and comments can read between the lines very skillfully. If you have conducted yourself reasonably in a transaction, that fact will probably emerge from the comments, even if the other party has the last word. Don't risk your reputation (and your sanity) by getting into a bickering contest.

Public or Private

You can choose to make your feedback public or private. Why would you do business with a person who kept his or her feedback private? Why would anyone do business with you, if you keep your feedback private?

Liability for Defamation

eBay's permanent public record of feedback will generate lawsuits. If you make false or derogatory statements about someone, you may find yourself at the wrong end of a lawsuit. However, truth is always a defense. As long as you make factual statements in your feedback, your risk of being sued is small. So, if you find yourself heading for the feedback section on eBay very angry at someone, you'd better stop and cool off before you type in something you'll regret later.

Evaluating a Person's Reputation

It's easy and quick to evaluate a person's reputation. Just read his or her ratings. Start with the negative ratings. Then read some of the positive ratings. You will probably get a good idea pretty quickly of whether you want to do business with the individual.

Buyers Beware

When reading negative ratings, I am always struck by how many seem to be about high bidders who just didn't understand their obligations and made unreasonable demands on the sellers, mostly out of ignorance. That leads me to advise that if you're a buyer, read the auction ad carefully, and don't complain if a careless reading gets you into a bind.

To fine-tune your analysis of a buyer or seller, pay attention to the percentage of transactions that are auctions and the percentage that are purchases. Then look specifically at the feedback for each. It's possible that a person can be a great seller but a lousy buyer, or vice versa.

If you're a buyer, remember that you're going to send the seller a check. The risk of the transaction is yours. If the seller is not reputable, you're the one who's out the cash. However, this is something you must decide before you bid. Reviewing the seller's reputation and refusing to pay after you've won the bidding will expose you to a justifiable negative rating.

If you're a seller, remember that if the buyer doesn't pay, you will waste your time and energy and become frustrated. In the end, you will have to put the item up for auction again with the requisite delay in selling the item. Also, remember that you don't have to sell to anyone so long as you have an acceptable reason. You may have to state that reason in response to feedback to defend yourself. If the winning bidder has a poor reputation, you can sell to the next-highest bidder. Should you decide to do so, however, you should advise the winning bidder of your reasons and remind him or her of your right to refuse a sale. Be tactful. Keep in mind also that the second-highest bidder has no obligation to buy.

SafeHarbor

eBay's SafeHarbor program exists to ensure that buyers and sellers can carry on commerce with the confidence that they will not experience an unreasonable level of the risk of fraud. The Feedback Forum, eBay's reputation program, is part of the SafeHarbor program. Take a look at the SafeHarbor program to see what else is there. Go *SafeHarbor* in the links at the bottom of any eBay Web page, or go *Services, safeharbor*.

Conclusion

This chapter deals with a lot of negative situations. Does that mean they're all going to happen to you sooner or later? Not necessarily. Most transactions resulting from eBay auctions close sooner or later despite occasional neglect or slow performance by one or the other party. Most people are reasonable, communicate competently, and have the skills to conclude a long-distance transaction. Most deals close, and presumably the parties walk away happy. eBay is a great way to sell stuff and buy stuff. But as for every public activity, there are rules of conduct. When a person flagrantly violates those rules, the eBay community should be warned about such an individual.

8

Reporting and Recourse

Report to eBay on your transactions, and ask the other party to report on you. That's how you build up your eBay reputation. Most transactions go smoothly, and this is your chance to pat the other party on the back and receive the same in return. Occasionally, however, transactions go bad. Chapter 7 covers eBay reputation and feedback, and this chapter doesn't repeat that information. This chapter reports on what else you can do to deal with the other party if you are not treated fairly or are a victim of fraud.

Most People Are Honest, But ...

Most people are honest, but occasionally a real loser comes along and grabs your money (or merchandise) and runs. There have been scams in the past on eBay. There are scams today. There will be scams in the future. Kind of reminds you of real life, doesn't it? Well, cyberlife ain't what it used to be.

If You Are a Bidder

How can you get taken? Let me count the ways:

1. Merchandise damaged in shipment
2. Merchandise lost in shipment
3. Defective merchandise
4. Merchandise not in the condition represented
5. Merchandise substituted without your approval
6. No merchandise delivered

A few of these you should foresee and take the necessary precautions. For instance, merchandise lost or damaged in shipment can be covered by insurance.

If You Are a Seller

What can happen? After all, presumably, you control the transaction by withholding the merchandise until payment has been assured. But there are a four things:

1. Insufficient funds for a check. You can get a report about a person's checking account (whether there has been prior trouble), but you will never know whether there are sufficient funds until the check clears.

2. Credit card charge-back. Any buyer can have his or her credit card bank nullify a purchase for good reason within a 90-day period. Many banks extend that period up to a year.

3. Forged or phony financial instrument (e.g., money order).

4. Shill bidding (see below).

Usually, prior trouble with a bank account warns you about a bad check; but when there is no prior trouble, you can still get stung when there are insufficient funds to cover your check. If a buyer does a charge-back on his or her credit card, you may have trouble getting your money or even getting the merchandise back. Then, of course, there's always a problem with stolen credit cards. Forged financial instruments are a large problem offline. Online, where forgers are easier to trace, it's not such a large problem; but beware.

Fraud Online

Interestingly enough, although fraud rates are about the same online as offline, more criminals get caught online than offine. They are simply easier to trace online.

Shill Bidding

Shill bidding can be collusion between two or more bidders working an auction. Online, it can be one bidder working with two ISP (and eBay) accounts. Unfortunately, this probably happens more than anyone is willing to admit. If you suspect shill bidding, report it to eBay.

Adverse to Buyers

Shill bidding affects bidders when the seller (with two ISP and eBay accounts) is bidding up the price on an item. This is illegal and not permitted by eBay. Nonetheless, many people have a second or third ISP account (and eBay account). A seller with more than one eBay account can bid up an item without being discovered. If you have good reason to think this is happening, report it to eBay.

Adverse to Sellers

Shill bidding affects a seller when the first bidder bids up the item to a high price to smoke out the reserve amount (the lowest price you are willing to accept) and to preempt honest bidders. The first bidder then retracts his or her bid late in the auction. The second bidder (who can be the same person using a different account) then bids slightly over the reserve. You are left with the second bidder's lower bid. Anytime a high bidder retracts a bid, make an analysis to determine if it's a shill bidding situation. If you think it is, report it to eBay.

Negotiate

Should you find yourself in a situation where you have a problem, negotiate. Don't get mad. Don't make unreasonable demands. Don't threaten. Just keep asking the other party to do what he said he would do. Be monotonous. Discuss whatever, but always return to asking the other party to do what he said they would do. That means do what he advertised or what he represented he would do.

In the alternative, ask for a refund and offer to return the item auctioned (buyer); or offer a refund and ask that the item auctioned be returned (seller).

It doesn't pay to quibble. As you will see from the remainder of this chapter, your remedies may not work well or be cost-effective. Consequently, if the other party is disagreeable, you may have to make the best of a bad situation and cut your losses. eBay is not a moral forum; it's a commercial milieu. If you want to fight, blame, or determine right and wrong, you are probably better off someplace else on the Web. If you want to be a buyer or seller, the marketplace has always been fraught with risk. eBay is no different. You have to roll with the punches. This is not to suggest that you should not stand firm and insist that the other party perform as agreed, but you have to take a practical approach due to the difficulty of finding an adequate remedy. For instance, you can't march down to small claims court and expect to get the matter effectively resolved when the other party lives 2,000 miles away in another state.

Remedies

When negotiations fail to reach an acceptable solution to whatever problems arise, you must consider taking other action. This section covers some things you can do.

Receipt

A receipt can protect each party to a transaction. It should specify the seller, the buyer, the date, the price, and the merchandise. The merchandise should be specified in detail and should match the merchandise described in the eBay auction ad.

Absent a receipt, what do you have? Well, you have eBay's email notification regarding the winning bid for the auction. And you have the eBay auction ad itself. These are documents that establish the terms of the transaction absent a receipt.

Buyer's View

From the buyer's point of view, the receipt is a legal instrument that summarizes the transaction. If you have to go to court, it's handy to have. Always check the receipt to make sure it's accurate, especially in regard to the specification of the merchandise and the price.

The best practice is to archive (save) all information in regard to the transaction, including the receipt. That means the eBay auction ad, the eBay email notification, and email correspondence. Alas, that's difficult to remember to do, but if you find yourself in a jam, you'll wish that you had done it.

Seller's View

Always provide a receipt that accurately summarizes the transaction. If a buyer does not dispute the accuracy of the receipt within a reasonable time, the receipt may come in handy later when a buyer starts making unreasonable demands. It also makes you look like a prudent and honest businessperson.

Just as for the buyer, the best practice is for you to save your eBay auction ad, the email notification, and all other information in regard to the transaction, such as any exchange of email.

Refund and Return

When there's dissatisfaction, a refund and a return of the merchandise often become a good remedy for both buyers and sellers.

Buyer's View

If something goes wrong with the transaction that is unacceptable to you, and the seller is uncooperative, try to get back to the starting line. That means request a refund and return the item. Don't quibble about who is going to pay the shipping (but there's a difference between asking and quibbling). Make sure the item, when sent back, is in the condition in which you received it, if possible. This is often a disappointing remedy, but it's far more practical than some of the others available.

Seller's View

Sure there are unreasonable buyers. Nonetheless, the best way to preserve your reputation and build a following of loyal customers is to offer a refund when problems arise. That is not to say that if problems arise you shouldn't try to get them resolved in other ways, if possible. But a dissatisfied and determined customer will waste your time and sap your energy.

Occasional Seller

Even if you are an occasional seller on eBay, you may have to act like a retailer to preserve your reputation. Your auctioning of 15 or 20 items over the next five years makes you look like a retailer once the time element is removed.

Oddly enough, it is the seller who usually suggests a refund and return. It's just a good way to resolve a problem, keep everyone happy, and reserve your energy for other business endeavors.

The tough case is when you've sold something in an "as is" condition with a stipulation that it is defective in some way, and then the buyer wants to return it because it doesn't work due to the defect mentioned. In this circumstance, you have plenty of reason to hang tough with the buyer. But it may be more trouble to hang tough than to just make a refund.

When you offer or agree to make a refund, always insist that the item be returned as a condition to making the refund, even in those occasional cases where you don't want to get the item back. Faced with having to ship the item, the buyer may decide the perceived problem isn't quite as bad as imagined. Just offering to make a refund often defuses the buyer's anger and sets the stage for resolving the situation in another way.

Mediation

When you can't resolve a dispute, sometimes mediation helps. Now we have e-mediation? Well, whatever. Actually, SquareTrade (*http://www.squaretrade.com*) provides dispute resolution. It uses some online techniques to resolve disputes, but if such techniques don't work, SquareTrade stands ready to use a hands-on effort to resolve arguments. There is an upfront fee; that is, you must pay the fee for SquareTrade before the auction ends. Thus, it's like buying insurance. You pay in advance for each auction, but you may never use the service. This is an excellent service. Give serious consideration to using it on large transactions.

Report to eBay

Negotiated remedies don't always work, and sometimes you have to take action. In addition, there are cases of nonperformance by one party; that is, a buyer doesn't pay or a seller doesn't ship the merchandise.

Unresolved Dispute

When you have a dispute that you cannot resolve, you have to decide what you are willing to do about it. Making a negative feedback that affects the other party's reputation on eBay may be appropriate, but it is not a remedy. However, it may force the other party to resolve the dispute just to make a credible reply to your negative feedback.

Another step in seeking a remedy is to report the problem to eBay. However, eBay isn't interested in resolving commercial disputes. That's up to the parties. Only when there is an act that clearly amounts to criminal behavior, or at least to a shady business practice, will eBay be interested in hearing from you. Its action against the other party, if any, is not a remedy for you unless it somehow forces the other party to resolve the dispute.

Non-Performance

If non-performance is due to one party changing his mind about buying or selling in spite of the occurrence of a valid auction, you will usually be able to convince the other party to perform just by standing firm and insisting. If non-performance is due to fraud or deliberate contracting with no intent to perform, you probably won't hear from the other party (i.e., they won't answer you).

Non-performance is a deliberate act. In some cases, it may be a criminal act. It is unacceptable behavior, and you should make a negative feedback comment. In addition, if you think it's criminal behavior, you should report it to eBay.

Not Optional

Don't think of reporting non-performance as an option. It's your duty as a good eBay citizen, so to speak, to report such behavior. Most (99.99 percent) of the people who use eBay are honest and reasonable people. If eBay is going to work for you, you have an obligation to make it work for other people. Your feedback on non-performance is a warning to eBay members. Your report to eBay on non-performance (in the case of suspected criminal behavior) may help eBay eliminate bad actors sooner rather than later.

Whether such a report to eBay will result in a remedy for you is not certain. In some cases, it may force the other party to perform. In other cases, it will simply result in the other party being barred from participation in eBay or in no action at all.

Insurance

eBay does provide insurance (Lloyd's of London) against fraud. The limit is $200 with $25 deductible. Although this insurance doesn't cover very inexpensive items, it does cover moderately inexpensive items that normally aren't worth taking a lot of precautions against loss. For items over $200, eBay probably figures that the parties can and will protect themselves adequately in regard to these more expensive items. This seems a reasonable assumption.

The insurance is automatic, and you collect on a loss by filing a claim. This is similar to filing a complaint, but unlike a complaint a claim comes with a cash remedy. It's too bad that the upper limit isn't $1,000 instead of $200.

This insurance doesn't cover damage in shipment. You need to purchase shipping insurance to cover such a potential loss.

Better Business Bureau

Although not the appropriate place to register a complaint against an individual, the Better Business Bureau (*http://bbb.org*) provides a mechanism for filing a complaint against a company. First, you will be referred to a local Bureau organization if one exists in the locale where the company operates. Not being a governmental agency, the Bureau has limited power to pursue complaints, but for grievances against established businesses, this is an alternative that might work.

Civil and Criminal Liability

Before the discussion of remedies goes further, it's important to distinguish between civil and criminal liability.

Civil Claim

A civil claim is one between the parties to an eBay auction transaction. A court will resolve the dispute between the parties if one of the parties files a complaint. This is the basis on which most transactional disputes will be resolved, if resolved by a court. The end result, if the claiming party wins, is a remedy, usually an award of money to compensate for damages incurred.

Criminal Complaint

Where one party commits fraud or theft, the act is an offense against the public (based on the victim's complaint). Once a criminal complaint is filed, it's out of the hands of the victim. Only the prosecuting attorney (district attorney or DA) has the authority to prosecute or not to prosecute the complaint.

As a practical matter, the DA will probably not prosecute your complaint should you withdraw it. After all, you may be the only witness; if you are not a cooperating witness, the complaint may not be worth pursuing for the DA. If you do not withdraw your complaint, the DA might decide not to prosecute it for lack of adequate evidence or other reasons. Nonetheless, much of the time your criminal complaint will result in an arrest warrant for the other party.

No Threats

Before discussing legal actions, it is important to remind you not to threaten the other party. Courts like reasonable people. Courts take a dim view of unreasonable people. You want to make sure a court always sees you as a reasonable person. This presents a dilemma: You always want to let the other party know that you intend to file suit; it may entice him or her to be more reasonable. But you don't want to threaten the other party because it will make you look unreasonable. Thus, you have to walk a fine line. In other words, tone down your threats so they seem like reasonable statements.

Improper: If you don't send my refund immediately, I'm going to sue you for everything you've got and report you to the Better Business Bureau.

Proper: Your refusal to be fair is forcing me into a situation where I feel I may have to seek other remedies.

If you feel this low-key approach has had no effect, repeating it may make it more convincing to the other party.

In many states, the improper statement above is unethical for an attorney. The following statement would be proper for an attorney:

Proper (for an attorney): If you continue to refuse to be fair, you will leave me no choice but to recommend to my client that she file a lawsuit.

Remember, reasonable people file lawsuits only as a last resort.

Although not making threats is important in civil cases, it is particularly important in criminal cases. Judges are not favorably impressed by people who threaten to make criminal complaints if the other party doesn't do this or that. Never overtly threaten to file a criminal complaint against someone if he or she doesn't agree to your terms. It will sound like you're abusing the criminal justice system for your own advantage. Be very subtle; the other party won't miss the point you are making.

If you threaten, however subtly, to make a criminal complaint against the other party where such a complaint is not justified, it may have the opposite effect intended. The other party may become indignant and prove even more difficult to negotiate with. Moreover, as long as you can communicate with the other party routinely, chances are that criminal action is not justified. Real criminals tend to disappear or become incommunicado.

Civil Suit

You can file a suit against the other party in your local small claims court without hiring an attorney. This is a cost-efficient way of suing someone, if you have the time to handle the case yourself. This kind of legal action can be particularly effective against a resident of your state because when you get a judgment (award of money), it will be easier to collect. As mentioned earlier in the chapter, however, small claims suits may not be effective against a party in another state.

To conduct your own case in small claims court, buy a book on doing so. Nolo Press (*http://www.nolo.com*) publishes a series of self-help legal books that can assist you.

Small claims courts have an upper limit on the jurisdictional amount. In other words, if the case is over a certain amount, you cannot get full satisfaction in small claims court. For instance, suppose you seek a refund of $4,000 and the small claims court has financial jurisdiction for $3,000. The most you can collect in the small claims court is $3,000. To recover the entire $4,000, you will have to hire an attorney and file your case in regular court.

Attorneys can be expensive. You need to make a determination as to whether it's worth it to pursue a lawsuit requiring the services of an attorney. If there is enough at stake, it may make sense. Otherwise a legal remedy may not be a cost-effective option.

Criminal Prosecution

When the other party makes a blatant misrepresentation or does not perform at all, it might be a criminal act. Criminal acts require criminal intent.

Suppose the seller represents that a computer printer prints at 12 pages per minute. It turns out the printer prints at only 4 pages per minute. The seller got the information from the manufacturer and then passed it on to bidders and potential bidders. There might be misrepresentation, but presumably there is no intent to misrepresent on the part of the seller. Without intent, there's no crime. This points out that you have to be very careful before you accuse anyone of a criminal act.

Suppose you send a check for the computer printer after exchanging email messages with the seller. You don't receive the printer in two weeks and you try to get in touch with the seller to no avail. How long do you wait to take action? Suppose the seller is an individual who happened to go on vacation for three weeks just after your check arrived and was deposited, and the printer was mistakenly not sent. It may not be a good business practice to close the doors, in effect, for three weeks, but it's not criminal.

You need to be very careful before you file a criminal complaint against someone. Make sure he or she has committed a criminal act, not just done something with which you don't agree. Make sure he or she intended to commit the act. Don't take filing a criminal complaint lightly. Keep in mind, too, that unless you have convincing evidence that the other party has committed fraud, the police are unlikely to be motivated to take action.

However, when you've been had by someone, sooner or later it becomes painfully obvious. Don't be reluctant to file a criminal complaint. In this case, it's not only your duty as a good eBay citizen; it's your duty as a good citizen of society. Usually, you will find that you are not the first victim. If you are the first victim, though, perhaps your complaint will save others the pain of being defrauded.

Is a criminal case a remedy for you? It's probably best used as a threat, albeit a subtle threat as explained earlier in the No Threats subsection. The end result of a criminal case, however, is a penalty like a jail sentence, and that will not necessarily benefit you.

Out of Touch

If someone defrauds you, he will almost certainly take the money (merchandise) and run. He will be out of touch, and your biggest clue that you've been bamboozled will be that you can't communicate with him. Can law enforcement eventually catch up with him? Apparently criminals online are easier to catch than those offline, but it will take aggressive law enforcement to catch such criminals in any event. Whether you can enlist such aggressive law-enforcement investigators on your behalf is the question.

Eventually, people on the Internet will use digital signatures. Such electronic identities will be bound (a technical term) to documentary identities (e.g., birth certificates) in such a way as to ensure that a person online is who he says he is. This will not keep people from committing fraud, but it will make it even easier to catch them than it is now.

Across State Lines

Conducting a lawsuit or even filing a criminal complaint across state lines is likely to be more complicated than filing one at home. It's probably not worth your time unless a large amount of money is involved. Attorneys typically charge over $100 per hour.

State Court

For instance, suppose you are in Michigan and file a claim in small claims court against the other party who lives in New Mexico. You get a judgment in Michigan. What are you going to do next? You may have to file an action (which requires a hearing) in court in New Mexico in order to enforce the judgment in New Mexico. This will probably require an attorney. Then you have to collect the judgment, which is often the most difficult part of the process. And you have to do all this over a thousand miles from home. Note, too, that in some cases a small claims court judgment may not be enforceable in another state.

Suppose you want to file a criminal complaint against the other party in New Mexico. You will file the complaint from a long ways away. To get a conviction, the local DA will have to trust that you will travel to New Mexico to testify. The local DA may not be enthusiastic about prosecuting such a case. Even if the person is prosecuted, a criminal conviction does not necessarily resolve the problems in the transaction (i.e., you don't get a remedy).

Federal Agencies

Under federal statutes you can file a formal complaint against the other party with the US Postal Inspection Service (if US mail was used by the other party—*http://www.framed.usps.com/postalinspectors*), the Federal Trade Commission (FTC—*http://www.ftc.gov*), or the Attorney General. Again, this might result in penalties to the other party but no benefit to you. The subtle threat of doing so, however, may have an effect on the other party, if such a complaint is justified.

You can also file a report with the National Fraud Information Center (*http://www.fraud.org*). The report is transmitted to the National Fraud Database maintained by the FTC and also to the National Association of Attorneys General. Where this will lead is anyone's guess, but it beats doing nothing if criminal behavior is apparent.

Federal Court

One place to conduct a lawsuit between parties from different states is in federal court. You will need an attorney, however, and conducting a lawsuit in the federal court tends to be more expensive than doing the same in a state court. To justify the expenses to conduct such a suit, the amount to be recovered must be large.

You can also file a criminal complaint in the federal court via the FBI if you believe that federal criminal laws have been broken. Whether the federal DA will pursue the case is out of your hands, but often this is the most realistic way to prosecute criminals who operate across state lines.

eBay

Request information via email for reporting fraud to eBay at *safe-harbor@ebay.com* with *fraud* in the subject line. It is particularly important to report fraud to eBay. It's the best way to protect your fellow eBay members and maintain eBay as a viable marketplace.

Collecting a Judgment

Just because you get a judgment against someone doesn't mean that you realize a remedy. You still have to collect the judgment. Often that is impossible.

- The other party disappears.
- The other party's assets disappear.
- The other party has no assets.
- The other party is difficult to locate.

You can go to all the expense of conducting a lawsuit (e.g., attorney fees), get a judgment, and then never collect a dime. This is a sobering thought when you consider initiating a lawsuit.

Prevention

This chapter will probably not be of much help to you except to make you realize that prevention is your best defense against an unfair or fraudulent transaction. If you will recall, this book recommends that you never bid more than you can afford to lose. If you bid more than that, make sure that you protect yourself with a transaction in escrow. If you are a seller, never deliver the merchandise until you've been paid.

Unfortunately, all risk cannot be eliminated. You can only take commonsense precautions. If you go overboard as a buyer, you may be asking for negative feedback. For instance, if you insist on paying by credit card when a seller has stated that the only acceptable payment method is by money order, you're asking for trouble. The seller may not even have a credit card merchant account.

If you go overboard as a seller, you will put a damper on your business. For instance, if you take only money orders, you don't run the risk of charge-backs on credit cards, but you eliminate a lot of honest potential bidders who want or need to pay by credit card. And money orders have their own risk. My bank (huge national bank) issues money orders that I wouldn't take. They are very plain and are printed on a laser printer. They don't even have a seal or a prominent logo. It looks as if anyone with a computer and a laser printer could easily forge such a money order. However, most money orders are notoriously easy to forge, even ones with complex designs, particularly when ostensibly issued by a non-standard source (e.g., First International Monetary and Exchange Bank of Escalante). With a misleading bank routing number, a forged money order could take several days (or weeks) to bounce. By then most sellers would have sent the merchandise.

Although precautions are not an absolute guarantee, they will considerably reduce your chances of becoming a victim of an unfair or fraudulent transaction. So, practice prevention as your best remedy for the acts of those unsavory predators lurking on the auction grounds.

Forget It

There comes a time when you may just have to forget it and get on with your life, not a pleasant thought when someone has treated you unfairly or defrauded you. But as you have learned from reading this chapter, conducting a lawsuit is expensive and time-consuming with negligible chances of collecting in most cases.

If you do get taken by someone, report it to all the proper places, but be prepared to absorb the loss.

eBay Offenses

eBay lists a number of prohibited offenses in its SafeHarbor section of the eBay website (use link at the bottom of each eBay Web page). See *SafeHarbor* for more detailed information. Some of these actions may constitute criminal activities. Some may not. Regardless, eBay will take action (e.g., indefinite suspension of an offender) on any of these offenses reported. The following subsections list some of the eBay offenses (see a redundant list worded differently in Appendix V).

Feedback Offenses

You cannot use second registrations or associates for the filing of positive feedback to boost your own feedback record (shill feedback).

You cannot use second registrations or associates for the filing of negative feedback to impact the feedback record of another person (shill feedback).

You cannot threaten negative feedback to demand from another person some undeserved action (feedback extortion).

You cannot offer to sell, trade, or buy feedback (feedback solicitation).

Bidding Offenses

You cannot use second registrations or associates to artificially raise the level of bidding to extremely high levels temporarily in order to protect the low bid of an associate (bid shielding).

You cannot email the bidders in a currently open auction to offer the same or similar item at a lower price (bid siphoning).

You cannot email bidders in a currently open auction to warn them away from a seller or item (auction interference).

You cannot retract a bid to manipulate the bidding.

You cannot use second registrations or associates to artificially raise the number of bids to the level required for a "HOT" designation.

You cannot chronically bid on items without completing the transactions for which you are the high bidder.

You cannot persist to bid on a seller's items after a warning from seller that your bids are not welcome (e.g., seller doesn't want to do business with you due to your negative feedback rating).

Selling Offenses

You cannot use second registrations or associates to artificially raise the bidding on your item up for auction (shill bidding).

You cannot represent yourself as an eBay seller (another person) and intercept the ended auctions of that seller for the purpose of accepting payment (auction interception).

You cannot manipulate the system to avoid paying fees.

You cannot sell items (accept payments) and not complete the transactions (not deliver the items).

Contact Information–Identity Offenses

You cannot represent yourself as an eBay employee.

You cannot represent yourself as another eBay user.

You cannot provide false information such as name, address, and telephone number to eBay.

You cannot use an invalid email address.

You cannot be an eBay user if you are under age 18.

Miscellaneous Offenses

You cannot use any device, software, or procedure to interfere with the proper operation of eBay.

You cannot send unsolicited email to past bidders or buyers.

You cannot threaten another eBay user with bodily harm via email.

You cannot publish the contact information of another eBay user on any online public area.

You cannot offer pirated intellectual property or illegal items for sale.

You cannot use profane, vulgar, racist, hateful, sexual, or obscene language on any online public area.

Verified Rights Owner Program

eBay operates a program with publishers (software publishers as well as publishers of other intellectual property) that helps keep counterfeit materials off eBay: Verified Rights Owner (VeRO) program. If you are a victim of a fraud involving a counterfeit product (e.g., pirated software), a complaint to eBay (or to the copyright holder that is a VeRO) should result in some action.

Summary

This chapter does not attempt to define every transaction on eBay that is unfair or fraudulent. Indeed, when it comes to fraud, some criminals are ingenious. Nor does it attempt to define everything you can do to prevent someone from defrauding you or otherwise dealing with you unfairly. The chapter simply explores the potential of resorting to eBay or the legal system for a remedy. Unless large amounts of money are at stake, however, the prospects do not look good for recovering a loss through the legal system. Therefore, you have to be conscious that prevention is your best remedy for losses you would certainly suffer, sooner or later, by being careless. But don't be so overly careful that you reduce your potential for making an auction transaction that's beneficial to you.

There are millions of people using eBay each week. There are bound to be a few crooks who do their best to prey on others for their own personal gain. But overall, eBay activity is thoroughly populated by nice people like you and me who just want to make mutually beneficial transactions.

III

Bidding Strategies

9

Timely Bidding

There are no bidding guarantees, only strategies and tactics. This chapter will help you develop an eBay strategy and give you some tactics that will improve your bidding success.

Realities

The truth is that no bidding practices will guarantee that you will win an auction, except perhaps overbidding by a considerable margin. Another bidder can come in and outbid you at any time by offering a price that you're not willing to match. At times eBay slows down, making the precise timing of bids difficult. When you get set up ahead of time to carry on a last-minute bidding frenzy, you may unexpectedly get called away to do something more important and thereby miss the final minutes of the auction. This has happened to me on numerous occasions. The bidding process itself may yield information about the item being offered—information that provides a basis for changing your bid limit at the last minute—but you may be unavailable or unprepared to make the adjustment necessary to win the bidding. Or, you may be overwhelmed by the bidding process in the heat of the last moments; it's sometimes difficult to make decisions when the window of opportunity is measured in seconds.

The underlying assumptions of the prior paragraph are:

That you will have bidding competition. The size of eBay tends to guarantee that you will. Nonetheless, you will find plenty of auctions where the expected competition does not materialize. You can often pick up valuable goods for even less than the minimum price you anticipated.

That your bidding competition will be tough, knowledgeable competitors. In fact, not everyone takes the time to bone up on eBay bidding, and your competitors may do some dumb things.

That your competitors who have already made competitive bids will also be there in the last few minutes of the auction. In fact, most bidders cannot be at the finale of every auction they enter. Some of your competition may be missing during those last few minutes.

Thus, there are no guarantees, but there are opportunities to buy at significant savings.

Strategies

What is your strategy for making purchases on eBay? For most people it will be one of the following five purposes:

1. Buying goods (e.g., camera equipment) for less money than elsewhere. This is a money-saving strategy.

2. Buying from a large selection of goods (e.g., offbeat brands). This is a consumer strategy.

3. Buying goods not otherwise available conveniently (e.g., old items). This is a time-saving strategy.

4. Buying for resale (e.g., buy at or below wholesale and sell retail). This is a profit strategy.

5. Having fun (e.g., last-minute bidding). This is an emotional strategy.

Many people on eBay buy collectibles. In doing so, they have a variety of motivations. Consequently, they act the same way as other people do. Some buy on eBay to save money, some to get a bigger selection, some to save time, some to profit, and some to have fun. In other words, there seems to be no reason to designate buying collectibles as a special strategy. (This is mentioned only because eBay got its start with collectibles, and such auctions are still a significant percentage of eBay activity.)

Buy Low

I can't speak for anyone else, but I can tell you my general strategies for buying on eBay.

- New items: These must sell at 40–55 percent of list price (i.e., a 45–60 percent discount). If you can't get the merchandise at such prices on eBay, you should buy it at a discount store; it's less risky. You know the discount store, you know where it is, and the discount store usually has a liberal return policy. When you deal with a seller on eBay, you usually don't get the same assurances.

- Factory-refurbished items: These are almost the same as new goods if they come in a factory-sealed box with a warranty. I will pay almost as much for these goods as for new goods (i.e., discounted price) under two conditions. First, the refurbished items are not generally available. If they are, the price should be lower than new goods. The scarcity of factory-refurbished goods makes them almost as valuable as new goods (i.e., sold with a deep price discount). Second, the item is soon to be obsolete (within a few years). For example, a hard drive will last for ten years in a home office. You will use it for only three before you buy a bigger one. What difference does it make if you buy a factory-refurbished one instead of a new one?

- Used items in excellent condition: These must sell at 35 percent of list price (i.e., a 65 percent discount). When anyone can buy an item new at a discount store for 60 percent of list price, used items even in excellent condition usually aren't worth as much as one would think. Most people given the choice between buying a new item at 60 percent of list and a used item at 40–60 percent of list will choose the new item. Realistically, the market value for most used goods is normally below 40 percent of list (i.e., more than a 60 percent discount).

I won't pay more than the above guidelines indicate. That's my strategy. Of course, there are plenty of situations on eBay that do not meet my general guidelines. Often there is one leading brand in a category that everyone wants (e.g., Marantz for high-end stereo components). Items with the hot brand name often sell on eBay for what you might pay for them in a discount store, or even higher. This doesn't make sense, but it happens. You won't find me making such a purchase on eBay. However, I live in a metro area of 7 million people with scores of specialty discount stores. I'm sure I would feel differently if I lived in a place where the nearest specialty discount store was 250 miles away.

Some used goods are rare but in high demand. They can go at surprisingly high prices relative to their original list price (e.g., Leica cameras). For such goods, if I needed them, I would certainly bend my guidelines. But generally speaking, you can say that my strategy for buying on eBay is to pay less than I would pay elsewhere.

Large Selection

Many people live in rural areas where their local retailers don't offer the range of choices they would have in metro areas. They can find a wider range of choices on eBay. Catalog sales have thrived on this reality for over a century. Indeed, catalog sales are high even in metro areas where people are too busy to shop or the specialty discount store is miles away on the other side of town. Keep in mind that a significant amount of the merchandise people sell on eBay is new. It's not all old stuff. The strategy here is to get a large selection. A consideration to keep in mind is that low price isn't as important for this strategy as it is for the Buy Low strategy outlined above.

Saving Time

You have an old Shure microphone you bought ten years ago. Now you need an exact match for a special vocal performance that your singing group is going to give. But Shure doesn't make that model any longer. Where do you get it? You can hang out at the local rock band store or the audio equipment store hoping that a duplicate will turn up in the used equipment department. But eBay will offer a wider choice of used goods than is available locally, and it provides you with a good opportunity to find what you're looking for.

For this type of item, you have to price it at what it's worth to you, or you may waste a lot of your time. In other words, don't use your guidelines for money-saving purchases. This is a time-saving purchase. Are you really going to turn down a high price on eBay and continue to look for a cheaper price? For instance, suppose the Shure microphone listed for $150 ten years ago. Today even in excellent condition, theoretically it should be worth about ten cents on the dollar (i.e., 10 percent of original list price). If you find one at 70 percent of list value ($105) on eBay, how much longer are you going to look around to find one cheaper? In fact, good microphones don't necessarily deteriorate if maintained properly and used properly, and the list price on a comparable microphone today might be $250. So, as a practical matter, what you think *should* be the price (about $15) and what you are willing to pay (you need the duplicate) will probably be different. The thing to keep in mind is that eBay may be the only place where you can find this item without a lot of time-consuming searching. So, the strategy here is saving time. It's quick and easy to find it on eBay (if it's there).

Resale

This is strictly a profit strategy. For buying, you need to buy low, just as with the Buy Low strategy, and sell at a profit. For arbitrage, you need to be confident that you can sell immediately at a higher price.

Retail

If you can buy new goods at or below wholesale on eBay and resell at retail, you can make a profit. However, presumably the risk of buying on eBay is higher than buying from a distributor. Thus, the price of new goods on eBay will normally have to be significantly lower than wholesale to justify the risk. Thus, the strategy is virtually identical to the Buy Low strategy.

The exception is for goods that are in high demand and may be temporarily unavailable from distributors or manufacturers. If you can buy such goods on eBay, even for a premium above wholesale, and resell at retail (or above), you can make a profit that you otherwise wouldn't be able to make. Here the strategy is to get the merchandise; but it's not that simple. You still have to get the goods at a low enough price to make a reasonable profit selling at retail.

It's a little different for used goods. Some retailers enjoy a healthy market for used goods but cannot find enough inventory to buy for resale (e.g., antique dealers). However, eBay provides them with a major source of used goods that they can depend on for acquiring inventory. Here the strategy is to build up your used inventory; but you still have to get the goods at a discount deep enough to enable you to resell the goods and make a reasonable profit.

Arbitrage

Arbitrage is buying in one market and selling immediately in another market where the price is a little higher. In other words, if you can buy something on eBay and sell it immediately at a higher price somewhere else (another market that's not as efficient), you can make a small profit. Certainly, other online auctions are not as efficient as eBay; that is, they do not have the volume to determine a stable price for a particular item. If you can be sure of selling something immediately for a higher price on another auction, buy it on eBay where it's likely to sell cheaper, and then resell it on the other auction.

Arbitrage is a stock market technique. It does not work as well for the more erratic and less efficient goods market. The cost of transfer for stocks is small. The cost of transfer for goods involves shipping and sometimes sales tax and other costs. Nonetheless, where prices are out of sync enough and a resale is assured, arbitrage can be profitable even though the profits are usually small.

Arbitrage Is Not Retail

Buying at low prices on eBay and selling at retail is not the same as arbitrage. If you can buy at wholesale prices or below on eBay, which is quite possible, then you can sell at retail offline without having to sell immediately. There's more profit in a retail sale, so you don't have to make an immediate sale to minimize your holding costs.

Arbitrage can work two ways for you with eBay. First, you can buy elsewhere and sell on eBay, or you can buy on eBay and sell elsewhere. The principle is simply that the resale must be certain, immediate, and profitable.

An example is baseball caps with official major league team insignias, about $8–$16 per cap at retail stores. If you can find a close-out purchase (in the closeout market) for $1 per cap and resell them easily to end users on eBay for $3 per cap, that's a retail operation. If you can resell them easily to sports distributors on eBay for $1.50 each (minimum order seven cartons—1,008 caps), that's more like arbitrage (between the closeout market and eBay). The sale to the sports distributors is certain because they normally pay about $4 per cap and would rather pay only $1.50, and the caps are always in demand. After all, the caps have the official major league team insignias.

In the example of selling to the distributors, you would not want to take delivery of the caps. You would want to make the resales to the distributors so quickly that you could have your seller ship directly to your buyers (distributors). In other words, you would be strictly a middleman.

For arbitrage, the buying strategy is to buy low, but it must be coupled with a resale plan that can be carried out immediately. In other words, the price you anticipate for the resale determines the upper limit for which you can buy the goods on eBay and still make a small profit on the immediate resale. With arbitrage you have to be careful because the volume is usually large and the profits normally small, and you can't afford to make a mistake.

I might also point out that arbitrage requires large transactions, often significant amounts of capital, and extensive knowledge of the markets. The profit is small, so the transaction must be large to make the deal worthwhile. And unless you have excellent knowledge of the markets in which you are dealing, arbitrage is financially suicidal.

Fun

Online auctions can be fun. They're like a game. It's perfectly legitimate to pursue participation just for the fun of it. Don't forget, though, that legally an auction is not a game. It forms a legal contract between the seller and the high bidder. If you are the high bidder, you are legally obligated to buy the item. If you're not willing to complete the contract (i.e., pay for the item), don't play the game. Read Chapters 7 and 8 carefully.

Tactics

Naturally, your tactics will be different for different strategies. If you want to save money or make money, you will behave differently than if you just want to save time or have fun.

Tactics are things you can do to reach the goals implicit in your strategies. Once you have taken some time to develop your eBay strategies, you will have a clearer idea of what you want to accomplish on eBay. From what you read in this book and your own experience, you will come up with things you can do to reach your objectives.

Research

Nothing beats research. If you want to use the Buy Low strategy, you have to know the list prices of the items you bid on. Then you can apply my percentage guidelines to estimate your high bid prices, or you can invent your own percentage guidelines. You can get list prices at manufacturers' websites, in online catalogs, and the like.

You also need to know what identical or similar items have sold for on eBay in the past. You can click on *Search Completed Items* at the top of a list of eBay auctions and view the completed transactions going back two weeks (with the highest bids displayed). With enough of these transactions, you can estimate what the high bid is likely to be for an item.

Know your offline markets too. It's silly to pay more for something on eBay when you can buy it with less risk locally. Yet, this is the case for many items. eBay is not 100 percent effective in providing the lowest prices for all merchandise.

Check out the seller. Check his or her feedback. Check his or her other eBay auctions. If there's a commerce website, check that. You never know what you might find out that will help you in your bidding.

Popular Items

For popular items you can try http://www.worthguide.com to get guidance on auction values.

Without research, not only will you be prone to making significant mistakes, but you will have a difficult time gauging success. Do your homework.

The Refresh

The Refresh is not only a tactic but a necessity. As you reach the final few minutes of an auction, you must keep informed of the bidding. The way you do so is to refresh (reload) the auction Web page by clicking on the refresh button on your Web browser (see Figure 9.1). This is the only way you can determine the latest high bid. The high bid amount for an auction in a list of auctions on eBay is hopelessly out of date—perhaps by hours. Keep this in mind when planning your last-minute tactics, and don't rely on the list of auctions for up-to-date bid information.

Figure 9.1   Click on the refresh button.

The Scare

This is a tactic to scare away potential bidders because they think the bidding is too intense. Suppose you are willing to bid as much as $85 on an item that currently reflects a high bid of $23. The high bidder has bid $52 (but you don't know this figure). If you bid $24, eBay raises the high bidder to $25 (automatic bidding or proxy bidding; see the Bay Way later). You are now the second-highest bidder. There are three bids.

You bid again, this time $26; eBay raises the high bidder to $27. You bid again, and this time it's $28; consequently, eBay raises the high bidder to $29. Now there are seven bids.

You can continue this procedure until you find the high bid. By the time you finally outbid the high bidder with a bid of $53, there will be 30 bids. That looks like a lot of activity, and eBay provides no way to analyze the auction except by looking at the number of bidders. Many potential bidders will not take the trouble to look beyond the number of bids, and many bargain hunters will not bother to bid because of the apparent intensity of the bidding.

This tactic works best for standard items for which it is easy to establish a value. Potential bidders know the item and are searching for a bargain price. That's why the bidding intensity might scare them away. They're afraid the price will go too high.

Bidding intensity, however, attracts the curiosity of many bidders, particularly regarding nonstandard items for which it is difficult to estimate market value. Bidders are curious to see what the intensity is all about. Therefore, this tactic may backfire for such items. The intensive bidding makes the items seem hot and attracts bidders rather than scares them off. Thus, this tactic works best for standard items such as merchandise with well-known brand names.

Legal?

Is this tactic in violation of eBay rules? The answer is no. However, if you are assisting the seller (or if you are the seller operating under a different alias), using this tactic as a means to artificially inflate the bidding not only is against eBay rules but is illegal in many states.

The Pass

Some items are just popular. Normally, new items sell for under the discount store price on eBay. But for a few popular items, the high bid often exceeds the discount store price. Why buy the item from a distant seller on eBay that you don't know? Pass. Buy it at your local discount store instead.

Other Auctions

This same idea applies to other online auctions. Such auctions simply don't have the critical mass of items that eBay does. Consequently, they don't attract as many buyers. The true market value is not as likely to establish itself as it will on eBay. There are not enough buyers and sellers. Additionally, these other auctions attract sellers who don't want to sell at the low prices established by a more efficient market (i.e., eBay). The result is that the sellers set high minimums. Either they sell to unknowledgeable buyers, or they don't sell.

Until another auction reaches a critical mass, do your bidding at eBay. So far, no other auction has reached such a critical mass except for a few small specialized auctions dealing in one or two categories of items.

The Bay Way

Set your highest price, and walk away. eBay has it set up so that you'll win the auction if your highest bid is higher than any other; but the eBay system will only reveal your bid as being one increment higher than the second-highest bid. What a deal! With this tactic, you don't have to be at your computer in the final minutes of the auction. You only have to bid once. You will pay only one increment higher than the second-highest bidder. This automatic bidding (proxy bidding) is built into the eBay system.

Suppose the highest bid is $22, and you bid $46. eBay will now show you as being the highest bidder at $23. Another bidder comes along and bids $24. eBay will automatically make you the highest bidder at $25. And so it goes. The only way someone can outbid you is by bidding more than $46.

This is a workable tactic when you are sure of yourself and sure of the value range. You know about how much the item will sell for, and you know definitely what you are willing to pay for it. If the value range is lower than you're willing to pay, you should win the bid in most instances. If the value range is higher than you're willing to pay, there will be some auctions, but not many, where you will have the highest bid. It's worth a shot; it doesn't take long to make one bid.

The Game

This is a nonfinancial tactic that enables you to enjoy the Fun strategy mentioned above. Because bidding on eBay can be fun, you can play it as a game. The goal is to win the bidding, but the primary goal is not necessarily to win with the lowest winning bid possible. It's to win without an excessively high bid but have some fun doing it, that is, have some fun bidding.

In reality, when you bid in the final minutes of the auction, you might switch into game mode whether you intend to or not. The excitement of the final minutes may lead you to bid more than the high limit you set for yourself. Presumably, however, you won't get excited enough to win at any cost. That could lead to a severe financial hangover.

If there is intense bidding in the final minutes and you're having fun, it's worth a few extra dollars to win. Go for it. The auction game is fun to play.

Don't, under any circumstances, bid on auctions that you don't intend to complete if you are the high bidder. You will end up getting kicked off eBay and lose what will almost certainly turn out to be a lifelong asset.

The Smoke Out

You use the Smoke Out before you use the Bay Way; it gives you a better idea of what the winning bid might be. Sometime well before the auction ends, you attempt to smoke out the price range of the final bidding. This is especially important when you have trouble estimating the value of the item.

Suppose you have a vague idea that the item might be worth about $120. You need it and don't have time to find it elsewhere. The current high bid is $42. When the final minutes of the auction come, you'll be across town on a business appointment. You don't have a snipe program (see the Snipe subsection later), so you'll make your final bid a few hours before the end of the auction.

The tactic is to bid in $5 increments until you have the high bid (assuming it's under $120). Do this early in the auction. Then wait to see if anyone outbids you. If not, you may have reached the range of value for the item. Unfortunately, you won't know for sure until the end of the auction. But if someone outbids you immediately, it may be an indication that you haven't reached the range of value.

On one hand, suppose you bid up in $5 increments to $75 to become the high bidder with three days to go. Two and a half days go by, and no one outbids you. That may be an indication that the value range is lower than the $120 you anticipated. For your final bid you might want to try $85.

On the other hand, suppose you do the same, but within a day someone outbids you. You again bid up in $5 increments to $95 to become the high bidder. Another day and a half goes by, and no one outbids you. Now, you might want to try $105 for your final bid.

In both of these cases, you're trying to smoke out the value range because you're not sure what the value is. If you know what the value range is, you don't have to use the Smoke Out. In both of these cases, you're making a higher bid at the end because you won't be around for the finale. You hope the higher bid will be enough to win in your absence.

Even if you're going to be present for the bidding in the last minutes, the Smoke Out can be a valuable tactic if you're not sure of the value range. It can help you anticipate the value range. For instance, if you're prepared to pay $120 and the value range turns out to be $90–$100, smoking out the value range early will give you confidence in the final bidding because you're psychologically prepared to pay the price.

If you smoke out the value range, however, and it turns out to be over $120, it gives you more information with which to further develop your tactics. You can drop out of the bidding and save what otherwise would be wasted time. Or, you can rethink your estimate of value. You may decide that a value range over $120 is not unreasonable. In that case, you'll be psychologically prepared to bid higher and stay in the game.

Obviously, the Smoke Out is not a perfect tactic. But it can be a helpful one in many circumstances. It's another way of gathering information to prepare yourself before the final minutes of the auction.

The Snipe

The pure sniper never appears before the final minutes or seconds. Then he or she places the winning bid out of the blue at the last possible moment.

With Software

Many snipers use special software to do their sniping. You can buy it at various eBay auctions. The software places a winning bid at a certain time before the auction ends, say 30 seconds before. In the software setup for the Snipe, you can put an upper limit on the bid so that you don't spend more than you want to.

Using the software seems like a foolproof way to win an auction. When you think about it, however, it doesn't do any more for you than the Bay Way, except it might come as a surprise to other bidders. In other words, using Snipe software, you can't change your tactic at the last minute, and the software is not infallible. If you set the software to make a bid in the last 15 seconds before the end of the auction and eBay takes 45 seconds to accept the bid, you're out of luck. There are plenty of times during the week (e.g., Saturday evening) when eBay will take 30 seconds or longer to crank out Web pages. So, you set the software to make a bid 90 seconds before the end of the auction. If eBay happens to be working fast at that time, you've given your competitors plenty of time to place higher bids within the last 90 seconds.

Without Software

If you don't use software to snipe, you have to be at your computer ready to roll during those final moments. You don't know whether your last-minute bid will work because you don't know what the highest bid is. What you're sure of is that the highest bid is at least one increment higher than the second-highest bid, but you don't know how much higher because of the way the eBay proxy system works. Consequently, the Snipe is theoretically a one-shot tactic. Maybe it'll work. Maybe it won't.

However, you can combine the Snipe with the Smoke Out for a very effective last-minute tactic. Perhaps it should be called the Last-Minute Smoke Out and Snipe. Give yourself a few minutes. You smoke out the value range in a hurry by making a series of quick bids. Once you've found the value range, you have to make a decision as to what your last-moment bid will be and how long it will take to submit it (based on eBay's current operational speed).

No Smoke

If there is spirited bidding but there appears to be no proxy bidding, you won't have to do a Smoke Out. You can watch and then do a last-second Snipe.

Unfortunately, eBay runs at different speeds at different times. Weekend evenings seem to be extra busy, and eBay may take up to a minute or more to deliver each new Web page. When you are trying to snipe where timing is crucial, this lag time can be frustrating. You will have to test the response, estimate the lag time, and make your bids accordingly. For instance, suppose you test the response time and it seems to be about 45 seconds. You want to snipe within 20 seconds of the close of the auction. Under these circumstances, you need to make your final bid about 65 seconds before the end of the auction.

Refresh

Remember the Refresh? Refreshing the eBay auction Web page is the only way you can keep up with the bidding. This is not a problem when eBay is fast. When eBay is slow, it compounds your sniping problems.

If you run into competition, you'll be in the middle of a bidding war. The difference between this and a normal bidding war is that you will be a surprise competitor, perhaps disrupting the expectations of the other bidder(s). You will have to be ready to submit additional bids instantly in response to the competing bidders.

The perfect Snipe is one that wins with 0 seconds left. With eBay's varying speed and with such precise control normally out of reach, it will be difficult to win with 0 seconds left. But you might win with 10 seconds left under normal conditions.

The Double Window

How can you best submit those last-minute bids efficiently and responsively? Use double browser windows. Open your browser, go to eBay, and open the auction at which you will bid. Next, for

Netscape Navigator 6.0, go *File, New Navigator Window* to create a new and fully functional browser window that is, in effect, a second browser. For Microsoft Internet Explorer 5.5, go *File, New, Window.* Now, as Figure 9.2 shows, you have two browser windows (two browsers, in effect) to make quick bids.

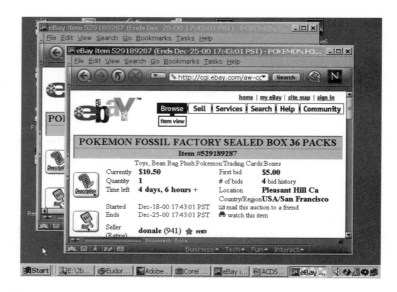

Figure 9.2   Two browser windows.

Actually, you can make as many browser windows as you want. I usually make about six to prepare for last-moment bidding. You add the bid price as you use each browser window to bid (see Figures 9.3 and 9.4).

Now, when you're in a hurry in the final moments of the auction competing with other bidders, you can make a bid fast. After every bid you make, discard the window you've just used, and move on to a fresh browser window (i.e., one that's been prepared ahead of time). This works very effectively. You don't have to go backwards. (It worked more effectively before eBay changed the bidding sequence in the summer of 1999 from alias and password in the first window and price in the second window to the reverse. Apparently eBay did this either to slow down the intensity of the last-minute bidding or to prevent the more knowledgeable bidders from gaining an advantage.)

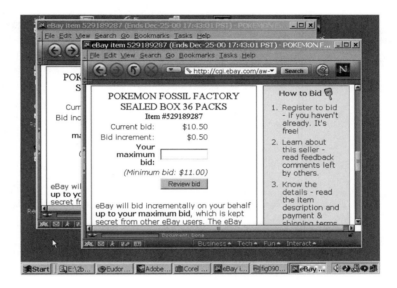

Figure 9.3   Two browser windows set up to bid.

The last few minutes of a hot auction can get very intense, and the Double Window tactic keeps you in the bidding. Don't worry about snipers. You can snipe better than any program can.

Sign In to Save Time

See Chapter 5 for information on signing in. If you sign in and elect bidding as a sign-in preference, you don't have to enter your ID and password when you bid. This gives you an advantage in the final minutes of a hot auction because you can save the time it takes to enter an ID and password and respond more quickly to sniping. Click on the sign-in link in the upper right-hand corner of any eBay page.

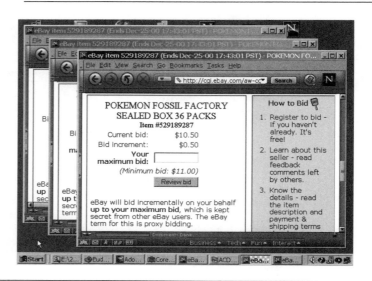

Figure 9.4   Three browser windows set up to bid.

The Ten Cents Difference

In order to make a bid, you must increase the amount of your bid by the requisite eBay increment (see Chapter 5). Presumably, most people submit a bid based on one or more increments. But you don't have to do it that way.

Suppose you bid $28 but are automatically preempted by a bid of $29 via eBay proxy by someone who has bid $32. You want to smoke out the high bidder. You bid $30. The eBay proxy bids $31. If you bid $32, you will be tied with the high bidder, but the high bidder—being first—will win the auction. If you bid $32.01, you will be high bidder and will win the auction. Thus, it's a good idea to always bid at lease one increment plus a penny. I always bid at least one increment plus 10 cents.

Turn the above scenario around. Suppose you made the high bid at $32.10, and someone else is trying to outbid you in the last moments of an auction. They bid $32. You win by a dime.

Why bother with a few cents? Why not bid an extra dollar instead? The nickels and dimes add up. Look at the overhead for a buyer (see Chapter 2). You can get nickeled and dimed to impoverishment. Win the bidding by 10 cents and save 90 cents wherever you can.

The Routine Check

This puts the time-saving strategy into action. You will find eBay especially valuable if you can wait. Suppose you need the Shure microphone (in the Saving Time subsection example) for a Christmas performance, but it's now August. You might not be able to find it today, but check every week. It'll turn up sooner or later. If you want to be diligent, you can check every three days because there are some three-day auctions. But check at least once a week. It takes little time to check the current auctions. When the Shure microphone does appear, keep in mind your strategy and act accordingly.

This is actually a good tactic to use for any merchandise, and I've used it to save money. But it's perhaps most valuable for the time-saving strategy. After all, for the time-saving strategy, there may be no viable alternative to the Routine Check.

The Multiple-Auction Finesse

Sometimes you bid multiple auctions on the same item that end within a short time of one another. It seems to me this is dumb on the part of a seller. As a seller, you want to give the bidders plenty of opportunity and time to concentrate and bid on each auction. Yet I've seen three or four Dutch auctions, with the same items offered by the same seller, end within 40 seconds of each other. And we've all seen two or three auctions with the same item offered by the same seller end within a short time of each other. If you're a bidder, how do you handle this situation?

There are two rules. The first rule is forget the first auction (ends first). The person willing to bid the highest is going to win that auction. Why be high bidder if there is more than one auction? The second rule is figure out the most difficult thing to do, and do it. Everyone else will tend to pick easier tactics. If you pick the most difficult tactic, you have a good chance of winning.

The necessity for the Multiple-Auction Finesse, of course, depends on competition. If you don't have competition, you don't need the Finesse.

Two Auctions

Because you're not going to bid the first auction, what do you do about the second auction? Well, you see the first auction through to the end, even though you don't bid on it. You need to know the winning bid amount. You have a pretty good idea of the value range because you witnessed the end of the first auction. The best tactic is to snipe the second auction. You're in a good position to snipe because you set up to snipe the second auction ahead of time. Don't forget the Double Window tactic. Presumably, your competition is frustrated and busy trying to regroup in the short time between auctions. You're not frustrated. You're ready to wrestle. It seems to me that you have the advantage. In this case, the most significant thing is to plan ahead.

Three Auctions

The most difficult thing for bidders is to regroup for a second auction right after the final frenzy of the first auction. Again, you watch the first auction to the end. The bidders will tend to take the easiest path to winning a bid by skipping the second auction and bidding the third. That leaves the second auction with no competition or light competition. Because you set up to bid the second auction ahead of time, you have a good chance of winning the bid. The third auction will be a replay of the first, with higher bidding than the second. In this case, the most significant tactic is to bid the second auction.

If you don't win the second auction by some horrible accident of fate, you're in a good position to snipe the third because you set up to bid the third auction ahead of time. Again, don't forget the Double Window tactic.

Why?

The intervals between auctions must be small for the Finesse tactic to work (under two minutes). Why would a seller schedule auctions of the same item this close together? It might be ignorance. It might be the result of a bulk upload. It might be the result of a hurried entry of auctions. Whatever the reason, it happens more often than you might think.

If the intervals are too long, the bidders will be able to regroup more easily and bid more effectively. Then the Finesse doesn't work as well.

Dutch Auction Bids

As explained earlier, at a Dutch auction, the high bidder wins but pays only the amount of the lowest successful bid. Suppose there are five items available and five bidders bidding on one item each. The bids in the last few minutes are as follows:

$77

$74

$73

$70

$68

If you bid $69, and no one enters another bid, you will be a winner and buy at $69. But if someone else bids, you're likely to get knocked out of the winner's circle because you're at the bottom of the winner's circle. However, if you bid $74, and no one enters another bid, you will be a winner and buy for a price of $70 (you knocked out the $68 bidder). But if someone else bids, you're not likely to get knocked of the winner's circle, and the final low successful bid (price to you) may be lower than your bid of $74. Thus, the tactic is to bid a little above the middle of the pack and hope for a successful low bid that is less than your bid.

Organization

For one auction, you don't need much organization. You can keep everything under control just by following a plan and improvising. However, if you bid on multiple auctions, you need to devise a systematic way of keeping track of your bids.

First, you don't want to bid on multiple separate auctions for the same item. You could become doubly successful (triply successful perhaps) and have to buy more than one item or possibly suffer negative feedback for the items you didn't buy.

Second, you can't count on eBay's email notification system to keep track for you. While such a system is handy in certain ways, particularly for your after-auction records, it's not going to help much for successfully bidding on multiple unrelated items and for avoiding costly mistakes. I've bid as many as three different unrelated items at the same time. Even with just three auctions to manage, things start to get out of control without some kind of at least informal auction management system.

Summary

Think about what strategy you will follow for bidding on eBay. Then pick and choose your tactics to carry out your strategy. Invent some tactics of your own. There is never a guarantee that you will win an auction, but with a clear strategy and some useful tactics, you will do as well as you can on eBay.

IV

Software

10

Software for Bidding and Selling

You will find much software available in auctions on eBay each week designed for either selling (auctioning) or buying (bidding) items on eBay, keeping track of items, or handling graphics. This book is not the appropriate place to evaluate all of the eBay software available—magazines and newsletters do a better job and are current—but it's appropriate to make some general comments on eBay software.

Software Developers

Someone who creates software and markets it is generally referred to as a software developer (can be a company too). The software covered in this chapter (prior to the last section) is not software developed by eBay. It is software published by software developers independent from eBay. Because the market is limited (compared to the general overall software market), the software developers tend to be individual programmers or small companies.

I find the eBay bidding software generally unnecessary, except for convenience in some cases. In regard to eBay programs that create auction ads, it seems to me they are as difficult to learn as the underlying technology, perhaps more difficult. If you have a difficult time with eBay auctions or are not competent at HTML or handling graphics, I encourage you to give some eBay software a try. You might have a different point of view than I do.

My Point of View

Although not a programmer, I am a sophisticated user and can use HTML competently.

Learning how to use eBay is not difficult. There are certainly many aids to learning on eBay including tutorials, bulletin boards, and customer service. You may find that your time is best spent with them rather than using software that does something simple for you. HTML is easy to learn, and you should consider learning it as a viable alternative to learning software that helps you create eBay auction ads (Web pages). If the software is more difficult to learn than HTML, it seems to defeat the purpose of using the software. Graphics editing programs are easy to use to do simple tasks, and handling graphics is not difficult. There are dozens of general graphics programs that are adequate for use in handling photographs for eBay. It's doubtful that you need anything special.

In fairness to the software developers, some of the software goes beyond handling the simple bidding processes. For instance, the software may keep a permanent record of all your transactions as well as assist you on eBay. If the software is easy to use, the extras could be a benefit.

What's Wrong with eBay Software?

Keep in mind that general observations do not apply to each program, and there are programs that I have not tried. General observations, however, do help you become a better and more discriminating buyer. My general observations about eBay software, I hope, will make you more wary.

First, the quality of eBay software varies. Some seems amateurish. Some seems polished. Second, some of the polished software seems poorly tested. Perhaps it works well on Windows 95, 98, or Me, but it doesn't work on Windows 2000, which I use. Third, some of the auction ad software is lackluster. It does a competent job, but aesthetically it's unappealing and does not offer much design flexibility. Fourth, most software that does anything worthwhile takes awhile to learn. In the case of eBay, it seems to me that it's easier to learn basic skills that will enable you to do the things that many of the programs do.

Don't take my word for it, though. Generally, eBay software isn't too expensive. Try some, if you think it will help you. If it doesn't, you're only out a few bucks plus the time it takes to give it a trial run.

What to Avoid in eBay Software

If you're going to buy eBay software, *buy eBay software*. That is, don't buy a CD with everything else in the world on it. CDs with everything in the world on them are known in the industry as *shovelware*. You can get a shovelware CD on eBay or at a local computer show for $4–$8. That's what shovelware is worth. If you want to buy an eBay program on a CD with shovelware, subtract $4–$8 and you'll know what the eBay program by itself is selling for.

Ironically, you can probably find the software and information contained in most shovelware CDs, if you use the search engines briefly, someplace on the Web for free.

Anything offered as part of a shovelware package is suspect. If the eBay software seems to get lost in the hyped benefits of the shovelware package, it's probably not worth much.

Chapter 9 discusses how you can beat any sniping program. Therefore, if a sniping program only offers sniping, it may not be worth much without offering additional features such as convenience.

What to Look for in eBay Software

If a software developer sells a program that has plenty of detailed information on how the program works, perhaps even a tutorial, and the promotional literature seems professionally done, chances are the software is worthwhile. This is particularly true if the software developer provides a money-back guarantee.

If you can use a trial version (e.g., 30-day version), that will be the proof of the pudding. Shareware is particularly attractive because you can use it before you make a buying decision. Look for trial versions and shareware because they have, in effect, money-back guarantees.

Hidden Cost?

Freeware is presumably even more attractive than shareware because you can use it without paying, right? Not necessarily. Don't forget, the software can potentially soak up your valuable time in a long learning experience only to turn out not to be very useful. The software may be free, but the cost to you is high.

This is true of any software, however, regardless of price. Always keep in mind the learning cost of the software you buy. If you can anticipate the learning cost before you buy, so much the better.

If a software developer sells a program solely on the strength of the program and not with shovelware, that's usually a good sign that the program may be worthwhile.

Sniping programs that offer extras that enhance convenience are likely to be more useful than ones that offer only sniping.

Although I'm a little skeptical that eBay software can do things better than you can, some eBay software offers a considerable degree of convenience, assuming it works properly. If convenience is what you look for, then check out the eBay programs that offer to do something more conveniently than you can do it for yourself. And don't lose sight of the fact that the eBay phenomenon is in its formative years. Look for new eBay features and new killer software that might appear anytime. Check out the following:

AuctionAmigo (*http://invenna.com*)

AuctionAssistant (*http://www.blackthornesw.com*)

Auction Wizard (*http://www.standingwavesoftware.com*)

BeyondSolutions (*http://www.beyondsolutions*)

ePoster 2000 (*http://auctiva.com*)

TurboBid (*http://etusa.com*)

Virtual Auction Ad Pro (*http://virtualnotions.com*)

Websabre (*http://websabre.com*)

Services

You will find services on the Web that claim to do more than a software program to help you with your eBay auctions. Many of these are oriented toward assisting sellers to keep track of a high volume of auctions. They include:

Andale (*http://www.andale.com*)

AuctionFlow (*http://www.auctionflow.com*)

AuctionHelper (*http://www.auctionhelper.com*)

AuctionWatch (*http://www.auctionwatch.com*)

Auctionworks (*http://auctionworks.com*)

GoTo Auctions (*http://auctions.goto.com*)

ManageAuctions (*http://www.manageauctions.com*)

Also consider PayPal and Billpoint covered in Chapter 16. These are payment services that also provide transaction tracking services for sellers. Billpoint is an eBay-owned service.

This Book

This book offers an alternative to eBay software. (So, take everything in this chapter with a grain of salt.)

Chapter 9 provides you with bidding tactics that can outmaneuver any eBay software. In particular, Chapter 9 provides you with specific tactics for sniping.

Chapter 13 features extensive information on using an HTML (Web page) template for your auction ads. If you don't like my simple templates—and I am not a graphics designer—you can use what you learn in Chapter 13 together with some HTML skills to make your own templates that you can use over and over again.

Good Programs That Do the Wrong Things

Some software developers may sell good software, but the software does the wrong things. For instance, software that focuses on adding frills to eBay auction ads and ignores good typesetting principles may be good software, but it will lead you in a wrong direction (see Chapter 13).

Chapter 20 covers using free, easy-to-use Web page authoring programs (e.g., Netscape Composer) to create Web pages and auction ads. You can use such authoring programs with templates too.

Chapters 12 and 21 will give you a grasp on handling graphics that will enable you to seek, find, and use competent general graphics editing software.

Chapters 14, 15, and 18 provide you with the basic knowledge to use a common desktop database program (e.g., Microsoft Access) to control inventory, to generate auction ads in bulk, and to build a catalog on a commerce website. This relatively simple (for capable

PC users) technology can provide you with a powerful retailing system.

The book provides you with a great deal of information on getting done what you need to get done to be successful on eBay. Nonetheless, I encourage you to try whatever eBay software seems like it might work for you. For a good start in finding eBay software, go to the auction categories *Computers, Software, General,* or *Utilities.*

eBay eBay Software

What is eBay eBay software? It's software that's part of the eBay website and that provides extracurricular eBay services. In other words, it's built-in software created by eBay, not by independent software developers.

For instance, the eBay proxy bidding (see Chapter 9) is built into the system and provides a solid service to the current high bidder in an auction. In addition, eBay provides services that enable you to keep track of your activities on eBay. My eBay provides you with an automatic record of all your activities on eBay. A search on your name provides you with a record of your current auctions in *Seller Search* or your current bids in *Bidder Search*. Consequently, any independent eBay software you consider buying should offer more than these built-in eBay devices.

Summary

Look for software that isn't packaged with shovelware, software that offers extra benefits above and beyond performing simple eBay tasks. Make sure eBay doesn't offer a program or service that meets your needs before buying other software. Look through this book to see what you can learn that will enable you to forgo buying software that may turn out to be unnecessary. Whenever you can, get trial software or shareware that enables you to try it before you buy it.

V

Selling Strategies

11

Customer Service

Even today it is not unusual for a business to open a website to sell to the public and to neglect to be ready to handle the orders. Here's how *not* to sell on the Web:

1. Hire a Web developer to build a website.

2. Get some inventory on the website.

3. Sit back and wait for the orders to roll in.

Why doesn't this work? Because it's likely that the customers will come, and the typical business isn't ready for them. This scenario works better:

1. Hire a Web developer to build a website.

2. Get some inventory on the website.

3. Organize your business to handle the customers you will get from your website.

4. Test the website, the order-handling procedures, and the transaction processes.

5. Provide for ongoing website maintenance.

6. Handle the orders promptly as they come in.

The commerce website is a business by itself and should be treated as such.

What's the point of this chapter opening in regard to eBay sellers? It's simply this. The most important selling strategy for eBay is customer service.

Business at eBay Auctions

It doesn't matter whether you run five auctions a year, five auctions a week, or twenty-five auctions a day, the better you treat your customers, the more bids you will get and the higher the final bids will be. Consequently, this section of the book begins with a chapter on customer service, not with a chapter on auctioning techniques. The Web is an interactive medium that gives you the chance to serve your customers (bidders) well.

The Occasional Seller

Put yourself in a buyer's shoes. You want to make a bid for $620 on a used telephone system (retails for $1,849) for your small office. The seller represents the system as in excellent condition and wants a money order for the final bid price (no escrow).

You are faced with sending a money order for $620 to someone you don't know. You don't know whether you will receive anything for your money. If you do receive something, you don't know what kind of condition it will be in. Will you make the bid? Try the following four scenarios:

1. The seller has no history (i.e., no sales or purchases).

2. The seller has a history of 5 transactions, all rated neutral.

3. The seller has a history of 7 transactions, all rated positive.

4. The seller has a history of 153 transactions, 3 rated negative and the remainder rated positive.

How are you going to vote with your $620? Chances are you'll pass on number one, too much of an unknown. Number two looks as though he or she will be trouble of some sort; that's a pass. Number three looks like a reasonable risk. Number four looks like a very low risk.

Each of the above sellers will lose a certain percentage of the potential market. Number one will get some bidders, but because of the high price, many potential bidders will pass because the risk is high. Few potential bidders will think it's worth the time and trouble to deal with number two, who obviously isn't making anyone happy. Although number three looks good, the information is a little thin, and some potential bidders will pass. Virtually all potential bidders will feel comfortable with number four; they've probably got more favorable information on number four than they do on many retailers in their own communities.

The point here is that your reputation is important as a seller, and your reputation depends on your customer service. Make your customers happy, and you'll build a good reputation. A good reputation will bring more bids. More bids will bring a higher price.

Now, *as the seller*, what can you do to improve customer service for the auction of the used telephone system? Here are four options:

1. Accept a credit card (or PayPal or Billpoint).
2. Offer to put the transaction in escrow.
3. Provide a warranty.
4. Throw in a gift certificate for a book at Borders on how to install and operate a small office telephone system.

If you accept a credit card, a person dissatisfied with the transaction can do a charge-back on the credit card transaction. That provides a buyer with a potential remedy. That will increase your bids. If you offer to put the transaction in escrow, it makes everyone feel more comfortable because it lowers the risk. You'll get more bids. If you provide a warranty, it doesn't necessarily lower the risk, but it makes everyone feel more comfortable, and you'll get more bids. Even the book will broaden the appeal of the auctioned item. Consequently, with a little customer service, you increase your potential for making more money. The four customer services listed above are a few among many you can offer.

Credit Cards

About 90 percent of buyers on eBay use credit cards where sellers accept them. Debit cards via MasterCard and Visa are now a part of the credit card system, for all practical purposes, and many people with only checking accounts can therefore

"charge" just like people with credit cards. (I was sent a MasterCard debit card by my bank without requesting it. I use it
more than I use my credit card.)

Perhaps the best, but most common, customer service you can
provide is accepting credit cards. There are dozens more ways
to get merchant accounts for Web commerce in 2001 than
there were just three years ago. Get yourself a merchant
account, and start accepting credit cards.

If you are an occasional seller, you need to read about PayPal
and Billpoint in Chapter 16.

What can you do as an occasional seller to increase customer service? Respond to communications (e.g., email) promptly. Be prepared to ship promptly the item you sell. Think of yourself as a
seller, and exercise common sense. Follow some of the suggestions
in the remainder of this book in regard to providing convenience
for potential bidders.

The Part-Time eBay Business

If you have a part-time business on eBay auctioning merchandise
at retail, pay close attention to customer service. Some of the
things you can do follow:

- Follow the guidelines in this book for running your auctions
  and conducting your eBay business.

- Promptly respond to communications from potential bidders
  and customers.

- Organize a responsive follow-up system to track your customers through the transaction process.

- Run your shipping operation in a professional manner.

- Accept payment in as many ways as possible.

- Provide guarantees where practical.

- Listen to your customers.

If you summarize the above list, it boils down to one idea. Get organized! Don't take selling on eBay lightly. Even selling just a few items a week can get out of control before you know it, if you're not prepared. If things do get out of control, you will have some unhappy high bidders and other unhappy eBay members; that does not bode well for life on eBay.

You can't conduct a part-time eBay business haphazardly and expect it to be as successful as possible. If you take it seriously and provide good customer service, your business may grow into something to which you can eventually devote your full time and energy; then you can quit your job.

Independent Contractors

If you have a full-time job and you are trying to supplement your income by selling on eBay, you may find it difficult to provide the customer service you need to maximize your success. Hiring employees to do some of the work is out of the question. Just the paperwork to employ a person is too demanding. One way to improve your customer service, when you don't have the time, is to hire independent contractors.

Shipping is a good example of something you can *outsource* (have done for you by another business). Some small businesses specialize in shipping merchandise for customers. Shipping is a chore. Have a shipping company do it for you. That will leave you time to spend on other customer service activities that you can do better, more efficiently, more quickly, or more easily. Obviously, the shipping company is an independent contractor.

Not so obvious is having a friend, neighbor, or acquaintance do your shipping for you as an independent contractor (e.g., out of his or her garage). Potentially, this can be a better service to you at less expense while providing more convenience. However, you need to consult the part of the tax laws that defines the difference between employees and independent contractors to make sure you can't be deemed by the IRS or state agencies to have an employee. Essentially, you will have to hand over your merchandise with a mailing label and let the shipping person do the rest. You can't exercise control. But this could be good part-time work for someone who is at home or who wants an extra part-time job for evenings or weekends.

If you don't follow the tax laws (and the labor guidelines of other governmental agencies), no one will ever catch you, right? Actually, that may not be the case. You'll get reported by the person you contracted with. Potentially, it will happen a couple of ways. First, the IRS will get after the person for not paying income taxes, and the person will say that he or she thought you were withholding taxes (a lie, but that won't stop the IRS from coming after you). Second, the person will file for unemployment benefits after you stop doing business with him. Third, the person will file for workmen's compensation after getting injured in his own garage with his own equipment while doing your shipping. So, it pays to make sure that you really establish an independent contractor's relationship with the person you contract with to do the shipping.

The details of this particular relationship are beyond the scope of this book, but it pays to research it thoroughly. You need to research it because outsourcing via independent contracting can be a very practicable and cost-effective way for you to do business, and it will become even more viable in the future as more people work at home.

Fulfillment

Filling the order (the sale from the auction) is one of the most important functions you will provide as part of your customer service. Fulfillment means processing the order and getting the merchandise shipped in a timely manner. You need to have a speedy procedure to handle fulfillment. Today people expect things they have purchased to arrive quickly. You are not excluded from this expectation just because you don't have a website storefront.

If you have a part-time retail business on eBay, you can't wait until the weekend to do your shipping. You have to ship as soon as payment is secured, or you will have some irritated customers. That's why the shipping example in the subsection above is a realistic one. If you can't do the shipping part of the fulfillment every day, find someone to do it for you.

Drop Shipping

One clever way to do your fulfillment is drop shipping. Drop shipping means having your wholesaler ship the merchandise directly to your customer. Many wholesalers are set up to do this. Today, to be competitive many wholesalers give quick shipping service. Hence, drop shipping can solve your fulfillment problem at the same time that it eliminates your inventory warehousing problem. The only questions are, How much does it cost, and can you do it more cost-effectively yourself?

Don't use drop shipping and then forget about the fulfillment service to your customers. It's your responsibility to make sure your customers get good fulfillment service via your drop shipping arrangements. That means you have to follow up with customer satisfaction surveys or otherwise test the quality of service that your customers are receiving. You'll always hear from customers if the quality of your service is bad. But if your service (via the drop shipper) is just mediocre, you may not get the complaints that alert you that something is wrong. Therefore, you have to stay alert and keep testing to ascertain the quality of your drop shipper's service to your customers.

The drop shipper is no different from an independent contractor in regard to quality. The difference is that you can usually check up on a local independent contractor more easily than you can a faraway wholesaler. As a result, you have to use other techniques to check up on the drop shipper.

If You're Small

If you're small, doesn't it mean that you can get away with not worrying about fast fulfillment and other customer service? The answer is yes, if you don't want to get bigger. But if you want to develop a good business or expand your business, you have to provide good customer service today regardless of size.

The Full-Time eBay Business

If you operate a full-time business that conducts business on eBay, you will be expected to provide excellent customer service because there is too much Web commerce that does provide first-rate customer service. From dealing with Amazon.com and the like, people's expectations are high. If you do not provide such service, you will be an ongoing irritant to your customers, hardly an enviable position considering the eBay feedback system.

With a Website

If you sell at retail full-time on eBay as a business or if you are a retailer who sells a fair amount on eBay but who has a bricks-and-mortar store too, you might seriously consider operating a commerce website. The question is, What is a commerce website? The following are some characteristics:

- Website catalog with inventory for sale

- Transaction system that takes orders, arranges payments, arranges shipping, and hands off the order to the fulfillment process

- Set up to receive payment in a variety of ways

- Organized to provide easy ways for people to communicate in regard to their orders or otherwise

- Attractive website with easy-to-use navigation

Perhaps the best commerce website of all in my opinion is Amazon.com. The story of Amazon is one of pure customer service. The Amazon website won't win any awards for aesthetics or for technical flamboyance. But it sure creates an easy, interesting, and convenient experience to buy a book online.

If you have a commerce website that functions intelligently, you can weave it into your eBay business. Here are some things you can do:

Link to your commerce website from your eBay auctions to generate extra business.

Link to your eBay auctions from your commerce website to generate extra business.

Refer winning bidders at your eBay auctions to your website for routine, reliable, and convenient transaction processing.

Extend your customer service activities at your commerce website to your eBay bidders and even to potential bidders.

Link to your commerce website from your eBay auctions to provide extra in-depth information on the merchandise being auctioned.

In other words, if you are a successful Web retailer with a commerce website, you probably already offer competent customer service. Why not extend it to your eBay customers too?

Likewise, if you are a successful eBay retailer with a high sales volume, why not establish a commerce website where you can offer more extensive and more convenient customer service than is generally possible by other means?

Without a Website

If you do not operate a commerce website, you have to ask yourself how you can provide comparable services. The first reaction you might have is that you can communicate by telephone, "snail mail" (i.e., US mail), and email. It seems to me the telephone may not work well. For instance, does someone whose only contact with you is via the Web, and possibly email, really want to start talking with you on the phone? Here are some reasons that it may not work:

Customer doesn't like to pay for long-distance phone calls. (Who does?)

Customer isn't available to talk on the phone during business hours.

Customer doesn't like to talk on the phone.

Customer wants a written record of entire transaction process.

A few of these things you can handle. You can get an 800 number so that the customer doesn't have to pay for the long-distance call. You can extend your business hours to cover evenings. Both are somewhat expensive, but your business volume may warrant such practices.

What about snail mail? Too slow. That leaves email as a primary means of communicating with customers. And that leaves you with the question, How can you provide customer service by email? After all, the customer came to you (on eBay) via the Internet.

There is no simple answer to this question. Email is a capable, powerful, and even flexible means of communication. Certainly, you can use email efficiently to conduct business. Indeed, it's just people talking to people, but not in real time. What are some techniques you can use with email communication?

Send a form email, like a form letter. This is very important for handling routine matters.

Attach a file (e.g., word processor file) to an email message.

Transfer lots of text into an email message via copy and paste.

Put links to websites into an email message.

Set up auto-responders to send automatic replies to certain email informational requests.

You may find, however, that having a commerce website instead can save you a lot of time and energy.

A Little Bit More

As a retail seller, exceed expectations. Go the extra mile. Do a little bit more than you said you would. For instance, communication is so important. As soon as a buyer's check clears and you ship the merchandise, send an email notifying the buyer that the merchandise has been sent. It's not required, but it will be appreciated. If you are well organized, you can do it easily.

Guarantee

There's nothing like a good old-fashioned guarantee. Why not offer one to your eBay customers? Many national retailers do. If you're serious about retailing on eBay, why not? Naturally, for used merchandise, you may need to be selective in offering a guarantee. But for new or refurbished merchandise, consider offering a blanket guarantee. Sure it will cost something, but it will also give potential bidders the confidence to become actual bidders. And the more bidders, the higher the price. The guarantee works well for many retail sellers on eBay.

Packaging

Bidders probably don't expect much from occasional sellers. But from retailers on eBay, they expect a professional job of presentation and packaging. That means an item needs to be cleaned and shined and then carefully packaged for shipment. If you don't do this, you will not maximize your retail business on eBay.

Goods That Don't Work

Many sellers sell merchandise in "as is" condition with no representation that the item will function or with a disclosure that the item does not function. Presumably such goods sell at low purchase prices because they are not in working condition. Clearly, eBay is an appropriate place to sell such goods, and buyers obtain such goods for parts or with the expectation that they can be repaired. However, if you're a retailer, you will do well to avoid such goods and only sell goods that function properly. Let someone else sell merchandise that doesn't work.

The Gift

Don't overlook the gift program that eBay operates. For $1 you can add a gift icon to your auction listing. Presumably you will reserve the use of this program for items that will make good gifts (almost anything) for the occasion. You have your choice of many icons representing different occasions, such as St. Patrick's Day, Mother's Day, and weddings. The items will be located in a special gift section as well as in the normal auction category.

The gift! Macy's, Neiman Marcus, Marshall Field's, Hudson's, and Nordstrom's. Does this ring a bell? Yes! Offer gift wrapping. Offer to enclose a card. Offer to ship direct to the gift recipient with some documentation sent to the buyer that the item was shipped in a timely manner. Offer a gift service. That's a nice touch for customer service.

Payment

The acceptance of payment in convenient ways for buyers is an important customer service. For eBay, the more ways you accept payment, the better for your customers (bidders). Because this is so important, it is treated separately in its own chapter, Chapter 16.

Response Times

As you know, if you sell much on eBay, there are deadbeat high bidders (bidders who never pay). To protect yourself, you must deal with each buyer systematically. Depending on your eBay selling experience, you may want to give deadlines for responses. For instance, you may want to send a form email to winning bidders informing them that they have won, requesting payment, and setting a deadline for a reply (e.g., three days). If you don't hear from them via email in three days, you automatically send another email requesting a response within three days. If there's no response to the second email within three days, you might send a last, more strongly worded email. Most sellers seem to quit at three requests. Then it's time to relist the item or offer it to the second-highest bidder (and be sure to report negative feedback on the deadbeat buyer).

Is this customer service? Sure it is. You give every buyer a reasonable chance to perform because you're a reasonable person. This seems like common sense, but you'd be surprised at the number of sellers who have a short fuse and relist an item (or sell to another) when they haven't heard from a buyer within two or three days.

The Other Side of the Story

As the winning bidder you're ecstatic. You just won. It's something of an ego trip, particularly when the bidding was heated and you feel you got a good price anyway. Then you have to wait three days for the seller to contact you. This is a big no-no on the part of the seller.

As a seller, you need to contact the winning bidder(s) as soon as possible after the close of the auction, certainly no more than one day later and ideally in less than three hours. This is essential customer service. You've got a hot prospect who's ready to pay. All you have to do is arrange payment. Don't dally. As the transaction cools down, your chances of completing it (and getting paid) diminish. Be prompt in your communication to winning bidders.

Shipping and Handling

If you simply charge for shipping, then you have to wait until after the auction to quote a charge (depending on how far away the buyer lives). The buyer remains uncertain about what the charge will be until he or she receives a quote. If you quote a *shipping* charge in the auction ad and collect it, the buyer may be angry when the actual shipping charge turns out to be less.

One way to get around this frustration is to charge for *shipping and handling*. No one knows what handling is. It probably should be covered in your overhead. Yet, many people charge it. My policy is to quote a shipping and handling charge in the auction ad. That gives the buyer certainty. My shipping and handling charge is enough to cover shipping anywhere in the US, but no more. If the actual shipping charge to a place close to where I live is less than the shipping and handling charge, the buyer has no grounds for complaint. This is less trouble for both parties.

Some people make their profit on shipping and handling. They charge a lower price for the item and a high price for shipping and handling. So long as the charge is stated in the auction ad, buyers have little grounds for complaint. Still, this practice is irritating to buyers and not recommended.

If you state no shipping or handling price in the auction ad, you'd better be ready to justify your charge. Otherwise you may get into a shouting match with the buyer.

Packaging

Package well to minimize your shipping problems. Most people overpackage perhaps. I've never received an item damaged that I've bought on eBay. But it's better to overpackage than to have to deal with damaged goods, collect insurance, and other nasty details.

Naturally, eBay is a fertile ground for selling packaging materials. Consequently, you do not have to look beyond eBay to find materials you need to package well at good prices. Also ask your shipper what is provided free in the way of shipping materials (e.g., containers). The following are also sources of packaging materials and containers:

Bubblefast (*http://www.bubblefast.com*)

Mail Boxes Etc (*http://www.mbe.com*)

Moving Unlimited (*http://movewithus.com*)

OfficeMax (*http://www.officemax.com*)

ShippingSupply.com (*http://www.shippingsupply.com*)

Staples (*http://www.staples.com*)

Uline (*http://uline.com*)

If It Doesn't Get There

What if you send it, and it doesn't get there? Who is responsible, the buyer or seller (you)? One way is to put the responsibility on the buyer and offer the buyer the opportunity to buy insurance. But what if the buyer doesn't buy insurance and it doesn't get there? Who is responsible, the buyer or seller (you)? Clearly, the buyer is responsible because that's the way you set up your sales requirements. This is terrible customer service, however, and you had better figure out another way to handle the missing package.

One way is to self-insure. If a package isn't delivered, you simply send another at your cost. Don't worry about getting and paying for insurance. Another way is to require mandatory insurance and

either pay for it or require that the buyer pay for it. A third way is
to use shippers that provide a minimal level of insurance (e.g.,
$100) at no extra cost. Whatever your solution, don't overlook this
aspect of doing business on eBay. And don't put the buyer in a losing situation.

Shippers

Any analysis of the different ways to ship that includes current
costs would be instantly outdated. So, I will leave you to figure
that out for yourself. Keep in mind the following, however, in evaluating shippers:

Convenience How convenient is it for you to use a particular
shipper? This is different for everybody. The shipper itself may
offer different convenience options. How much paperwork
does the shipper require?

Size and Weight What are the maximums? How do the maximums relate to what you need to ship?

Cost How much does it cost? Is it a flat fee or a fee based on
distance?

Included? What does the shipping service include? Pickup?
Insurance? Package tracking? Guaranteed delivery?

Reliability How reliable is the shipper? I believe FedEx is at
one end of the spectrum and the Postal Service is at the other
end. How far apart are they?

Customer Service If you ship 1 item a month, customer service may not be important. If you ship 100 items a month, the
shipper's customer service will be an important factor in your
business. A shipper's website where you can can monitor your
shipping reliably yourself 24 × 7 may be important for you.

Shipping is currently very competitive and changes continually. Keep up to date on the options available to you. The less hassle your shipper causes, the more smoothly your fulfillment operation will function.

There are other reliable shippers, but most people use one of the following:

Airborne Express (*http://www.airborne-express.com*)

DHL (*http://www.dhl-usa.com/index*)

Federal Express, aka FedEx (*http://fedex.com/us*)

United Parcel Service, aka UPS (*http://ups.com*)

US Postal Service, aka Post Office (*http://usps.com*)

Postage

Postage meters are a must for those who use the Postal Service and have a busy fullfillment operation. Or, you might try instead one of the Web postage services; you can print out postage on your computer printer.

E-stamp (*http://www.e-stamp.com*—may be defunct)

Pitney Bowes (*http://www.pitneybowes.com*)

Pitney Works (*http://www.pitneyworks.com*)

Trades

If you care to negotiate with buyers, you can start to wheel and deal. That means you can do creative transactions that benefit both parties to the transaction. For instance, you can do trades or partial trades rather than outright sales. When you do a trade, each party is both buyer and seller. Don't lose sight of that fact and become careless in playing the role of the party that you don't normally play.

Communication

Communication is the lubricant of the eBay mechanism. If you can stay in communication with the other party, you can usually work out almost any difficulties. Treat communication as a customer service.

Communication is time-consuming. Hope that you don't have to do anything but the routine communications (form emails) for every buyer. But when problems arise that need special treatment (special communication), and they do occasionally, be ready to spring into action and exchange email messages.

Offer to Communicate

Take the initiative in your initial email to winning bidders. Invite them to communicate with you if there are any problems. Be ready to handle those communications in a timely and efficient manner. The better organized and more systematic you are in handling your auctions and winning bidders, the fewer the problems and the less need for communications.

How to Get Organized

How do you get organized? That's a question you have to answer within the scope of your skills and knowledge or the skills and knowledge of your employees. Some ideas follow, but you know far better than I what's best for you.

Spreadsheet

A spreadsheet such as Excel or Lotus 1-2-3 can help you account for your transactions. What you should know is that you often use the database capabilities of the spreadsheet program rather than the calculation capabilities. Why not use a database manager instead?

I don't recommend the use of a spreadsheet unless you are a spreadsheet expert and don't know or don't want to know how to use a database manager. eBay attempted to devise a spreadsheet solution to the bulk upload situation (Master Lister) and finally backed off. Spreadsheets are great for calculations but not so adroit for accounting systems.

Database Manager

Desktop database managers such as Corel Paradox, FileMaker, and Microsoft Access are fabulous and powerful programs. You will find them easy to use. They offer great potential, and you will find them very handy for keeping track of your inventory, auctions, and transactions. There's nothing better than a compelling project with which to cut your teeth on a new program. You can learn quickly and get better organized in the process. Learn some general database principles, usually available in books on the various programs, and forge ahead to build a custom application for yourself using one of the desktop database managers. You won't regret it.

The best approach is to build one table into which you enter all your basic data as well as your follow-up data. When the table is open in front of you, you can easily and quickly go directly to the appropriate fields (column cells) and input data, delete data, or change data. You can cover a lot of territory in a short time. Or, a data entry and maintenance employee can do a lot of work in a short time.

Eventually, you may find yourself graduating to greater functionality by creating related tables (relational database) and doing all sorts of clever database things. But starting out with one easy-to-build table is an easy step to take, and a productive one.

On Paper

Does anyone still use paper? Ultimately, pushing paper is not as productive as pumping electrons. But sometimes the best move is one that's comfortable for you. A total paper system to handle Web commerce is insanity. But a hybrid system (paper–electronic) makes sense. The goal is to get as close to 100 percent electronic as is practical. Nonetheless, you don't have to get there immediately. Work toward that goal at a comfortable pace while still using some of your paper practices.

PowerSellers

The eBay PowerSellers program is for people who are doing a lot of retail auctions on eBay. It provides certain customer service benefits to you as an eBay customer. For example, as a PowerSeller, you can display the PowerSellers logo, which identifies you, in effect, as a high-volume eBay retailer.

This is likely to instill more confidence and trust in you by bidders than you would otherwise receive.

The program has monthly minimum sales requirements and three levels of participation (bronze, silver, and gold) based on sales. This program is evolving into something quite valuable for eBay retailers. Check it out at *Services, buying & selling, PowerSellers*.

This is not a small program. eBay has 20,000–25,000 PowerSellers according to the *San Francisco Examiner* (August 20, 2000, p. C-6). It's certainly something to aspire to if you are a high-volume eBay seller. Your PowerSellers logo shows that you are doing business successfully on eBay and therefore implies that you provide acceptable customer service.

Where the Gold Is

In every gold strike (California, Colorado, Alaska), it never seems to be the miners who get rich. It's the store owners in the gold-mining towns that spring up who make the money. Similarly, you might consider providing services to eBay retailers. I know of an antique dealer in the Bay Area who provides the following package of services to other antique dealers she knows:

1. Puts their antiques up for auction on eBay

2. Conducts the auction and communicates with bidders

3. Receives the purchase payment

4. Ships the antiques

All an antique dealer has to do is stop by and leave the antique off at her office. She gets a percentage of the selling price. In other words, she does not only the fulfillment but also the auctioning.

Is this a good business? Hard to tell, but the man who owns the local photography shop in my town has someone sell his cameras on eBay for him. Think of customer services you can perform for serious eBay auctioneers, and make a business out of it.

Check out my eZsale (*http://myezsale.com*), a business serving eBay sellers (and other online auction sellers) at various locations, primarily in Colorado and two other states, and Craters & Freighters (*http://cratersandfreighters.com*) with shipping from 60 locations nationally.

On-Site Auctions

On-site auctions are the latest rage. You can purchase software from $1,500 to $150,000 for conducting online auctions at your website. But it's a lot of trouble to operate such auctions. Your chances of building the critical mass to make your on-site auctions profitable are remote. eBay provides you with a great opportunity to bring your auctions on eBay to your website via links. It's not exactly like having an auction at your website, but it doesn't cost anything extra either. With proper linking, it provides your customers with added convenience. See Chapter 18 for information on linking eBay to your website. Don't forget to follow the eBay rules in the eBay User Agreement in regard to linking to your website from your eBay auction ads.

Amazon.com

If you want to maximize customer service at your website, study Amazon. Everything at Amazon is aimed at making it easy for customers to make purchasing decisions about books (and other merchandise) and then to easily purchase them. And sometimes at a discount! Navigation is easy. Searching is easy. Information access is easy. And ordering requires only one click.

One click does everything! It puts the book in your shopping basket and checks you out automatically. If you order another book within two hours, Amazon makes sure that both books (or more) are shipped together, if possible, to save shipping costs. It doesn't get any easier than one click.

This didn't happen haphazardly. The Amazon founder, his wife, and a few employees spent a year designing and testing their website system before they opened on the Web for business. That means they spent a year on customer service before they took their first customer.

Can you afford to do this? Perhaps not. Nonetheless, there are dozens of website commerce programs available today that provide some of the functions of customer service found at Amazon. (Starbase-21 even has an Amazon-like affiliate module for Miva Merchant that enables you to develop a referral mechanism—see Chapter 18.) Many commerce programs are inexpensive to set up and operate. There's no excuse for not providing enhanced customer service at your website.

Try Lands' End (*http://www.landsend.com*), which enables you to try on clothes at its website via *My Virtual Model* (a model of yourself). Now that's customer service!

Benchmarks of Customer Service

Your eBay auctions are not somehow magically exempt from the need for customer service. Indeed, the secret to success in auctioning merchandise on eBay is excellent and speedy customer service any way you can provide it. Of the Web we will know in 2020, probably only 3 percent has been invented yet. Invent something you can do to improve your customer service on eBay (and be sure to let me know).

Even if you are an occasional seller, you need to provide good customer service. It affects your reputation. Moreover, you have your own set of interests. The things you sell over the years will reflect those interests. The people you sell them to will tend to have similar interests. Despite the huge number of people using eBay, you may run across some of the same people in your eBay auctioning activities from time to time, if not regularly. If you are a regular seller on eBay, even if not a retailer, you will certainly run across many of the same people regularly in regard to your auction activities. Your reputation will count for something with such people.

So, to conclude, the following is offered as a baseline list of Web customer service benchmarks for commerce websites and eBay auctions:

- Easy and intuitive navigation
- Easily readable text
- Robust information on products for sale
- Guarantees
- Clear instructions on transaction procedures
- Multiple payment methods
- Quick service
- Professional fulfillment procedures
- Prompt communications

Don't feel comfortable with this list. It's a good beginning, but it's not enough. If the above is all you have, some of your competitors are already ahead of you. But if you meet all the benchmarks above, you're ahead of most of your competitors.

Summary

Customer service is the essence of selling on the Web, whether it's a commerce website or a series of auctions on eBay. As a seller, customer service should be in the front of your consciousness at all times. If a securities analyst on Wall Street can get together with a Web programmer and invent Amazon.com, you can probably come up with a few new ideas yourself for providing better customer service in regard to your eBay auctions.

12

Handling Images

Digital photographs sell merchandise. eBay enables you to embed images in your eBay auction ad. This is a wonderful opportunity to show what you're selling. People like to see the things they contemplate buying.

Photographs may seem unimportant for some products. For instance, how do you show software or other seemingly intangible products? It's simple. You show the box. Even showing the box will help you sell. In fact, showing the box or showing manufacturers' photographs and drawings will help you sell new products and even used products. Where the merchandise is used, blemished, scratched, or otherwise damaged, however slightly, a good close-up photograph of the item will provide potential bidders with the information they need to make a bidding decision. The more disclosure you make, the less trouble you will have from buyers. A photograph is often the best way to disclose exactly what you're selling.

Surprisingly often, a photograph assists a seller to make more accurate disclosure. If you advertise one model but show another in a photograph, some knowledgeable potential bidders will set you straight. It's not unusual at all for a potential bidder to be more knowledgeable than a seller in regard to an item, and you see sellers being set straight routinely. Better to learn about your mistake before the auction is finished than after.

Photography Tips

Product photography is something of an art, but you're not taking pictures for the Oldsmobile brochure, so don't worry about it too much. Do, however, take the little bit of extra time to ensure that your photographs are appealing. Here are some things you can do:

1. Photograph in color. Does anyone use B&W anymore?

2. Use outdoor light, if practical. Even outdoors, however, you may need a flash to fill in shadows.

3. Use a flash indoors. Mute the flash with a translucent cover, or bounce it off the ceiling, to avoid glare.

4. Use a plain, dull (not shiny), one-color background. Cloth backgrounds (e.g., tablecloths) work well.

5. Get as close to the item as possible. Use a closeup lens, if

appropriate. Fill the frame. But be careful of overexposure from a flash.

6. Take multiple photographs with different settings. Give yourself a choice.

7. Use a tripod, and focus carefully.

Take multiple photographs for items that deserve multiple photographs in your auction ad (e.g., vehicles). Don't forget to take photographs of blemishes and defects that bidders will want to see.

Digitizing Photographs

You have your choice of a variety of ways to digitize photographs so you can use them on eBay.

Kodak Photo CD

You can take photographs with a 35mm camera and send them for processing via Kodak Photo CD at virtually any photo finisher. It costs about $25 for the CD plus one roll of film developed (you get thumbnail prints and negatives too), but the CD can hold 100 images (4 rolls of 24, or almost 3 rolls of 36). You get back high-quality digital images (photographs) in six sizes each; but only the two smallest (or the third smallest, if you crop it) are suitable for eBay. The quality of Photo CD is much higher than you need for your eBay ad, but it's one method of digitizing your photographs.

Kodak Picture CD

Kodak Picture CD (available at most photo finishers) costs less and gives you less than Photo CD. But Picture CD is really all you need. It provides you with a JPEG image file you can use on the

Web, but only in one large size. You will need to use an image editor to reduce the size.

Kodak PhotoNet online

Kodak PhotoNet online (*http://www.kodak.com/US/en/photoNet/ aol/learn.shtml*) is a special service just for creating digital photographs and posting them on the Web. Go to the URL to get complete instructions.

Removes a Step

As you will read later, you need to upload your digital photographs to the Web in order to use them for an eBay auction. With this service, you do not have to upload the photographs to the Web yourself, thus eliminating a step. Kodak does it for you. Again, you use this service through photo finishers.

Scanner

You can digitize the photographs (prints) with a flatbed scanner. Such scanners are now inexpensive (under $90), and the quality is adequate for eBay. This is an excellent way for you to convert your snapshots into digital photographs.

Scan your photographs at the highest resolution possible for your scanner (usually better than 700 dots per inch (dpi). Although computer monitors typically display at about 92 dpi, you would not be happy with photographs scanned at 92 dpi or even 300 dpi. Consider 600 dpi a minimum for attractive images.

Not Just Photographs

You can also use a scanner to make images of documents, flat art, photographs printed in publications, and the like. Scanners work just like copy machines.

You can also go to a place like Kinko's to get a photograph scanned, but it's expensive.

Another alternative is to use a film scanner. A film scanner for 35mm film costs at least $350. You actually put the film negative or positive (slide) in the scanner, and the scanner makes a high-quality scan. This quality is higher than a consumer flatbed scanner and beyond the quality you need for eBay.

For all of these methods, the film must be developed. You need prints for the flatbed scanner and Kinko's, and negatives or slides for the film scanner.

Digital Camera

Inexpensive digital cameras (under $1,000) are not known for their high quality in comparison to film cameras, but they're perfectly adequate for eBay photos. If you do a lot of eBay auctions, using a digital camera is the least expensive, quickest, and most convenient way to create digital photographs. Just shoot the photographs and load them into your computer. It couldn't be easier.

The quality is adequate for most purposes. If you sell antique Japanese prints and want to capture the subtle colors, don't use an inexpensive digital camera. Use a 35mm camera and Picture CD. But most products do not require such quality, and a digital camera does just fine.

High-quality digital cameras in the over $3,000 price range will provide higher quality, if you need it. Lower-quality digital cameras in the $300 price range are perfectly adequate for most eBay purposes.

Make sure that any digital camera you buy has the capability of taking close-ups. This is a feature you will probably use a lot.

Camcorder

Some analog camcorders and many digital camcorders have the capability of taking digital snapshots (one frame at a time). Consult your owner's manual. If you can get such snapshots into your computer (via whatever means the manufacturer provides), you will have digital photographs you can use for eBay.

Size

Don't make your photographs large. Seldom is a photograph larger than 500 × 375 pixels justified for an eBay ad. Make it smaller. Digital images larger than 400 × 300 take longer to download, making your eBay ad photographs slow to appear, perhaps even slowing the download of your entire ad. They also may interfere with your auction Web page. However, don't think by recommending 400 x 300 that you should enlarge smaller photographs to that size. If you have smaller photographs, use them in their smaller size. Digital photographs don't enlarge well.

Typically, digital cameras use at least a 640 × 480 pixel format, and you don't want to use anything smaller. This is quite large. Since digital camera formats and the Picture CD format do not provide a proper size, you will have to shrink your digital photographs. One way to do it is via the image markup, but this doesn't change the download time. Another way to do it is to reduce the size of the image with a graphics editing program (covered in Chapter 21) to make the image file smaller to download.

Image Markup

Regardless of the actual size of the digital photograph, you can set the size that it will show on eBay in the image markup. Suppose the image is 640 × 480 pixels. You want to shrink it to 400 × 300. Use the image markup:

```
<img src="[URL]" width="400"
height="300">
```

The size of the digital photograph remains the same, but the browser reduces the image shown in the Web page (the ad) to 400 × 300. This does not reduce the download time but saves you the task of graphics editing. This is not a recommended procedure, primarily because it causes an unnecessarily long download time.

Photo Manipulation

You can use a photo manipulation (image editing) program such as Adobe PhotoShop to decrease the size of the image before you use it. PhotoShop is a well-known, high-end program, but hundreds of inexpensive photo editing programs can resize digital photographs and also do much more. Most will enable you to easily change the contrast, brightness, and gamma. In other words, these programs act like a digital darkroom. You can make better photographs than you took. Whether you want to go to all that trouble is a matter of judgment, but if you have to change the size, it's usually little additional trouble to adjust the contrast, brightness, and gamma. You can see the photograph change as you make the adjustments. Chapter 21 covers graphics editing.

Format

All digital images must be in the GIF, JPEG, or PNG format. If your digital photographs are not in one of these forms, you need to convert them. The photo editing programs enable you to make conversions, too, and are handy just for that.

Making Photographs Available

You store digital photographs on your hard disk. When you want to make them available to others via the Internet, you have to upload them to a hard disk that's on the Web (i.e., an ISP's hard disk).

Storing Photographs

Once your images are ready for publication, you must store them at a website. That gives them a URL.

Website

Suppose you store them at your website (*www.yourwebsite.com*). Your root directory at your website is:

```
/clients/yours/public_html
```

You can create a handy directory (folder) named *images* just to store your images:

```
/clients/yours/public_html/images
```

Suppose you need an image named item41.gif (in your auction ad at eBay) that you have stored on your website in the *images* directory. The image markup in the ad will look as follows:

```
<img src="http://
www.yourwebsite.com/images/
item41.gif">
```

Thus, your image stored on your website will appear magically in your eBay ad. (See Chapter 20 for ideas about using a Web authoring program to create your image markups.)

If you need help with creating directories and determining what the URL of your images will be, consult your Web host ISP (Internet service provider). In particular, America Online provides space for you to store files.

ISP Account

If you don't have a website, you may be able to store your images on your dial-up ISP's hard disk in the space reserved for you. Your ISP reserves space for your email messages. Most ISPs also enable you to use such space for Web pages. If you can put up a Web page, you can store images. Suppose your Web address is *http://www.isp.com/~yours*. You can create a directory named *images* and upload all your images for eBay auction ads to that directory. The image markup will be:

```
<img src="http:// www.isp.com/~yours/
images/item41.gif">
```

If you need help with creating directories and determining what the URL of your images will be, consult your dial-up ISP.

ISPs

If your dial-up and your Web host ISPs are the same, you have a combined dial-up plus Web host account.

Special Services

There are a number of Web services that cater to auction users. They will store your images for auction ads for free or for a fee. Go to their websites to get instructions:

- Auctionimage (*http://www.auctionimage.com*)
- The Best Shots (*http://www.thebestshots.com*)
- Honesty (*http://www.honesty.com*)
- Imagehost (*http://www.imagehost.com*)
- ImageHosting (*http://www.imagehosting.com*)
- Images R Us (*http://www.imagesrus.net*)
- ManageAuctions (*http://www.manageauctions.com*)
- PixHost (*http://www.pixhost.com*)
- Pongo's (*http://www.pongo.com*)
- Service For You (*http://www.images4u.net*)
- Twaze (*http://www.twaze.com*)
- WeppiHeka (*http://www.weppiheka.com*)

Make sure when you sign up with one of these services that you know how to upload your photographs to the service (to their website). Also make sure you know exactly what the URL of your image will be once you have uploaded the image. Many of these services also provide scanning and other image services.

Check Chapter 18 for a list of free websites where presumably you can store images in addition to creating a website.

eBay Picture Service

You don't have to use an outside service for storage. You can use the new eBay Picture Service (*http://pages.ebay.com/help/basics/pictureservices.html*). The first two photographs per auction are free. After that, it costs you. This is a handy service that you might want to try. The photographs are automatically deleted after your auction ends.

Uploading Photographs

To upload your photographs to your storage place (website), you use the File Transfer Protocol (FTP). Consequently, you will need an FTP client to upload the images. There are many freeware and shareware FTP clients available. Try *http://www.cnet.com* and look for *downloads*.

I upload with WS_FTP, which is easy to use. It enables you to show a directory (folder) on your own hard disk on the left and a directory on the hard disk of your website on the right. After getting online, you simply highlight the file(s) on the left and click on the arrow pointing right to make the upload. You can also download by highlighting the files on the right and clicking on the arrow pointing to the left (see Figure 12.1).

One of several places on the Web where you can get WS_FTP is at *http://www.ipswitch.com/_ebay/index.html*. This URL also provides special instructions for eBay users. Other FTP clients include:

- CuteFTP (*http://www.cuteftp.com*)
- Fetch (for Mac—*http://www.dartmouth.edu/pages/softdev/fetch.html*)
- FTP Voyager (*http://www.ftpvoyager.com*)

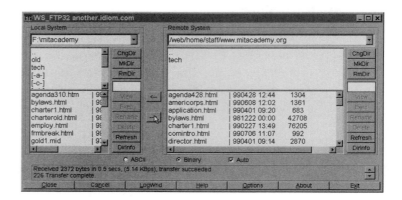

Figure 12.1   WS_FTP uploading files to a website.

Pulling In Photographs

Through the magic of links, you can pull media into your eBay auction ad from other servers on the Internet. This is a little different from a link to another Web page. A link to another Web page will take you to that Web page. But a media markup will bring the media into the eBay auction ad (which is a Web page). The media can be images, sound clips, or even video clips (see Figure 12.2).

But we are concerned primarily with images. Store the images at your website, in your ISP account storage space, or at one of the Web services that offer to store images. Then pull it into your eBay auction ad with the image markup.

Making It Happen

So, you've stored your photograph where it's accessible on the Web. You have its correct URL. What do you do next?

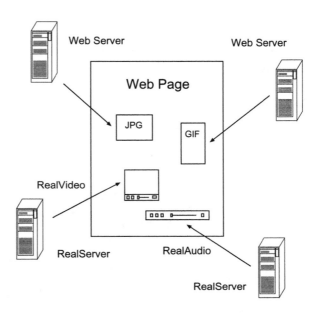

Figure 12.2   Media markups pull in media from across the Web.

At eBay

When you access the *Sell Your Item* form in the Sell section to enter your eBay auction ad, be ready to enter the URL of your image. The URL will start with *http://.*

If you don't add the URL at the time you enter the other information for your auction, you can add it later. If you add it later, however, the photograph will be tacked onto the bottom of the ad and will look like an add-on.

In the Template

In the template featured in Chapter 13, you add the URL of the photograph into the template. You then enter the entire template in the *Description* for the auction ad (i.e., at *Sell Your Item*). You do not enter the URL of the photograph into the *Picture URL* for the eBay auction ad when you use a template; just leave the *Picture URL* blank. The template places the photograph in a special place. The whole point of using a template is to create an attractive auction ad with the photograph well integrated (see Figure 12.3).

Figure 12.3   Photograph in auction ad made with template.

In the Bulk Upload

For bulk uploads, the URL for a photograph goes into the database. The URL then gets "mail merged" into the mail-merge template (which includes the Chapter 13 template). The result is exactly the same as for the Chapter 13 template, except that the templates are filled in by a bulk system (mass-produced) rather than filled in manually one template at a time.

Other People's Photographs

Other people may have photographs you can use. More specifically, you can use photographs from manufacturers' websites; simply right-click on the photograph. You will see the file name of the photograph, and you can also save the photograph to your own hard disk. Once you have saved it, you can use it as if it's one of your own; that is, you can upload it to your Web photograph storage place. Another way you can use it is to look at the Source for the Web page (Go *View, Source* in either the Netscape browser or the Microsoft browser) after right-clicking on the photograph to get the image file name (see Figure 12.4).

The source will show you the URL of the photograph. (Sometimes the URL is incomplete because it is a relative reference, and you will have to try to figure out the complete URL. This level of analysis is beyond the scope of this book, but this method is worth mentioning for readers who know HTML.) Once you have the correct and complete URL, you don't need to download the photograph and you don't need to store it at your Web photograph storage place; you only need to use it where it is. That is, you use the URL of the manufacturer's photograph at the manufacturer's website by putting the manufacturer's URL in the *Picture URL* in your eBay auction ad (i.e., *Sell Your Item*).

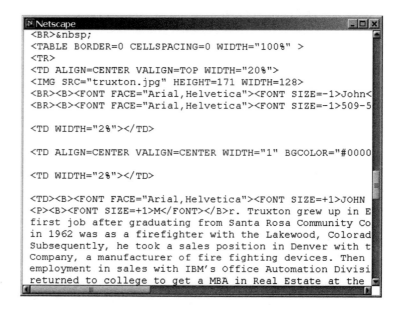

Figure 12.4   The source shows the entire Web page in HTML.

Now it's one thing to say you *can* use these techniques, but the fact that you can doesn't mean you should. In fact, you must consider everything on the Web to be copyrighted. If you use other people's copyrighted materials without permission, you are liable for copyright infringement. So, before you pull in (or download) a photograph or logo from a manufacturer's website into your eBay auction ad, first get permission from the webmaster at the manufacturer's website.

Graphics

A digital photograph is just a digital color graphic. You can use any color graphic just as if it were a digital photograph. Consequently, you may want to use a drawing or other art form rather than a photograph. Whatever graphic you use, however, you must first convert it to a GIF, JPEG, or PNG file format. Photographs are always best, but if you can't find a photograph or can't take one, a color graphic may be better than nothing.

Summary

A digital color photograph helps sell merchandise on eBay. It is well worth going to the trouble of taking one, developing it, digitizing it, editing it, and using it in your eBay ad. If you use a digital camera, you can skip developing it and digitizing it. The seemingly toughest part of the procedure, graphics editing, is really quite easy, and it's a step you need to take just to resize or crop your photograph, if nothing else. Once the digital photograph is ready, it's just a matter of posting it via FTP on a website and referencing its URL in your eBay auction ad—a pretty simple process, and a pretty powerful means of advertising.

13

Using a Template for eBay Ads

eBay provides you with a Web page space with which you can do almost anything to advertise the item you auction. Take advantage of this great opportunity. This is your chance to create some interest in your offering that will bring in a higher final bid.

eBay Advertising

Every medium has its own unique characteristics. The Web is an information medium. You can publish unlimited information on the Web at a small cost. It's not a medium like television where every time slot commands a premium price and where advertising is relatively expensive. Take advantage of the Web's strength and publish plenty of information on the item you auction.

Keep in mind that the Web (and eBay) is not a retail store where a customer can walk in, examine the merchandise, and talk to sales-people. What you publish is what the customer gets. Your eBay auction advertisement has to create interest, then inform, and finally, close the sale.

An eBay ad has two parts: the one-line title that goes in the listing and the Web page section that is part of the auction page. This chapter considers the one-line title at the end of the chapter, but let's start with the ad.

The First Goal

The first objective of the ad is to create interest. A little hype is OK here, so long as you can back up the hype with facts a little farther down the page. The top of the ad should always include:

1. The specific identification of the item being auctioned

2. Condition of the item

3. One or two major benefits of the item to potential bidders

Put your strongest benefits here. You may get only one chance to hook the bidder/reader. Give it your best shot at the top of the ad.

Clearly and specifically identify the item being sold here. Other-wise you will frustrate and anger potential bidders. Even worse, it may create a lot of unnecessary, undesirable, and time-consuming communication for you. If the item is a model XMT-5001 camcorder, not a model XMT-5011, you'd better get it right.

The condition of the item is important and should be stated at the top of the ad. New, mint, and excellent condition are prime selling points. Don't neglect to put them in up front. However, many people can't afford to buy a new product of the type you're selling. They look for bargains where the product is *in good working order but has a few cosmetic blemishes* (and other such descriptions). Express the condition as a prime feature, and you will draw potential bidders regardless of what the condition is.

Determine one or two major selling points that will draw the interest of the most likely bidders. Don't try to tell the whole story here. You have plenty of room later. Just mention one or two benefits to hook potential bidders.

Hook them into bidding? No. Your objective with the hype at the top of the ad is not to get them to make a bid. It's to get them to read more about your offering, that is, to get them to acquire enough facts on which to base a confident decision to bid.

> Wrong: ActionCatcher camcorder with picture stabilization, flicker reduction, digital zoom, review/retake functions, and random editing.

> Right: ActionCatcher camcorder XMT-5001, new, all automatic features, perfect for intermediate users and even novices.

What's wrong with the information in the first example? Nothing. But it's too much information, and it doesn't seem directly tied to benefits. There's plenty of space to mention such information below. ActionCatcher has many different models of camcorders ranging in price from $300 to many thousands of dollars. Which model is it?

What's right with the second example? It mentions that the item is new and clearly identifies exactly what's for sale. Then it adds a little hype. It's probably not going to interest expert users, but then they won't buy the XMT-5001 anyway. Novice and intermediate videographers will be likely to read more.

The Second Goal

The second part of the ad has two parts, the product information and the purchasing information.

Product Information

Now that you've hooked bidders into reading, provide them with the facts. The hype is over. Leave the hype to the television folks who only have a few seconds to hook potential buyers. And keep in mind that a television ad attempts to hook potential buyers into what? Into going to a local store to make a purchase, a local store where the potential buyer will interact with a salesperson. At eBay there is no salesperson. There's only your ad. Consequently, for the main body of your eBay ad, it's your job to supply the facts and benefits to enable the potential bidder to make a decision to bid (to buy).

At eBay, there's no limit on the ad. This circumstance requires facts. Provide as much factual data on the item for sale as you can find. Don't assume that anyone knows anything about the item. If you do, you'll be cutting out a significant percentage of your potential market.

What do you publish? Don't reinvent the wheel. A good place to start looking for information is the manufacturer's information and specifications. Get them off the box. Get them off the manufacturer's website. Get them out of the user's manual. Put in a link to the manufacturer's information and specification sheets on the manufacturer's website.

Hype, Information, and Specifications

The manufacturer's information and specifications usually contain some hype. Is that OK? Sure it is. So long as the ad is essentially informative, a little hype woven in is to be expected. Just a little hype, though. Overly hyped information loses credibility with potential bidders. Instead, they want facts and benefits.

A link to a manufacturer's website by itself is not enough. Such a link can cut your ad from seven paragraphs to one perhaps, but you still need a paragraph or two to keep readers involved in your ad. If you use a link, make sure it is a link directly to the specific Web page at the manufacturer's website that has the relevant information.

Express your personal enthusiasm for the item. If you have a positive opinion of the item, express it in terms of benefits to bidders. Honest opinions, even coming from the seller, are valuable. If you have a negative opinion of the item, don't say anything. Let the manufacturer speak for you. If the item is a lemon product, even if new, you better warn the bidders, albeit mildly. If you don't and you sell a lot of stuff on eBay, you may negatively affect your reputation. eBay is not a dumping ground for lemon products. If you treat it that way, you may adversely affect your reputation and fail to achieve your long-term commercial objectives on eBay. Lemons can be sold honestly, albeit at lower prices, with happy sellers and buyers, but only with disclosure up front.

Don't make the ad too long. You could put the full text of three magazine reviews on the product in your ad, but that would be too much in most cases. Link to them instead. Beyond 1,000 or 2,000 words, you're bound to start losing people. However, it's different for every product. Bidders probably don't need 2,000 words about an office file cabinet. But if you're selling a $19,000 timeshare at a Steamboat Springs, Colorado, ski resort, 2,000 words may not be enough.

Losing Your Market

I was looking for a new camcorder on eBay. One person was selling two or three each week of the model I had decided to buy. He provided a generous amount of information (all the text from the manufacturer's website), enough to inspire a decision. He was selling the same model over and over again for an average price of $550. I got ready to make my bid.

I reviewed what was being auctioned one last time. Surprisingly, I discovered another person selling the identical camcorder (also new). This person had posted very sparse information on the camcorder, only four sentences and few specifications. As a result, he had attracted few bidders. I put in my bid at this person's auction, won the bidding, and got the new camcorder for $450. The same day the other person sold three more identical camcorders at his Dutch auction for $550; the bids were $550, $600, and $600.

The moral of the story is that if you're a seller, it pays to provide plenty of information. If you're a buyer, it pays to look for lazy sellers.

Purchasing Information

To build the bidder's confidence in purchasing from you, you must give complete information on how the transaction can be closed. How can the buyer pay? The more ways, the better. But whatever the acceptable payment methods, state them clearly.

Don't forget shipping and handling. State specific amounts for such expenses up front. If your website states payment methods, you can say less in your eBay ad and put in a link to the complete statement of acceptable payment methods and policies on your website. If you do that, however, at least cover the basics in your eBay ad.

Payment Methods

You will sell more if you accept credit cards (or PayPal or Billpoint). Do you know that you can take checks via the Web or via telephone? This is not popular yet, but it will be, and it's easy for you to do. See Chapter 16.

This is a golden opportunity to put in a general link to your website where presumably you have the opportunity to sell something to potential bidders directly, outside of eBay. For some reason, a lot of sellers who should be doing this don't. Don't miss this opportunity; it doesn't cost anything extra.

Promote Yourself and Your Other Auctions

Promoting yourself works best after you have accumulated some proof that you're trustworthy. That is, as soon as you've built up some positive feedback, you can state, "Check my feedback." Make your self-promotion modest and factual. Do it, but don't overdo it. Also, use your auction ad to promote your other eBay auctions. You can put in a link in your auction ad to the eBay list of your other auctions.

The Third Goal

Ask for the order; that is, ask people to make a bid. Don't make a statement like "The lucky winning bidder will enjoy the CleanCut

Estate Mower for many years." Rather say something like "Make a bid now. I think you'll be satisfied with the quality of this mower if you're the winning bidder, and I appreciate your interest in my auction." What you say doesn't have to be long or elaborate, but do ask for the bid.

Unique Products

Certain products do not lend themselves neatly to the preceding format, which is designed essentially for mass-produced goods with which many potential bidders will be familiar. Unique products and custom products require more explanation. Not only that, but in many cases, it may be appropriate and worthwhile to provide information expressed in a creative way.

Suppose you want to sell custom two-week tours to the central Italian countryside via tourist bus. A canned tour might be comparable to a mass-produced product. People will compare the itineraries of the different tours available. The itineraries are like the specifications for a camcorder.

However, a tour to be customized to the desires of a group (e.g., the Northwest Atlanta Garden Club) is different. You might want to provide some information on alternatives for touring central Italy in order to provide a basis for the group leader to determine the custom itinerary. You might even provide excerpts from *Under the Tuscan Sun* (with permission), a book about Tuscany by Frances Mayes, for potential bidders to read.

Potential bidders who are looking for unique products will take the time to review a creative presentation of relevant information. It's difficult to imagine someone comparing camcorder specifications, which are much the same, taking the time to read a creative presentation on a camcorder. But for a custom tour, a creative presentation is necessary to make the sale. Thus, for unique products, the product information section (middle section) of the ad can be a creative presentation that doesn't necessarily follow a standard formula.

Presenting the Ad

What's the goal for your presentation of the ad? The same as for the ad itself. You want potential bidders to read the entire ad. The best way to do so is to make it easily readable.

Text

Text is your most important medium. Remember, the Web is an informational medium. The most efficient way to convey the requisite information to potential bidders in most cases is via words.

The following subsections outline the format for the text. The penalty for neglecting to follow these guidelines is shrinkage of your potential market. Each guideline you fail to follow will shrink your market more. At some point, there will be no market left, and potential bidders will ignore your auction. In addition, by doing a sloppy job of publishing your ad, you detract from your credibility as a seller.

Grammar

Write the ad well. Check your spelling. Don't use acronyms or abbreviations; at least half the bidders won't know what those mean. Even if you use what you think are commonly understood acronyms having to do with the product or procedures on eBay, you will lose a lot of bidders, and you will never know it. Use good grammar and complete sentences. You are not writing a classified ad for which you pay by the word. Write something that's readable.

Don't be afraid to make mistakes. We all make spelling and grammatical mistakes. These are understandable and forgivable. What is irritating is the intentional cutting of corners (abbreviations, acronyms, incomplete sentences) that makes reading more difficult for everyone and often makes the text incomprehensible.

Paragraphs

Divide your text into paragraphs. It astounds me that some people put 1,500 words of information in their ad, all in one paragraph. That makes the text very difficult to read and comprehend. For example:

The ActionCatcher XMT-5001 camcorder with LCD color monitor. MSRP is $1,399. Features include: Built-in still camera with 140,000 pixels. LCD color monitor with 290-degree screen rotation for high- and low-angle viewing. Quick 44X Zoom with close-up focus. Picture stabilizing that differentiates between intentional and unintentional camera movements. Six-head mechanism for precision recording. Built-in head cleaner. Automatic system for recording, including auto focus, white balance, and auto exposure. Flicker reduction, flying erase head, and random editing. Floodlight built in that automatically turns on or off as needed. Review and retake functions with indicators for remaining tape time and remaining battery time. Remote control, editing, and dubbing. Image transfer and recording software. Special effects and titling. Languages: English, French, Spanish, and German. Fog and ND filters. Mic input. S-Cable output. Lens cover, dew sensor, 3-way power supply. New, sealed in box.

You can easily divide the above paragraph into separate paragraphs by using the HTML paragraph markup *<p>* at the beginning of each paragraph:

```
The ActionCatcher XMT-5001 camcorder
with LCD color monitor. MSRP is
$1,399. Features include:<p>Built-in
still camera with 140,000
pixels.<p>LCD color monitor with 290-
degree screen rotation for high- and
low-angle viewing.<p>Quick 44X Zoom
with close-up focus.<p>Picture
stabilizing that differentiates
between intentional and unintentional
camera movements.<p>Six-head
mechanism for precision
recording.<p>Built-in head
cleaner.<p>Automatic system for
recording, including auto focus, white
balance, and auto exposure.<p>Flicker
reduction, flying erase head, and
random editing.<p>Floodlight built in
that automatically turns on or off as
needed.<p>Review and retake functions
with indicators for remaining tape
time and remaining battery
time.<p>Remote control, editing, and
dubbing.<p>Image transfer and
recording software.<p>Special effects
and titling.<p>Languages: English,
French, Spanish, and German.<p>Fog and
ND filters.<p>Mic input.<p>S-Cable
output.<p>Lens cover, dew sensor, 3-
way power supply.<p>New, sealed in
box.
```

After you do so, the presentation will be more readable in a Web browser:

> The ActionCatcher XMT-5001 camcorder with LCD color monitor. MSRP is $1,399. Features include:
>
> Built-in still camera with 140,000 pixels.
>
> LCD color monitor with 290-degree screen rotation for high- and low-angle viewing.
>
> Quick 44X Zoom with close-up focus.
>
> Picture stabilizing that differentiates between intentional and unintentional camera movements.
>
> Six-head mechanism for precision recording.
>
> Built-in head cleaner.
>
> Automatic system for recording, including auto focus, white balance, and auto exposure.
>
> Flicker reduction, flying erase head, and random editing.
>
> Floodlight built in that automatically turns on or off as needed.
>
> Review and retake functions with indicators for remaining tape time and remaining battery time.
>
> Remote control, editing, and dubbing.
>
> Image transfer and recording software.
>
> Special effects and titling.
>
> Languages: English, French, Spanish, and German.
>
> Fog and ND filters.
>
> Mic input.

S-Cable output.

Lens cover, dew sensor, 3-way power supply.

New, sealed in box.

Although the above presentation is not as attractive as it can be with additional HTML coding (it needs bullets), it is definitely more readable than a solid block of text. Anyone can add the *<p>* markup without knowing HTML.

To add bullets, you must use more HTML markups. The *<ul>* and *<li>* markups are simple but not as simple as *<p>*.

```
The ActionCatcher XMT-5001 camcorder
with LCD color monitor. MSRP is
$1,399. Features include:

<ul>

<p><li>Built-in still camera with
140,000 pixels.

<p><li>LCD color monitor with 290-
degree screen rotation for high- and
low-angle viewing.

<p><li>Quick 44X Zoom with close-up
focus.

<p><li>Picture stabilizing that
differentiates between intentional
and unintentional camera movements.

<p><li>Six-head mechanism for
precision recording.

<p><li>Built-in head cleaner.

<p><li>Automatic system for
recording, including auto focus, white
balance, and auto exposure.
```

```
<p><li>Flicker reduction, flying
erase head, and random editing.

<p><li>Floodlight built in that
automatically turns on or off as
needed.

<p><li>Review and retake functions
with indicators for remaining tape
time and remaining battery time.

<p><li>Remote control, editing, and
dubbing.

<p><li>Image transfer and recording
software.

<p><li>Special effects and titling.

<p><li>Languages: English, French,
Spanish, and German.

<p><li>Fog and ND filters.

<p><li>Mic input.

<p><li>S-Cable output.

<p><li>Lens cover, dew sensor, 3-way
power supply.

<p><li>New, sealed in box.

</ul>
```

When the browser displays the code immediately above, it will have bullets, as shown in Figure 13.1.

Copy Writing

What are we talking about here? We're talking about writing copy. Copywriters write copy. Some of the best copywriters working for large manufacturers, advertising agencies, and catalog companies make a lot of money just writing compelling copy correlating product features to consumer benefits. You can't expect to be a skilled copywriter without study and practice, but part of being a copywriter is writing clearly and in an organized manner. You can do that much.

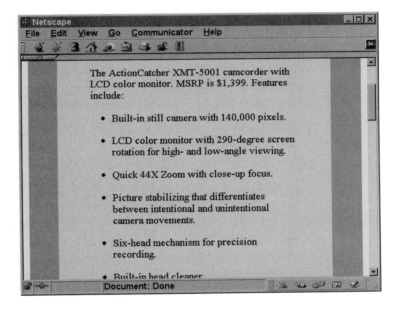

Figure 13.1   A bulleted list looks better than an unbulleted list for the presentation of this camcorder.

Typesetting

The choice of fonts is quite simple. Use the browser defaults.

PC: Times New Roman, serif; Arial, sanserif; and Courier New, monospaced

Mac: Times, serif; Helvetica, sanserif; and Courier, monospaced

If you don't do anything, the text will appear in the browser
default serif. This is your best choice. It's readable. It may be bor-
ing, because you see it all the time on the Web; but you're not trying to win a typesetting contest. You want your text to be readable
above all else. Times New Roman and Times are quite easy to
read.

If you use any font except the browser defaults, for the font to
work, the viewer will have to have the font installed on his or her
computer. Chances of that are nil. Therefore, your choices are limited to the fonts mentioned above.

Follow these seven standard typesetting guidelines:

1. Use italics for emphasis, not bold. Bold type is difficult to
    read through quickly. The use of bold for emphasis is justi-
    fied only for warnings for equipment- or life-threatening sit-
    uations and for similar uses.

2. Use lines between 50 and 70 characters wide. This provides
    optimal reading. Wider lines are difficult to read. Narrower
    lines are difficult to read without special typesetting treat-
    ment (e.g., smaller type).

3. Avoid small type. Use at least 12-point type. Reading on a
    monitor is difficult enough. Don't make it worse. Space is
    not limited. (Note: 12-point type is the Web browser default,
    so you don't have to do anything in regard to specifying the
    type size.)

4. Avoid large type for text. Oversize type is difficult to read
    quickly.

5. Avoid huge type for headings. Headings are great, but keep
    their size modest. Use bold type.

6. Avoid centered text. Centered text is difficult to read. Make all text left justified.

7. Avoid *all caps*. People cannot read all caps quickly. You don't need all caps for headings; you can use a larger-size font and bold.

These rules are simple but nonetheless necessary for a professional look and readable text.

Layout

The width of the browser maximized is too wide for text. You need to narrow the text column to an easily readable size. There are a number of ways to accomplish this with HTML. If you don't use a template, you will have to learn a way to narrow the text column. The following code provides you three ways.

First

```
<table width="500"
cellpadding="10"><tr><td>

[your text paragraphs]

</td></tr></table>
```

This is the best way to ensure an accurate size of text column. This keeps the column 500 pixels wide. You can adjust the pixel dimension according to your needs, but don't go over 520 pixels or your presentation may not fit in some special browsers such as those for WebTV and cable set-tops.

Second

```
<dl><dl><dl>

<dd> [your text paragraphs]

</dl></dl></dl>
```

This shrinks the width of the column by expanding the left margin but is not an absolute measurement. Therefore, the column will expand and contract depending on the size of the browser window.

Third

```
<blockquote><blockquote><blockquote>
```

[your text paragraphs]

```
</blockquote></blockquote></
blockquote>
```

This shrinks the width of the column by expanding both the left and right margins but is not an absolute measurement. Therefore, the column will expand and contract depending on the size of the browser window.

Each of your paragraphs should be marked with the $<p>$ markups. For example:

```
<p>The vase has a miniature hand
painting covering most of its
midsection. The painting has bright
colors, which have not faded,
indicating that the vase has been well
cared for over the years. This is a
vase that many museums would love to
have.</p>
```

This is the proper way to do paragraphs. However, as illustrated above in the Paragraphs subsection, the $<p>$ markup without the $</p>$ is enough to get the job done. Avoid fancy and complex text layouts. Simple is best. Don't try to win a design contest. Just make it readable.

Color

Color is a dangerous thing for Web pages if not controlled carefully and properly.

Background Color

Some people change the background color of their ad using the *<body bgcolor="...">* markup. The result is that no one can read the auction information and make a bid. eBay is not going to stop you from shooting yourself in the foot this way.

Don't interfere with eBay's color scheme. Don't use the *<body bgcolor="...">* markup. The eBay auction section, both above and below your ad, together with your ad, comprises one Web page. If you change eBay's color scheme, you make it difficult for bidders to understand what's going on. In many cases, the eBay information will be unreadable if you change the background color.

Ad Background Color

To change the background color just for your ad without affecting the eBay color scheme, use the *<table>* markup. This means putting your entire ad in an HTML table. Use the first layout scheme mentioned above in the Layout subsection and add background color:

```
<table width="500" cellpadding="10"
bgcolor="#000033">
```

This will confine the background color to your ad, and the eBay color scheme will remain the same, as it should.

Font Colors

To change the color of the type from the default black, you must use the *<font>* markup:

```
<font color="#ffff00">

[your text paragraphs]

</font>
```

Color Combinations

There is nothing wrong with having your own color scheme in your ad. In fact, it can be quite attractive, if properly designed. Remember, it's readability you seek. There must be contrast between the background color and the text (foreground) color. Here are some readable possibilities:

Black on white (default)

Black on red, yellow, or green (all light or medium)

Black on light blue

White, yellow, blue, or green (all light) on black

Browser-Safe Colors

Always use browser-safe colors. Not all colors appear the same in all browsers except the browser-safe colors. The browser-safe colors have the following pairs of hex numbers in them:

```
00, 33, 66, 99, cc, ff
```

Thus, the color #00ccff is browser-safe. The color #01ccff is not browser-safe. The hex numbers correspond to RGB numbers (see

Table 13.1). For a useful collection of browser-safe colors that makes good background colors for reading, see Table 13.2.

Table 13.1 Hex Numbers and RGB Numbers for Browser-Safe Colors

Hex #	RGB #
00	000
33	051
66	102
99	153
cc	204
ff	255

Color Numbers

Browsers use hex numbers. Graphics editing programs use RGB numbers (and in some cases hex numbers too). RGB stands for red, green, blue. RGB numbers are easier for people to understand. Total dark is 000, and total light is 255. Thus, 000,000,000 is black; 255,255,255 is white; 255,000,000 is red; 000,255,000 is green; and 000,000,255 is blue.

Recommendation

Unless you have experience as a Web page developer, stick with default black type. Use a light green (#ccffcc), light turquoise (#ccffff), light rose (#ffcccc), cream (#ffffcc), or another light browser-safe background color. Or, experiment to see what you like, always keeping readability in mind. Naturally, certain colors are more appropriate for some things than other, and maintaining good taste is always important. You don't want to get out of sync with your readers.

Table 13.2 Light Browser-Safe Colors That Provide a Good Background for Reading with Black Text (colors named by author, not official Netscape or Microsoft names)

Color	Hex #	RGB #
Cream	ffffcc	255,255,204
Tan	cccc99	204,204,153
Flesh	ffcc99	255,204,153
Light Grey	cccccc	204,204,204
Medium Grey	999999	153,153,153
Light Rose	ffcccc	255,204,204
Dark Rose	cc9999	204,153,153
Light Green	ccffcc	204,255,204
Fatigue Green	99cc99	153,204,153
Light Mauve	ffccff	255,204,255
Mauve	cc99cc	204,153,204
Light Purple	ccccff	204,204,255
Purple	9999cc	153,153,204
Light Turquoise	ccffff	204,255,255
Turquoise	99cccc	153,204,204
Light Blue	99ccff	153,204,255

Links

eBay offers you a wonderful opportunity to put links in your portion of your auction Web page. A link markup looks like this:

```
<a href=" [URL] "> [text] </a>
```

What are the possibilities? The possibilities are limitless, but you need to limit them to what's relevant to your auction. The purpose of an ad is not "show and tell." It's to sell the item being auctioned.

Your Website

You should include a link to your website in every ad. It's your chance to market your other merchandise. A person may not bid on your item being auctioned but nonetheless may buy something at your website. If you do not have a commerce website where you sell merchandise, then this idea is not relevant.

Manufacturer's Website

If you do not have (or do not want to type) the manufacturer's information on the product being auctioned, it might be posted on the manufacturer's website. If so, you can create a link from your ad to the place in the manufacturer's website where the information and specifications are posted. This relieves you of a lot of work in processing information for many products. But, in any event, you still need to put a short paragraph about the product in your ad.

Review Website

If a Web magazine or other entity has favorably reviewed the product being sold, put in a link to the review. Don't copy the review and include it in your ad. That's a copyright infringement and will make your ad too long. A link gets people who want to learn more directly to the review, and you don't have to get permission to publish the review.

Email

You might find it appropriate to provide an email link in your auction ad. This is a link that automatically pops up a potential bidder's email client with your email address already entered on the *To:* line. Although this provides a convenience to your potential bidders who want to contact you, it also has a tendency to clutter your auction ad with too many links. Experienced bidders know they can find your email address at the top of the auction in the eBay portion of the auction Web page. That's why it is not included in the template.

To add an email link, use the code that follows:

```
<a href="mailto:emailaddress">text</
a>
```

Here's how I like to do it:

```
<a
href="mailto:jt@sinclair.com">jt@sinc
lair.com</a>
```

This not only pops up an email client but also displays the email address (text) as a link.

Auction List

You can put in a link to a list of your current auctions on eBay (see Chapter 18). Again, this is a convenience to potential bidders, particularly if the other items you auction on eBay are similar to the item featured in your auction ad. But again, this link is left out of the template because experienced bidders know that they can find this link at the top of the auction in the eBay portion of the auction Web page. To put it in your auction ad may add unnecessary and unattractive clutter.

This is not a rigid rule, however, and you may want to experiment with cross-linking to your other auctions. Rather than putting in a link to your list of eBay auctions, try putting in links to your specific eBay auctions that are somehow relevant to the item being promoted by your auction ad.

Media

You can link to Web media too. This is a mixed blessing, as is explained in the media subsections that follow.

Spanning the Web

It's one thing to go to another website via a link. That's easy to understand and easy to do with the link markup mentioned above. In addition, you can also bring media , such as images and sound clips, into your ad (Web page). Such media doesn't have to be the same place as your ad at eBay. It can be anywhere on the Internet. Media is only a URL away. Thus, you can span the Web to retrieve your media. You can retrieve any media for which you have a URL, although the use of someone else's media is a copyright infringement.

Photographs

Photographs sell merchandise. Always use them. They will increase the number of buyers bidding on your item and are thereby likely to increase the high bid amount. You take the photograph. Then you digitize it into a GIF or JPEG format file. Finally, you make the file available at a place on the Web (a URL). You can retrieve it with the image markup:

```
<img src=" [URL] ">
```

The *src* is the *URL* of the image file. See Chapter 12 for a detailed overview of using photographs in your eBay auction ad.

Music

How about using a music clip in your ad? This is another download that may delay your ad and irritate potential bidders. It seldom adds anything relevant to your ad. It imposes your taste in music on potential bidders, probably irritating most. And it goes on and off as people load and upload your auction Web page, again irritating them. In short, it's a nuisance. Restrain yourself from using music. There may be some situations where music is relevant and appropriate, but they will be few and far between.

However, if your eBay ad is a place where you expect people to stay a long time because you are auctioning a unique item and have 5,000 words of information for potential bidders to read, tasteful music might be appropriate. However, if you provide music, give potential bidders a choice to listen or not. Do not make it play automatically.

Voice

Voice is even worse than music, right? Or is it? Certainly, no one wants to hear a vendor give a hype message about the virtues of a super-duper videocassette recorder (VCR). You can read the specifications and advertising faster than listen, and you can do your comparisons more easily and efficiently with text.

Promoting Unique Products

Nonetheless, you can promote certain kinds of products quite well with voice. These are unique products where the audio gives added value. For instance, suppose you look at a digital photograph of a painting by the renowned artist Pablo Painter up for auction. If you are interested in the painting, wouldn't you like to hear Mr. Painter talk about his painting? You would probably take the time to listen. It may be hype, but at least it's not the hype of an art gallery owner. It's coming directly from the artist. Figure 13.2 shows the temporary Web page of artist Sue Kooiman (courtesy of AlphaStudios.net) who makes jewelry, sells it on eBay, and makes a short, personal audio presentation to help sell individual items that are unique or have short production runs. The best way to present audio is to give potential bidders a choice of listening or not. Give them a link from the auction ad to a Web page somewhere (not at eBay) that you have set up for the audio presentation (e.g., at your commerce website). If they want to listen, they click on the link (see Figure 13.2).

There is a Return-to-eBay button at the bottom of the Butterfly Ring Web page (not shown). Don't leave your potential bidders out in cyberspace with no way home.

Figure 13.2   A link from an eBay auction brings up this Web page that plays a voice message directly from the artist.

Sound is beyond the scope of this book, but a visit to the RealNet-works website will give you all the information you need to produce and add sound to Web pages and websites. Visit *http://realnetworks.com* where there is free information in the developers' section (devzone).

Institutional Advertising

At your commerce website, you should publish information about your business. A voice message narrated by the owner or manager of the business is appropriate and can be effective if sincere and if relevant to customer service. A link in your auction ad to such a Web page where potential bidders can hear such a sound presentation makes a nice public relations touch. But don't make it compulsory. Always indicate exactly what it is and give potential bidders the choice of whether they want to access it and listen to it (i.e., whether they want to click on the link). A phrase like the following lets potential bidders know exactly what they're going to get if they click on the link (link underlined):

Click to hear a <u>welcome message</u> from our Internet Sales Manager Frank Frisbie.

Other Media

You can use other media in a Web page too. How about digital video, Shockwave movies, animated GIFs, or clip art? Like music, these are seldom justified, although your ad can incorporate them from your website just like digital photographs.

Dancing digital doodads can be very distracting. They diminish the impact of the text information that sells the item being auctioned. They brand you as a Web amateur. Don't use them unless they directly relate to what you sell and unless they add to the information on the product.

However, do use your business logo if you have one. It will add credibility to your ad. Use the logos of manufacturers, if you dare. They are trademarks, and you may be liable for violating owners' trademark rights, although I suppose that you can get away with this most of the time.

Consider the Bidders

Remember, unless you are running multiple auctions, you may have a tendency to fancy up your one auction page. This can prove disastrous. What you think is *cool* and attractive may be a reading impediment to potential bidders. Serious bidders survey the offerings before they bid. Often it's long, hard work. The faster and easier a potential bidder can glean the information from your auction ad, the happier he or she is and the more credibility you have as the seller. Potential bidders often read through dozens and dozens of auction offerings before they make a decision to bid. Before they make the decision, they invariably return to a few of the auction offerings to narrow the field. They make their decisions to bid based on adequate information, price, and the urgency of their need. They don't base their decisions on the coolness of your ad.

However, don't let me spoil your afternoon. If you want to run a cool auction ad because you're a would-be website developer without a website, lavish your attention on your ad. It's great fun. But in your quest to make your ad cool, don't forget to make it readable too.

Using an eBay Ad Template

If you have done some Web development, you will have no trouble creating your own ad. If not, and you want to learn, buy a basic book on HTML. You can learn to do your own ads quickly and easily. Otherwise, use ad templates.

What Is an Ad Template?

An eBay auction Web page is an ordinary Web page constructed with HTML. A Web page is an ASCII document, a plain text document. You mark up the plain text with simple markups that tell the browser how to display the text, incorporate media, and make links (hyperlinks). It's a simple, straightforward system.

An ad template is an HTML document, a template Web page. All the markups already exist. You just put in the text, and your ad is done. You're ready to go.

Using a Template

Using a template is easy. You just fill in the blanks. The template shows the blanks with the comment markup:

```
<!-- [instructions] -->
```

This markup provides instructions to you and has no other purpose. It does not show up in the Web page. By looking for this markup in the template, you will find the places where you need to enter text or URLs.

Sample Template

I created the following template for eBay auctions. Note that it has a comment line before and after every input.

```
</blockquote>
<table bgcolor="#99cccc"
width="100%"><tr><td>
<br>
<table bgcolor="#ccffff" width="520"
align="center"><tr><td>
<table width="400"
align="center"><tr><td>
<br> <br>
<!-- add your short description of the
item BELOW this line to replace the
xxx BELOW -->
<center><h3>xxx</h3></center>
<!-- add your short description of the
item ABOVE this line to replace the
xxx ABOVE -->
<br>
<!-- add your text for your ad BELOW
this line to replace the xxx BELOW -->
xxx
<!-- add your text for your ad ABOVE
this line to replace the xxx ABOVE -->
<br>
<!-- add your shipping charge to
replace the xxx in the paragraph BELOW
this line -->
<p>High Bidder pays $xxx.00 shipping
and handling delivered anywhere in 48
states. Higher outside the lower 48
```

```
states.</p>

<!-- add your shipping charge to
replace the xxx in the paragraph ABOVE
this line -->

<!-- add your boilerplate text BELOW
this line to replace the xxx BELOW -->

<p><b>Terms: </b>xxx</p>

<!-- add your boilerplate text ABOVE
this line to replace the xxx ABOVE -->

<br>

<table bgcolor="#99cccc"
cellpadding="2" width="304"
align="center"><tr><td><table
bgcolor="#ccffff" width="300"
cellpadding="12"
align="center"><tr><td>

<center><p><font size="-1"
face="Arial,Helvetica"><b>Visit our
website by clicking on the name
below.</b></font></p></center>

<!-- add your website URL BELOW this
line to replace the xxx and your
business name BELOW to replace the
zzz-->

<center><p><a href="xxx">zzz</a></
p></center>

<!-- add your website URL ABOVE this
line to replace the xxx and your
business name ABOVE to replace the
zzz-->

</td></tr></table></td></tr></
```

```
table></td></tr></table>

<br> <br>

</td></tr></table>

<br>

<table bgcolor="#ccffff"
cellpadding="20" align="center"
border="0"><tr><td align="center"
valign="middle">

<!-- Put the URL of the photograph to
replace the xxx BELOW this line-->

<img src="xxx" border=0>

<!-- Put the URL of the photograph to
replace the xxx ABOVE this line-->

</td></tr></table>

<br>

</td></tr></table>
```

The first *xxx* to replace is for the short description of your item for auction. The second *xxx* to replace is for the text of your ad. The third *xxx* to replace is the shipping and handling charges. The fourth *xxx* to replace is the boilerplate. What is boilerplate? It's what you want to appear in every ad regardless of what you're auctioning. The fifth *xxx* to replace is the URL for your website. The accompanying *zzz* to replace is the name of your business at your website. And the last *xxx* to replace is the URL of the digital photograph of the auctioned item.

You create your text in your word processor. Then you copy and paste it into the template. Save the template itself as a new file (e.g., *ad1.html*). Next test it; look at it with your browser. If it's

OK, you're ready to go to the next step. If not, go back and adjust it.

When you're ready, go to eBay. Enter the ad into the proper input that's part of setting up an auction (see Chapter 6). You simply open *ad1.html* and copy and paste the contents into the eBay input. It will appear on eBay just as it did in your browser.

Item for Auction

The first thing in the ad is a short description of the item for auction. This should match the one-line title of the auction, but it need not be as short. However, don't make it long either.

```
ActionCatcher camcorder XMT-5001,
new, all automatic features, perfect
for novices and intermediate users
```

This will appear in bold as a heading.

Body of Text

The body of the text is your opportunity to act as a salesperson. Give complete information. Anticipate questions, and provide the information that will answer the questions before they are asked.

```
XXXXXXXXXXXXXXXXXXXXXXXXXXXXXXXXXXXX
XXXXXXXXXXXXXXXXXXXXXXXXXXXXXXXXXXXX
XXXXXXXXXXXXXXXXXXXXXXXXXXXXXXXXXXXX
XXXXXXXXXXXXXXXXXXXXXXXXXXXXXXXXXXXX
XXXXXXXXXX

XXXXXXXXXXXXXXXXXXXXXXXXXXXXXXXXXXXX
XXXXXXXXXXXXXXXXXXXXXXXXXXXXXXXXXXXX
XXXXXXXXXXXXXXXXXXXXXXXXXXXXXXXXXXXX
XXXXXXXXXXXXXXXXXXXXXXXXXXXXXXXXXXXXX
XXXXXXXXXXXXXXXXXXXXXXXXXX
```

```
XXXXXXXXXXXXXXXXXXXXXXXXXXXXXXXXXXXXXXXX
XXXXXXXXXXXXXXXXXXXXXXXXXXXXXXXXXXXXXXXX
XXXXXXXXXXXXXXXXXXXXXXXXXXXXXXXXXXXXXXXX
XXXXXXXXXXXXXXXXXXXXXXXXXXXXXXXXXXXXXXXX
```

Boilerplate

The boilerplate is the administrative information you put in each ad. It covers procedures and policies.

```
We accept VISA, MC, PayPal, and
Billpoint. Michigan residents add
8.25% sales tax or send a copy of
valid resale certificate. Customers
from outside the United States are
welcome. We ship anywhere in the
world. High bidder must pay within 14
days of auction or the transaction is
canceled. We will post positive
feedback on all finished transactions
if the bidder posts feedback. Please
check out our other auctions too. Bid
now please, and thanks for your bid!
Camcorders for All, Inc.
```

Web Page Link

This is the URL of your business website. It must be a complete URL.

```
http://www.camcordersforall.com
```

Photograph Link

This is the URL of your digital photograph. It must be a complete URL.

```
http://www.camcordersforall.com/
images/cam5001.gif
```

Changing Colors

In the template the general background color is #99cccc, a medium shade of turquoise. The other background color is #ccffff, a light shade of turquoise. These background colors provide a neutral, unobtrusive appearance that does not detract from your information. Yet, they give your presentation a neat and professional look. If you want to change the colors, go through the template, find the numbers, and substitute your own hex numbers (colors). The subsection Color earlier in this chapter shows you how to use hex numbers.

Doing a Little HTML

You will notice that if you paste four paragraphs of text from your word processor into the body of the template, the paragraphs will merge together as one paragraph (browser view). You will have to add the HTML paragraph markups in your text.

```
<p>xxxxxxxxxxxxxxxxxxxxxxxxxxxxxxxxx
xxxxxxxxxxxxxxxxxxxxxxxxxxxxxxxxxxxx
xxxxxxxxxxxxxxxxxxxxxxxxxxxxxxxxxxxx
xxxxxxxxxxxxxxxxxxxxxxxxxxxxxxxxxxxx
xxxxxxxxxxxxx</p>

<p>xxxxxxxxxxxxxxxxxxxxxxxxxxxxxxxxx
xxxxxxxxxxxxxxxxxxxxxxxxxxxxxxxxxxxx
xxxxxxxxxxxxxxxxxxxxxxxxxxxxxxxxxxxx
xxxxxxxxxxxxxxxxxxxxxxxxxxxxxxxxxxxx
xxxxxxxxxxxxxxxxxxxxxxxxxxxxxx</p>

<p>xxxxxxxxxxxxxxxxxxxxxxxxxxxxxxxxx
xxxxxxxxxxxxxxxxxxxxxxxxxxxxxxxxxxxx
```

```
xxxxxxxxxxxxxxxxxxxxxxxxxxxxxxxxxxxxxxx
xxxxxxxxxxxxxxxxxxxxxxxxxxxxxxxxxxxxxxx
xxx</p>
```
This will display three paragraphs instead of one.

Special Features of the Template

Note that the template starts with the *</blockquote>* markup. This is to turn off the block quote formatting started by eBay (to provide small left and right margins for people running auctions). Because the template takes control of the middle section of the auction Web page, it is appropriate to turn off this particular eBay formatting. In the future, eBay may change its Web page formatting, and each template will have to be adjusted to enable you to take complete control of the midsection of the auction Web page.

The Ad

Voila! The ad completed using the template looks custom made. Note how the template adjusted the ad to the amount of the text and the size of the photograph (see Figures 13.3 and 13.4). With a template the design, layout, and typesetting are predetermined. You need only create the content that goes into the ad. Using any method of creating an auction ad, you still have to create the content; that is, you always have to write the ad and obtain or take the photograph.

Shortcut

A shortcut for creating your own auction ads is to use a Web authoring program instead of hand coding in HTML. See Chapter 20 and read my *Web Pages the Smart Way* (AMACOM, 2001).

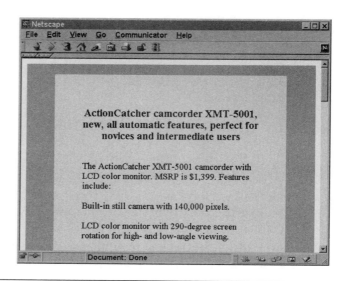

Figure 13.3   Top of eBay ad made with template.

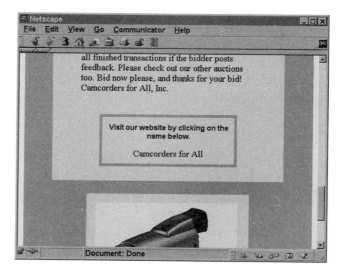

Figure 13.4   Bottom of eBay ad made with template.

Alternatives

Alternatives to templates exist. People offer programs that will generate attractive ads for sale on eBay. My experience with such programs is that, like most other programs, they may be difficult to learn, have bugs, or not work for some reason. They seem more trouble than they're worth. The use of templates seems easier and more practical. But most of the programs are not expensive, and it might be worth your time and money to give one a try.

You can make your own eBay ad templates look any way you want them to look. Their purpose is to save time and effort so you will be able to publish ads quickly. See Chapters 12 and 21 for details on how to handle the photograph.

You do not necessarily have to use the template in this chapter. You can design your own, you can find a Web developer to design a template for you, or you can simply alter whatever templates you can find to suit your purposes better. Also, go to *http://book-center.com* for more templates.

You can use templates with the Web authoring programs covered in Chapter 20. For the templates available on the website (*http://bookcenter.com*), you don't have to worry about HTML. You just replace the *xxx* (via copy and paste) with the appropriate text wherever you see the *xxx* in the Web page.

The One-Line Title

Finally, at the end of the chapter we get to the beginning of the auction Web page, the one-line title. This is the one-line heading that eBay uses both as a heading (title) for the auction Web page and for the auction listing. This line cannot be more than 45 characters long. The one-line title should:

- Include keywords for searches
- Clearly identify the item
- Be easy to read

Searches

Some people search through the lists of items for sale on eBay. Most probably use the eBay search engine to narrow the search first. People use keywords to search. If you're looking for a camcorder, life is simple. *Camcorder* is the keyword. The search result will be a list of camcorders for auction.

Word Order

The brand name, if it is important, should come first. The product should come second. The model identification should come third. Condition, if new or mint, should come last; if not, condition should not be included in the title.

```
ActionCatcher camcorder XMT-5001 new
```

A potential bidder probably searches on *camcorder*. He or she looks for known brands and known models. For an unbranded item, the most compelling characteristic of the product should come first. Use your judgment. Always put the most important feature a potential bidder might look for first.

```
Eighteenth-century vase with miniature
```

A potential bidder probably searches on *vase*. He or she is already in the Antiques section, so there's no need to include the word *antique*. *Eighteenth-century* immediately categorizes the vase, although a more specific date would be better. Mentioning *miniature* indicates the vase has hand-painted art.

The line must be easy to read and specifically identify the item for auction. Review the one-line title for the camcorder:

```
ActionCatcher camcorder XMT-5001 new
```

ActionCatcher is a well-recognized name. (Actually, it's a fictitious name. Imagine that it's a well-known brand.) The fact that the camcorder is new, not used, is important enough to include. People looking for camcorders will find this item easily. Do not jazz up your title. It just makes it more difficult to read. Don't use exclamation marks or all caps to draw attention to it. It will be more difficult to read and more frustrating for a reader (potential bidder). Remember, an average reader looks at two or three lines a second.

Some products are more difficult to write titles for than others. For instance, if you are auctioning a microphone, you have a keyword problem. People will search both on *microphone* and on *mic*, so you have to include both in your title:

```
Shure dynamic microphone mic SM58
```

Each product has its own characteristics and jargon that you must consider.

If the item is new, always include that fact at the end of the line. New items command a premium price. The newness is a motivating selling point. Some people, like me, often look for only new items.

Dressing

eBay would like to sell you bold or yellow highlight for your title. Don't waste your money. These impair readability. Bold and highlight are similar to using exclamation marks or all caps. They slow down potential bidders who can otherwise read quickly through auctions to find what they want. You are not going to sell someone something they're not looking for; to sell someone something they are looking for, you need to make the title as readable as possible.

At the End, the Beginning

The reason this section comes at the end of the chapter instead of the beginning is that it's the last thing you write. After you have thought through and have written your ad, you will usually have a better idea of what the title should say. Think about the keywords you will use. Think about exactly what potential bidders will be looking for. Then write the title.

Quite a few people do a good job of writing one-line titles for their auctions. Consequently, good examples are not scarce. Nonetheless, there are plenty of bad examples too, so write with care.

Purpose

The purpose of the title is not to hook people. It's to identify items for which some potential bidders are looking. If I'm not looking for a camcorder to buy, no matter what your title says, it won't interest me. If I am looking for a camcorder, you don't have to hook me to take a look. You just have to identify your item in such a way that I can find it easily (i.e., read it easily) on a list or via a search. Once I look at your ad, that's your opportunity to hook me on the particular product you have up for auction.

Summary

Your ad in your eBay auction listing provides you an opportunity to include all the information you need to sell one item effectively. Don't miss this opportunity. Present the information clearly and attractively. Don't overdo it with a lot of website frills. Above all the information must be easily readable on the screen. And don't forget the photograph; photographs help sell merchandise on eBay.

14

Conducting Auctions

Auctioning items one at a time may be fun and profitable, but it's no way to make a living, unless each item has a high price and a large profit. Most people who make a living on eBay make money by running multiple, simultaneous auctions, the more the better. Some retailers are running hundreds of auctions a week. So, for those who want to use eBay more productively, this chapter will cover the handling of multiple auctions. For people who will run only one auction at a time, this chapter will also cover general auctioning strategies.

General Auction Techniques

Although the general techniques this chapter covers below appear to pertain primarily to individual auctions, these techniques also apply to multiple auctions. Successful multiple auctions are always a collection of individual auctions that work well.

Timing

You do not enter an auction when it is convenient for you if you want to generate the most bidding action. You enter an auction so that it ends at a time when the most potential bidders will be online to pay attention to it. Consequently, if you think the most potential bidders will be online between 5 PM and 9 PM on Saturday evening, start your auction so that's when it ends.

This is easy to do because the auction will end at the exact time you entered it, either three days, five days, seven days, or ten days later. In other words, if you want a three-day auction to end Saturday at 7:30 PM, enter it at 7:30 PM on Wednesday evening.

Needless to say, there are complications. For instance, 7:30 PM where? There is a three-hour difference between New York and Los Angeles. There is an eight-hour difference between London and Los Angeles. Keep in mind, too, that eBay runs on Pacific Standard Time (PST), that is, the time in San Jose, California, where eBay headquarters is located (see Table 14.1).

Table 14.1   eBay Time and US, Japan, and Britain Time Zones

Japan	Hawaii	eBay	Pacific	Mountain	Central	Eastern	Britain
5:00	10:00	**0:00**	**12:00**	1:00	2:00	3:00	8:00
6:00	11:00	1:00	1:00	2:00	3:00	4:00	9:00
7:00	**12:00**	2:00	2:00	3:00	4:00	5:00	10:00
8:00	1:00	3:00	3:00	4:00	5:00	6:00	11:00
9:00	2:00	4:00	4:00	5:00	6:00	7:00	**12:00**
10:00	3:00	5:00	5:00	6:00	7:00	8:00	1:00
11:00	4:00	6:00	6:00	7:00	8:00	9:00	2:00
12:00	5:00	7:00	7:00	8:00	9:00	10:00	3:00
1:00	6:00	8:00	8:00	9:00	10:00	11:00	4:00
2:00	7:00	9:00	9:00	10:00	11:00	**12:00**	5:00
3:00	8:00	10:00	10:00	11:00	**12:00**	1:00	6:00
4:00	9:00	11:00	11:00	**12:00**	1:00	2:00	7:00
5:00	10:00	**12:00**	**12:00**	1:00	2:00	3:00	8:00
6:00	11:00	13:00	1:00	2:00	3:00	4:00	9:00
7:00	**12:00**	14:00	2:00	3:00	4:00	5:00	10:00
8:00	1:00	15:00	3:00	4:00	5:00	6:00	11:00
9:00	2:00	16:00	4:00	5:00	6:00	7:00	**12:00**
10:00	3:00	17:00	5:00	6:00	7:00	8:00	1:00
11:00	4:00	18:00	6:00	7:00	8:00	9:00	2:00
12:00	5:00	19:00	7:00	8:00	9:00	10:00	3:00
1:00	6:00	20:00	8:00	9:00	10:00	11:00	4:00
2:00	7:00	21:00	9:00	10:00	11:00	**12:00**	5:00
3:00	8:00	22:00	10:00	11:00	**12:00**	1:00	6:00
4:00	9:00	23:00	11:00	**12:00**	1:00	2:00	7:00

As you can see in Table 14.1, eBay uses military time. And why not? It's unambiguous time; that is, it numbers each hour of the day uniquely. Thus, 19:00 hours (eBay time) is 7:00 PM Pacific time, 10:00 PM Eastern time, and 3:00 AM Britain time.

Greenwich Mean Time

PST is Greenwich Mean Time (GMT) less eight hours. GMT is a standard reference that you can use to calculate the difference in hours between a place (time zone) and PST.

Now, what if you are selling cases of Dr. Pepstop's Anti-Insomnia Elixir? The middle of the night might be a good time to have your auction end. Therefore, you have to enter it in the middle of the night.

Or, suppose you want to sell Arizona cacti (souvenir of the Old West) to Europeans. You might want to enter your three-day auction at about 11 AM PST on Wednesday. That puts the ending after dinner Saturday evening in Europe.

To set your computer clock, or your regular watch or clock, go *eBay Official Time* on the eBay Site Map accessed via the *site map* link over the navigation bar.

System Maintenance

The eBay system is usually down for maintenance during the night on some days. This is not a time to enter auctions. Check to see the current maintenance schedule so that you can plan to avoid that period for posting your auctions. Go *Community, overview, News, Announcements*.

Best Times

Most eBay sellers will tell you that evenings and the weekends, particularly the weekends—when people are home from work—

are the best times to have an auction come to a close. Are there any good times of the month? Most offline retailers will tell you that sales are good around paycheck times. However, on eBay that phenomenon may not hold up. After all, someone can be the winning bidder on eBay and not have to buy a money order or write a check for several days after the end of the auction. Therefore, several days before payday (first and fifteenth) might work well in theory. And several days after payday may be prime selling time too.

Best Time of Year

What about time of year? Avoid holidays? Too many people traveling, right? But what about all those people who aren't traveling and who stay home looking for something to do? And I remember, while on vacation, rushing to use someone's PC to make my final bid on an item. This leads me to think that holidays might be OK for eBay auction action.

But tax time in April is always a tough time for most offline retailers. It's probably not a good time to auction your item on eBay either. The Christmas season, of course, is prime time to sell merchandise, especially an item that makes a good gift (just about anything). For the mail-order catalogs, the Christmas season starts in September or October. The closer to Christmas, the more success you'll likely have on eBay.

The Right Time

In truth, the right time depends on the item and the circumstances. A dozen authors can voice a dozen different opinions and you might even be able to get general statistics from eBay, but in the end each item has its own set of potential bidders that may or may not follow the normal bidding patterns in regard to timing.

Who's There?

In reality, there is no one there in the final minutes of many auctions no matter when they end. People make their bids earlier and forget about it. There is no last-minute frenzy. In such cases, the time the auction ends is irrelevant. All the theory, speculation, and observations of authors and other cognoscenti are for naught. There are definitely some auctions, however, that do have a lot of action in the last minutes.

Convenience

The bottom line is that your best bet for timing may be an evening on the weekend with a seven-day auction. But that's a congested, and sometimes frustrating, time for everyone because eBay is so busy. It may bring you the most bids, but the additional bids may produce negligible results on items that are not "hot." For many items, catering to your own convenience rather than to the perceived convenience of the potential bidders may bring a final bid almost as high. And if your convenience means more to you than the highest possible bid, enter your auction when it's convenient for you.

Multiple Auctions

Some people have run multiple auctions (same item) instead of a Dutch auction. That's not a bad idea. It gets bidders fired up. If they don't win the first auction, they still have more chances left. Where I've seen it done, however, it was obvious that the seller conveniently entered the auctions one after another within a short time. Consequently, the auctions end very close together, usually within two minutes of each other. That does not allow enough time for losing bidders to regroup for a renewed bidding effort. As a result, the second and third items often have fewer bidders and often go for less than the first item. It is important to give bidders some breathing room. Multiple auctions for the same item should be spaced at least five minutes apart.

How Long?

The answer to How long should an auction be? is another question: What's the purpose? If your primary purpose is advertising, the longest auction (ten-day auction) is for you. You're up the longest time for the least trouble and get the most exposure for the dollar.

What if you want to get the most bidders? The theory goes that the ten-day auction is the best because your auction is up longer and attracts more potential bidders. Hey! Enter your auction at 7:30 PM Wednesday evening and get exposure on two Saturdays. What a deal! This definitely appeals to a certain group of potential bidders, bidders with patience.

Another class of bidders, however, those without patience, will more likely bid on an auction with a shorter deadline. Whether because of circumstances or personal character, they can't wait. A ten-day auction goes well beyond their horizon.

The nice thing about the ten-day auction is that you rope in the patient bidders for the first seven days and the impatient bidders for the last three days and get the best of both worlds. That's why the ten-day auction makes good sense.

But what about you? You may not want to wait ten days. You need the money right now. Or, you've got to get the stuff out of the garage right now before it drives you nuts. Or, your landlord just gave you a ten-day notice and you can't take your giraffe with you to your next apartment (no large pets allowed). There are lots of legitimate reasons to do shorter auctions, but most of them have to do with your wants, needs, or convenience rather than the quest to generate the most bids.

A general rule is that the more popular the item, the shorter the auction. In other words, a popular item (e.g., a recognized brand) will bring plenty of bidders in a short time. An obscure item needs all the time it can get to attract bidders. On one hand, suppose you're selling a currently popular portable Sony television in the $150 price range. You will attract many bidders if the offering is attractive. On the other hand, if you're selling an antique wooden soup spoon manufactured in Houghton, Michigan, you may have to wait longer than three days for a significant number of bidders to materialize.

Seller Control

In a real sense, a bidder's situation is out of his or her control. There are other uncontrolled competitive bidders with whom a bidder is sometimes funneled into a short bidding frenzy. In contrast, a seller has complete control over the setup of the auction. eBay's liberal policy of *anything goes* in the auction page provides a seller with a great opportunity to skillfully promote his or her merchandise. As Chapter 13 explains in detail, everything you do properly works to attract more potential bidders (e.g., readable text). Everything you do improperly works to reduce the number of potential bidders (e.g., background colors that make text unreadable). Consequently, it pays to learn something about writing copy, advertising, typesetting, using HTML, and editing digital photographs if you're going to be a regular seller on eBay.

And never forget your reputation, which is also in your control. Would you send a money order for $750 to a seller who had obvious problems getting along with bidders and may even have cheated a few people? Would you send a money order for $750 to a seller who made all his or her bidders happy?

Pricing

Presumably, your objective is to get the highest possible bid. To do so, you usually have to inspire some competitive bidding. How do you price your auction?

Low Minimum with a Reserve

The thing to keep in mind is that in the end, a bidder will bid only so much for an item. The price you set at the beginning has little effect on this reality. Low prices probably attract rookie eBay bidders, but rookies soon catch on that a low price in the beginning does not necessarily mean a low price at the end of the auction. Once rookie bidders realize their initial misconceptions, they look for signs that a seller is being reasonable.

A reserve, until it is met, is a hidden minimum allowable bid and doesn't tell bidders anything simply because it is hidden. If you use a reserve, bidders don't know whether you're for real or just another unreasonable seller. (Many auctions do not get any bidders.) The low minimum also adds an aura of unreality that may not be inviting to potential bidders. It's better to send a strong signal that you're for real. See High Minimum Bid (next section).

When does it make sense to use a low minimum bid and a reserve? When you want to test the market. You're not sure of the probable high bid, and you want the market (the bidders) to decide for you. If you set a high reserve, you won't sell the item and won't learn anything. But if you set a low reserve and get bids over the reserve, you may get a strong indication of the market value. You can use that knowledge in your next auction.

High Minimum Bid

If you want to maximize the high bid, do your homework. Research what identical or similar items have sold for in past auctions. Chances are you're not going to get a bid that's higher. So, set your auction with a minimum bid (no reserve) that attracts potential bidders. It must be high enough to live with should there be an abnormally low number of bidders and an abnormally low winning bid. It should be low enough to lure potential bidders to make a bid. It sends a message that you're serious about selling the item.

Being realistic about selling something is tough. You buy an item for 20 percent off list, use it once and decide it's not for you (although it's a popular item), and put it up for auction on eBay at 30 percent off list. You're an unreasonable seller because many people can buy the item for 35 percent off list at a discount store. To sell it on eBay new will probably require a price of 50 percent off list, but it's not new (maybe *like new*).

People selling items at retail on eBay are realistic about their prices. They have to be, or they couldn't stay in business. You compete with them. Thus, unrealistic pricing just wastes your time.

Research the market first. If you're not happy with the potential high bid, sell your item some other way. Or don't sell it.

Plenty of Stuff Not for Sale

I have plenty of expensive but small high-quality stuff in the garage that I won't sell. It seems more rational to keep it, with the thought that I might need it again someday, than to sell it for the low price I know it will bring on eBay or anywhere else. However, one has more incentive to get rid of the large expensive stuff that takes up a lot of space.

Your main goal is to convey the message to people that you're a reasonable seller. They can buy from you at a reasonable price and deal with a reasonable person to complete the transaction. Everyone is looking for a steal. Everyone finds one occasionally. But most of the time people pay a reasonable price for merchandise, and that's something they're willing to do.

Your auction setup, your advertising, your reputation, and the services you offer bidders all work to convey a message to potential bidders. That message should spell *reasonable*. The high minimum bid that's still lower than a reasonable price is the best way to attract bidders because it's reasonable.

The Market

Keep in mind that you don't decide price. The market does. For eBay, the market is eBay auctions; that is, eBay auctions for identical or similar items determine the market value of an item. It really doesn't matter what the price of an item *should* be. It doesn't matter what I think it should be according to my magic formulas expressed in this book. It really doesn't matter what you think the price should be. And it really doesn't matter what the price would be in a St. Louis flea market. The only thing that matters is what the market value is on eBay.

Research

The most important technique you can use as a selling strategy is research. Research the market value of the item you want to sell. Use past eBay auctions to do an appraisal. Use offline data. Use list price as a reference for items that aren't very old. Use whatever reliable information you can find. At *http://www.worthguide.com* you can find auction data on some popular items. Using market price is all-important.

Anomalies

Despite the fact that eBay has a high volume of both auctions and bidders and is a rational market, there will always be eBay market anomalies. How do you explain commonly available items selling auction after auction for 10 percent more than people would have to pay for them in a discount store? How do you explain a first-rate branded item selling new for as little as 70 percent off list price? These anomalies happen by chance or due to some undiscernible force in the marketplace. Anomalies create the risk that no matter how careful your research, you won't get the high bid for your item that you aim for.

Dutch Auctions

Selling in quantity makes sense sometimes, but not all the time. A Dutch auction offers something special.

Special Attraction

For instance, if you have a dozen new outboard motors (list $10,000 each) to sell at a high auction price (40 percent off list—i.e., 60 percent of list price), an eBay Dutch auction is probably not your best bet. But if you want to sell the outboard motors at a rock-bottom price (e.g., 70 percent off list—i.e., 30 percent of list price), a Dutch auction might work well.

A Dutch auction should offer something special to bidders so that it attracts enough bidders to be successful—that is, the auction sells the multiple items. If there is nothing special about the offer, you are better off selling the item in separate auctions over a span of time that enables the eBay market to absorb the offering.

Storefront

Sellers also use Dutch auctions in a special way. They use them as storefronts. What about a Dutch auction that offers 30 Agfa film packs every week at a minimum bid of $10.95 each but never sells more than a dozen? This is not an auction. This is a storefront on eBay. The price is always $10.95. The Dutch auction is run week in and week out. It's a store where you stop in to buy an Agfa film pack (ten rolls) whenever you need to take some photographs.

This offers you a real opportunity to sell large quantities at a fixed price. Always offer more items than the eBay market can absorb so that the price never goes up with competitive bidding. The special attraction of your Dutch auction is the low price for which you sell your items, and you don't want the price to go up even temporarily.

Featured Auctions

For a substantial extra fee, you can have your auction featured. For $99.95 you can have your auction featured on eBay. For $19.95 you can have your auction featured in its category. The featured auction appears in the *Browse* section on eBay or at the top of its category. It also appears in the regular auction listings in bold.

Is it worth it? Probably not for most items. When potential bidders look for something specific, they probably don't look in the featured sections. Impulse items, however, may sell well in the featured sections. Many people visiting the featured sections are just out browsing around looking for something, anything, to buy.

If an item is difficult to search for (difficult to identify with keywords) and it's on a long list of auctions, the featured section may be your best shot at selling it. If you are selling to novice eBay users, many of whom do not know how to search effectively, you might have some luck with the featured sections. And if you are selling a popular consumer item, you may sell well in the featured sections too.

Changing Auctions

You can always change your auction ad (*Description*). The change will appear tacked on the bottom of your auction ad. However, don't make changes that will upset bidders. You may get negative feedback. For instance, don't auction a Cadillac Seville and then change it to a Mercury Tracer near the end of the auction.

Check the Buyer

You don't have to sell to anyone you don't want to sell to. If you don't like the buyer, don't sell to him or her. Not selling to someone, though, has its consequences. For instance, suppose you check out the high bidder at your auction, and he has a feedback rating of +2 in eight transactions (i.e., five positive and three negative). You decide you don't want to do business with this guy. You refuse. On one hand, you may be saving yourself a lot of trouble. On the other hand, you may get negative feedback from the jilted high bidder. Sure, you can explain the feedback. But do you want to go through that process?

If you don't want to sell to someone, make sure you tell him or her before the auction is over, not after.

Notify High Bidder and Set Deadline

As the seller, don't ever leave things ambiguous. Notify the high bidder (buyer) what to do and when to do it. If the buyer doesn't meet deadlines, send reminders via email. Many people seem to agree, if you don't get any reaction from the buyer after two reminders (the initial email message plus two reminder messages reasonably spaced), consider the auction canceled. Perhaps you can sell to the second highest-bidder.

It's even better to announce your terms and deadlines in your auction ad (i.e., prior to the completion of the auction). That way a buyer has little grounds for claiming that one of your policies is out of line.

The After-Auction Auction

Need to auction something, but there is a current auction offering an identical item? No reason to flood the market. Wait until the current auction comes to a close and immediately put your item up for auction. You might even contact the active losing bidders by email to inform them that your item is now up for auction. However, make sure you don't initiate email contact before the current auction has been completed, or you'll be guilty of bid siphoning, a forbidden practice on eBay.

You might note that this practice applies to your own auctions too. Unless you have a valid reason to auction multiple identical items at the same time, you may get better prices if you auction them off in sequence. It will take much more time, but it may result in higher gross sales revenue.

Follow-Up

Chapter 11 on customer service covers follow-up for your auctions, and this chapter will not repeat such information except to say that systematic follow-up is the most important part of your auctioning activity. There is a special type of follow-up, however, that can add retail sales.

If you have additional identical items to sell, you can contact all the losing bidders via email after the auction and offer to sell them the item at a fixed price (above your auction reserve or minimum bid). Assuming the price is attractive, this will often generate additional sales to people who are, presumably, predisposed to buy your merchandise. However, you will want to look closely at the current eBay rules to make sure you don't violate any guidelines with such follow-up.

Trades

For certain types of goods such as collectibles, you may be more interested in trading than in selling. This is easy to do just by attempting to communicate and negotiate with the high bidder. Don't attempt to force a trade on an unwilling high bidder, however. You may get negative feedback.

Database Techniques

You can enter multiple auctions in eBay by hand, but it's tedious and takes a lot of time. The more auctions you create, the more you have to keep track of. Pretty quickly things get out of control.

Multiple Individual Auctions

Although databases and other tools enable you to handle multiple auctions with efficiency and profit, you cannot forget that each individual auction must stand on its own and use the general techniques for auctions outlined earlier.

There's no reason to suffer such a demanding routine. A desktop database can make your life easier.

What should you include in your database? That's a matter of personal style and organization. Whatever works for you. This chapter provides a simple database to get you started thinking about how you might organize your own database. But every business is different, and there's no simple "one formula fits all."

This book takes the point of view that you can create your own database to keep track of your auctions much better than anything a book can show you. What this chapter shows you is how to begin to create a database for other uses (e.g., inventory control) and then add data for eBay use. Moreover, many businesses already use inventory control programs that include databases, accounting programs that include databases, and other business software that includes databases. You can use data in such databases for eBay use, and you can add data to such databases for eBay use. This chapter provides the conceptual basis for doing so.

After you go to the trouble to create and maintain a database, you will find at the end of the chapter several ways to work with your database to make the operation of your multiple eBay auctions easier and to do the follow-up necessary to complete the transactions successfully.

A real benefit of getting organized is the capability your database will give you to upload multiple auctions to eBay simultaneously. Chapter 15 covers the procedures for doing so, but you can't get to the next chapter without a database, so this chapter is your first stop. Create or augment your existing database here and learn to create useful database queries, and then you'll be ready for bulk uploads.

But the benefits don't end in Chapter 15. Chapter 18 shows you an example of using Web commerce software to operate a catalog on your own commerce website. Databases drive Web commerce software. Without a database, you can't make a commerce website work efficiently. Consequently, you can augment your database a little more and then easily accommodate a robust Web commerce system.

Tables

A database table is simply a series of rows (records) and columns (fields). For instance, each row can represent a product, and each column can represent a piece of information about that product. So, let's get started building a database to keep track of inventory. The following are some columns you might want to include to keep track of your merchandise:

Column	Column Name
Product	product
Manufacturer	manufacturer
Wholesale cost	cost
Shipping weight	shipwt
Number received	received
Number sold	sold
Number in stock	instock

That seems simple enough, a table with seven columns. When you receive products, you can increase the number in the received column. When you sell products, you can increase the number in the sold column. The difference between the two columns is the number in stock, the last column.

Automatic Calculations

Database applications will do calculations automatically for you. For instance, the instock number above can be automatically calculated from the received and sold columns.

This table is a simple database, but useful nonetheless. By generating a subset of information, you can create a lot of useful data for managing your business. This is the process of making a *query* to the database. Suppose you query the database to give you a list of all the items made by a specific manufacturer. That will give you a pretty good idea of how much business you are doing with that manufacturer.

You can make simple queries or complex queries. For instance, a more complex query would be to ask for a list of all the items made by a specific manufacturer that have a cost over $300. If your merchandise typically sold for $10 to $500, such a query would give you a good idea of how many big-ticket items the manufacturer is supplying to you. But you don't have to get that fancy. Just keeping track of inventory in the table above is useful.

Not a Database Book

This book provides some powerful ideas for using database technology to run your website and eBay commerce. It even provides some details for implementing database ideas. But it is not a database book and does not pretend to be your database primer. If you are interested in putting these database commerce ideas to work, bone up on using database software. If you are more than a novice computer user, you will find a database like Microsoft Access, or its competitors, easy to use.

Using Microsoft Access

Access is simple to use. Just create a table by creating some columns (see Figures 14.1 and 14.2).

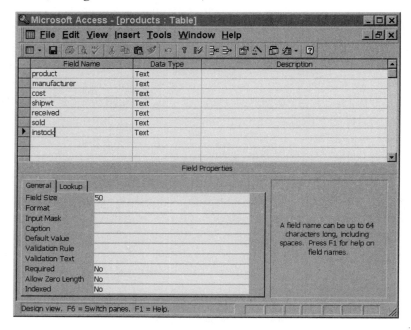

Figure 14.1   Creating columns in Access 97.

You give each column a name and a data type. The data type is usually *text*. In addition, you can assign each column individual characteristics. Suppose you've designed your table by listing your columns on a piece of paper (e.g., a napkin). You can create your table in Access in a matter of seconds.

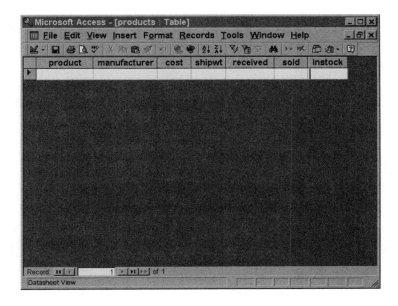

Figure 14.2   Displaying a table in an Access 97 database.

Using an Existing Database

What about using an existing database to do the inventory control? That depends. If the existing database is easy to use, then you can add the columns to tables to enable it to keep track of inventory too. If the existing database is difficult to use because it is a specialized and dedicated system, you can create a database in Access and then export the data from the existing database to the new Access database. This gets the new Access database off to a good start with plenty of data readily installed. Unfortunately, this is not advisable. Maintaining overlapping data in two different and unconnected database applications is not an efficient practice.

Adding Data for eBay Auctions

Whatever columns you need for your database system, you will
need the following for the eBay bulk auction upload system and
your auction ads:

Column	Column Name
One-line title	title
Category	ebaycat
Bold type	bold
Category featured	featurecat
Featured	feature
Location	location
Quantity	quantity
Reserve	reserve
Minimum bid	minbid
Duration	duration
Private	private
Product	product
Manufacturer	manufacturer
Opening line	open
Ad body	ad
Shipping cost	shipcost
Terms	boilerplate
Website URL	weburl
Image URL	imageurl

As you can see, you already have *product* and *manufacturer* in your existing database. You need to add only the remainder. Now your table looks like this:

Column	Column Name
Product	product
Manufacturer	manufacturer
Wholesale cost	cost
Shipping weight	shipwt
Number received	received
Number sold	sold
Number in stock	instock
One-line title	title
Category	ebaycat
Bold type	bold
Category featured	featurecat
Featured	feature
Location	location
Quantity	quantity
Reserve	reserve
Minimum bid	minbid
Duration	duration
Private	private
Opening line	open
Ad body	ad

Shipping cost	shipcost
Terms	boilerplate
Website URL	weburl
Image URL	imageurl

This contains both your inventory control columns and your eBay columns.

Queries

A query is a process that enables you to request and receive a subset of data from a table or series of tables.

Extracting Data from a Database

When you make a query to create the subset of data needed for the eBay bulk upload system, you will be extracting information from the following columns:

Table		eBay Query
Table		**eBay Query**
product		
manufacturer		
cost		
shipwt		
received		
sold		
instock		
title	—>	title
ebaycat	—>	ebaycat

bold	—>	bold
featurecat	—>	featurecat
feature	—>	feature
location	—>	location
quantity	—>	quantity
reserve	—>	reserve
minbid	—>	minbid
duration	—>	duration
private	—>	private
open	—>	open
ad	—>	ad
shipcost	—>	shipcost
boilerplate	—>	boilerplate
weburl	—>	weburl
imageurl	—>	imageurl

The end result of the query (eBay Query) is a set of data you can export to eBay for a bulk upload of auctions. Each row represents one item to be sold (one auction). Only the data in the columns you selected for the eBay Query will be exported (be extracted) from your database; the eBay Query will not include the columns *product*, *manufacturer*, *cost*, *shipwt*, *received*, *sold*, and *instock*.

Boilerplate

Shouldn't the terms of the sale (boilerplate) go right into the template instead of being a database column? That's true when the terms of the sale are the same for all products in the catalog. In that case, there's no reason to have a separate boiler-plate entry for each product. Often, however, certain subgroups of products within the catalog have their own set of standard terms on which they are sold. In that case, you will need a database column to store such terms of sale. Because such terms are the same within a subgroup, you can copy and paste the terms into the column from a word processor for each item in the subgroup (i.e., you don't have to type the terms individually for each item).

The Template

Do you remember the template from Chapter 13? It has a place to enter a one-line title for use in the eBay auction listing. It has a place for you to enter the text of your ad. It has a place for you to enter the URL of your commerce website. And it has a place for you to enter the URL of your image. The bad news is that it's a lot of work to enter all that information. The good news is that you can do it automatically with your database. You enter the data once in your database, and you can generate auctions using templates routinely and automatically again and again.

What do queries look like? The following subsection will give you an idea.

Making the eBay Query to Access

With Access, you will find it easy to make a query. Remember, you are simply creating a subset of the data. In Access, you use a visual interface to create the query (see Figures 14.3 and 14.4).

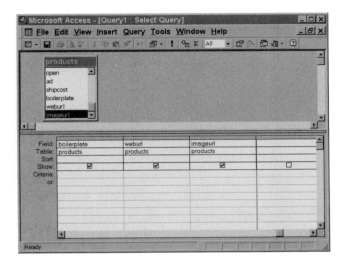

Figure 14.3   Making a query in Access 97.

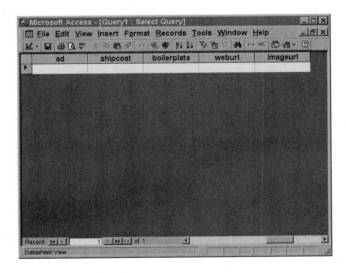

Figure 14.4   Displaying a query (subset) in Access 97 with no data entered.

Making the Miva Merchant Query to Access

As you will read in Chapter 18, a database is the key to operating a full-fledged commerce website efficiently. Consequently, you will need another query to your database to extract the information for Miva Merchant, the Web commerce software featured as an example in Chapter 18. With that in mind, Chapter 18 will pick up where this section leaves off; that is, Chapter 18 will start its demonstration with the Miva Merchant query. It will show how to fill an online catalog easily and quickly with data from a database.

Exporting Data from Access

When you have generated the subset of data (query) you need, how do you get it out of the database to use it elsewhere? You can export it in a delimited format (i.e., a simple file format that other software can use). See Figure 14.5.

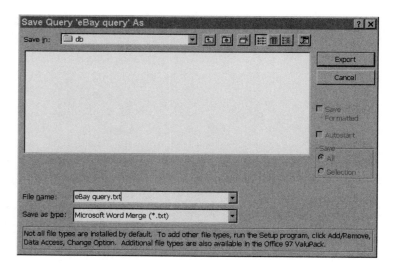

Figure 14.5   Exporting a subset of data resulting from a query.

Using Your Table

Using your Access table is easier, faster, and more fun than the alternatives. The eBay process for entering auctions is slow and tedious. The Miva Merchant process for entering or changing products in the online catalog is slow and tedious. Using your Access table instead is fun (by comparison).

The table is open. You can see many rows at a time and many columns at a time. You can scroll up and down or back and forth quickly and easily. You can move around freely and cover a lot of territory in a short time. It's fast and efficient to make data entries and changes.

Add

You can add new products easily just by filling the columns as you move horizontally across the row for the new product. Remember, this table will provide the necessary data for eBay auctions as well as for the catalog on your commerce website. You must fill in all the columns necessary to provide adequate information for each product. Then you have to decide whether to include an item in the products to be auctioned and whether to include the item in the website catalog (you do so by adding an *x* in the appropriate column).

Subtract

To subtract something from the bulk auction upload or the website catalog, you do not have to subtract it from the database. You merely remove the *x* from the appropriate column or columns, and the product will no longer be included. But it's still in the database for possible use later.

Control Column

You can add a column named include. When you put an x in the include column, the item is included in your subset for uploading to eBay. If the x is not in the include column, the item is not included in the subset for uploading. Thus, you control whether or not to include any particular item.

If you want to get rid of a product completely, you simply delete it from the database. Make sure before you do so that you are not going to use it any longer.

Change

It's easy to change something. Just find the proper row and column and type over what's in the column. You can also copy and paste into the column. That is, you can copy something somewhere else (e.g., in another program) by highlighting it and copying it to the clipboard. Then you can paste it into a column. Copying and pasting are especially handy when using large blocks of text that you do not want to retype. The capability of seeing large parts of the database by viewing the table makes it easy for you to make changes quickly.

The Whole Thing

Once you've made your additions, subtractions, and changes, you're ready to make your bulk upload to eBay or update your website catalog. To do so, read Chapter 15 on bulk uploads (Master Lister) and Chapter 18 on commerce websites.

Summary

Conduct your auctions intelligently. eBay does not require you to be a genius to do well. Just knowing how eBay works and observing eBay practices will give you a good idea of how you can make your auctions effective.

When your auction operation reaches a certain level, you're not a casual seller any longer. You're an eBay retailer. As such, you will probably find, sooner or later, that a desktop database is a good way to keep track of your retail operation. In addition, it enables you to upload multiple auctions at once on eBay. Chapter 15 explains this in more detail.

15

Uploading Auctions in Bulk

Usually to do a bulk upload of information, you use a data file; that is, you export data into a file from a desktop database manager (e.g., Microsoft Access). Then you import the data file into the application in which you need to use the data.

Chapter 18 Example

Chapter 18 outlines a good example of this. You keep all your data on your inventory in a desktop database manager (e.g., Access) where you can easily and quickly maintain the data. You will find Access and its competitors, such as Paradox and FileMaker, easy to use. Next you export the data into a data file (i.e., a delimited data file, explained in Chapter 18). You upload the data file into a Web commerce program at your website. The Web commerce program includes a catalog. The data file provides all the information to fill in the catalog. This process takes only a short time, three to five minutes depending on the size of the data file. The result is that the catalog suddenly has hundreds or thousands of items in it. It works pretty slick.

Unfortunately, eBay chose to have its Master Lister bulk upload process work differently. Instead of uploading a simple data file to eBay, eBay wants you to send all the data in an email message, a very long email message. *This makes things unnecessarily complicated.* Fortunately, complicated does not necessarily mean difficult. It means that you have to set up a process that you can go through step-by-step to be successful, and this chapter covers how to do so.

Database

It all starts with the database. Chapter 14 outlines how you can create a database—a simple table—that includes both data for inventory control and data for creating eBay auctions. You extract the data (subset) for eBay auctions by using a query (the eBay Query). The result is a data file that contains a subset of all the data. Such a subset is designed especially to provide the data for your eBay auctions.

Only eBay

You can, of course, create a database that is only for eBay auctions and nothing more. In that case, you export the data from the entire table for eBay auctions because the table does not contain any other data.

Wouldn't it be nice if you could just take your data file and upload it to eBay? Your job would be done, and in one upload you could create dozens or even hundreds of eBay auctions. Alas, there are a few more steps because eBay wants you to submit the data by email.

Why a Database?

Why maintain your data in a desktop database manager such as Access? It's simply easier. Desktop databases like Access are easy to use. That means that you can add, subtract, and change data easily, quickly, and conveniently on a desktop (or laptop) computer. You do this with the table open—where you can go directly to each column entry (field). Maintaining large amounts of data any other way is invariably more difficult. You can manage small amounts of data perhaps more easily in other ways, but desktop databases make managing large amounts of data easy even for untrained personnel.

If you're not quite sure you understand how we use databases, you might review Chapter 14 before you proceed in this chapter. Once that lightbulb over your head switches on, this stuff is pretty easy. Nonetheless, you still need to pay attention to the details.

Email

eBay wants us to submit our data in an eBay template via an email message. The instructions are in the Master Lister. Go *Services, buying & selling, Manage Your Items for Sale, Upload many items for listing*. eBay provides the template. One template must be filled with information for 1 eBay auction ad. If you submit 85 eBay auctions ads, you must use the template 85 times, and all filled-in eBay templates go in the same email message, up to 100 at one time. In other words, 400 auction ads will require four separate email messages, each containing 100 eBay auction ad templates filled with information (data). The question is, How do you use a database program to do this? This chapter answers that question.

Word Processor

Email is simply text. If you want to do things with text, what do you use? A word processor. In this case, we want to fill and refill the eBay template with information to create multiple auction ads. What does that sound like? It sounds like a mail merge. You can use the mail-merge function of a word processor together with a data file to generate multiple auction ads. Then you can highlight and copy all the generated auction ads to the clipboard and then paste them into an email message. Let's review this process:

1. Create a data file with a desktop database manager.

2. Put the eBay bulk upload template into a word processor.

3. Set up a mail merge using the template, the word processor mail-merge function, and the data file.

4. Run the mail merge.

5. Highlight and copy to the clipboard all the resulting auction

ads from the mail merge.

6. Paste the auction ads into an email message.

7. Send the message to eBay.

Overall, that sounds a little complicated, although each step is easy. It's your job to set it up. Once set up, it's easy and quick to use. It sure beats creating all those eBay auction ads one at a time.

No Print

Normally mail merging results in multiple printed documents (e.g., letters). In this case, the mail merge–generated templates remain in electronic form and are never printed.

Which Template?

You might ask, What about the template in Chapter 13 that makes eBay auction ads look good? Where does that fit in? Does the eBay template substitute for that?

These are good questions. If you use only the eBay template, your auction ads will look as if you entered them using just text (no HTML). In other words, they will have that plain look. Consequently, you will want to use the template from Chapter 13, too (or a template of your own design), to give your auction ads a little pizzazz. So, what are we talking about here? That's right. We need to use a template within a template.

Template Within a Template

The eBay template has places where you plug in information. One of those places is the information for the body of the auction ad (description of the item being auctioned). That's where you plug in the template from Chapter 13 (see Figure 15.1).

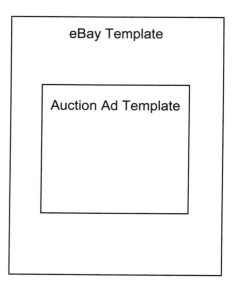

Figure 15.1   A template within a template.

One objective is to fill the eBay template with information (data) from the data file. Your other objective is to use the auction ad template from Chapter 13 to make your auction ad look better. Why not use the data file to fill that template too?

You can do this. The question is, Do you need to do this in two steps? Or can filling both of these templates with data be combined into one step? The answer is—happily—yes, you can combine them into one step; that is, one mail merge fills both templates at once (see Figure 15.2).

And now it's time to review mail merging. Read the documentation for your word processor in regard to the mail-merge function.

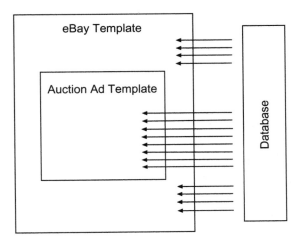

Figure 15.2 One mail merge fills both templates.

Mail Merge

A mail merge takes the data from a data file and fills in blank spaces in a template document. The classic case is a letter. At the top of a letter is the addressee:

```
Dear Mr. Smith,
```

You have a database with the information on 137 people in it, and you want to send them customized letters. But you don't want to individually address them. The title (e.g., Mr.) is in a column called *title*, and the last name is in a column called *lname*. The following letter template is simple:

```
Dear «title». «lname»,

XXXXX XX XXXXXXX XXX XXXXXX XXX XXX
XXXXXXX. XXXXX XX XXXXXXX XXX XXXXXX
XXX XXX XXXXXXX. XXXXX XX XXX XXXXXXX
XXX XXXXXX XXX XXXXXXX XXXX

etc.
```

The remainder of the letter is the same for each person. Only the addressee is different. Thus, when you mail merge the data file with the simple word processor letter template, you will get 137 letters exactly the same except for the addressee, which will be customized for each letter. That's a simple mail merge.

We use the same technique for mail merging data into the eBay template and the Chapter 13 template, but the data are not quite as simple. For instance, the description of the auction item is an entire paragraph (or multiple paragraphs), not just one word such as Smith.

For each record (row), each column of the database stores one word or number. Or it can store multiple words or numbers. It can even store a paragraph or multiple paragraphs. Whatever it stores will be deposited into the template during the mail merge.

The following examples use the Microsoft Word 97 mail-merge function. However, you can do the same easily with any word processor. Review the mail-merge portion of your word processor manual, and you will find it's easy to use the ideas in this chapter to make your own mail merge work.

The Templates

Now let's take another look at the templates. The templates seen one at a time make sense.

eBay Template

The eBay template follows:

```
<EBAY_BULK_ITEM>

<EBAY_BULK_ITEM_DESC>Description of
item that may span multiple lines

</EBAY_BULK_ITEM_DESC>

oneline^138^n^n^n^yourcity^http://
isp.com/graphics/
picture.gif^1^0.0^10.0^7^n

</EBAY_BULK_ITEM>
```

The template includes 12 fields (columns) separated by a delimiter:

Title (one-line title for auction)

Category (get category numbers from eBay)

Bold (**y** for yes, **n** for no; costs extra)

Category featured (**y** for yes, **n** for no; costs extra)

Featured (**y** for yes, **n** for no; costs extra)

Location (location of seller)

Picture (URL for photograph—use **http://** for blank)

Quantity (number of items being auctioned)

Reserve (a decimal is required even for zero)

Minimum bid (a decimal is required even for zero)

Duration (**3**, **5**, or **7** days)

Private (**y** for yes, **n** for no)

As you see, eBay wants you to fill in this template much as you would fill in the input forms at the auction entry in the Sellers section on the eBay website.

If you will recall from Chapter 14, you have all that information in a database. Use the data in the eBay Query from Chapter 14 to fill in the eBay template.

Table		eBay Query
Table		**eBay Query**
product		
manufacturer		
cost		
shipwt		
received		
sold		
instock		
title	—>	title
ebaycat	—>	ebaycat
bold	—>	bold
featurecat	—>	featurecat
feature	—>	feature
location	—>	location
quantity	—>	quantity
reserve	—>	reserve
minbid	—>	minbid
duration	—>	duration
private	—>	private

open	—>	open
ad	—>	ad
shipcost	—>	shipcost
boilerplate	—>	boilerplate
weburl	—>	weburl
imageurl	—>	imageurl (C13 template)

If you enter the column names into the eBay template as a symbol of the data required (instead of the actual data), you get the following (picture field is blank—use imageurl in C13 template):

```
<EBAY_BULK_ITEM>

<EBAY_BULK_ITEM_DESC>ad</
EBAY_BULK_ITEM_DESC>

title^ebaycat^bold^featurecat^feature
^location^http://
^quantity^reserve^minbid^duration^pri
vate

</EBAY_BULK_ITEM>
```

This is a mail-merge document. You have used only 11 columns (eBay Query) with the remainder for the Chapter 13 template.

Chapter 13 Template

The auction ad template from Chapter 13 follows:

```
</blockquote>

<table bgcolor="#99cccc"
width="100%"><tr><td>

<br>
```

```
<table bgcolor="#ccffff" width="520"
align="center"><tr><td>

<table width="400"
align="center"><tr><td>

<br> <br>

<!-- add your short description of the
item BELOW this line to replace the
xxx BELOW -->

<center><h3>xxx</h3></center>

<!-- add your short description of the
item ABOVE this line to replace the
xxx ABOVE -->

<br>

<!-- add your text for your ad BELOW
this line to replace the xxx BELOW -->

xxx

<!-- add your text for your ad ABOVE
this line to replace the xxx ABOVE -->

<br>

<!-- add your shipping charge to
replace the xxx in the paragraph BELOW
this line -->

<p>High Bidder pays $xxx.00 shipping
and handling delivered anywhere in 48
states. Higher outside the lower 48
states.</p>

<!-- add your shipping charge to
replace the xxx in the paragraph ABOVE
this line -->
```

```
<!-- add your boilerplate text BELOW
this line to replace the xxx BELOW -->

<p><b>Terms: </b>xxx</p>

<!-- add your boilerplate text ABOVE
this line to replace the xxx ABOVE -->

<br>

<table bgcolor="#99cccc"
cellpadding="2" width="304"
align="center"><tr><td><table
bgcolor="#ccffff" width="300"
cellpadding="12"
align="center"><tr><td>

<center><p><font size="-1"
face="Arial,Helvetica"><b>Visit our
website by clicking on the name
below.</b></font></p></center>

<!-- add your website URL BELOW this
line to replace the xxx and your
business name BELOW to replace the
zzz-->

<center><p><a href="xxx"> [your
business name] </a></ p></center>

<!-- add your website URL ABOVE this
line to replace the xxx and your
business name ABOVE to replace the
zzz-->

</td></tr></table></td></tr></
table></td></tr></table>

<br> <br>

</td></tr></table>
```

```
<br>

<table bgcolor="#ccffff"
cellpadding="20" align="center"
border="0"><tr><td align="center"
valign="middle">

<!-- Put the URL of the photograph to
replace the xxx BELOW this line-->

<img src="xxx" border=0>

<!-- Put the URL of the photograph to
replace the xxx ABOVE this line-->

</td></tr></table>

<br>

</td></tr></table>
```

Now we want to enter column names into this template in place of the *xxx*'s to create our mail-merge document. The result follows:

```
</blockquote>

<table bgcolor="#99cccc"
width="100%"><tr><td>

<br>

<table bgcolor="#ccffff" width="520"
align="center"><tr><td>

<table width="400"
align="center"><tr><td>

<br> <br>

<!-- add your short description of the
item BELOW this line to replace the
xxx BELOW -->

<center><h3>open</h3></center>
```

```
<!-- add your short description of the
item ABOVE this line to replace the
xxx ABOVE -->

<br>

<!-- add your text for your ad BELOW
this line to replace the xxx BELOW -->
ad
<!-- add your text for your ad ABOVE
this line to replace the xxx ABOVE -->

<br>

<!-- add your shipping charge to
replace the xxx in the paragraph BELOW
this line -->

<p>High Bidder pays $shipcost shipping
and handling delivered anywhere in 48
states. Higher outside the lower 48
states.</p>

<!-- add your shipping charge to
replace the xxx in the paragraph ABOVE
this line -->

<!-- add your boilerplate text BELOW
this line to replace the xxx BELOW -->

<p><b>Terms: </b>boilerplate</p>

<!-- add your boilerplate text ABOVE
this line to replace the xxx ABOVE -->

<br>

<table bgcolor="#99cccc"
cellpadding="2" width="304"
align="center"><tr><td><table
bgcolor="#ccffff" width="300"
```

```
cellpadding="12"
align="center"><tr><td>

<center><p><font size="-1"
face="Arial,Helvetica"><b>Visit our
website by clicking on the name
below.</b></font></p></center>

<!-- add your website URL BELOW this
line to replace the xxx and your
business name BELOW to replace the
zzz-->

<center><p><a href="weburl"> [your
business name] </a></ p></center>

<!-- add your website URL ABOVE this
line to replace the xxx and your
business name ABOVE to replace the
zzz-->

</td></tr></table></td></tr></
table></td></tr></table>

<br> <br>

</td></tr></table>

<br>

<table bgcolor="#ccffff"
cellpadding="20" align="center"
border="0"><tr><td align="center"
valign="middle">

<!-- Put the URL of the photograph to
replace the xxx BELOW this line-->

<img src="imageurl" border=0>

<!-- Put the URL of the photograph to
replace the xxx ABOVE this line-->
```

```
</td></tr></table>

<br>

</td></tr></table>
```

Now you have another mail-merge document.

Word Processing Template

The word processing template you will use is a combination of the preceding two templates. The eBay template requires a description for the body of the auction ad. Instead of entering a column here (i.e., the column *ad*), you enter the Chapter 13 template:

```
<EBAY_BULK_ITEM>

<EBAY_BULK_ITEM_DESC>

[entire Chapter 13 template complete
with column names goes here (not shown
to save space)]

</EBAY_BULK_ITEM_DESC>

title^ebaycat^bold^featurecat^feature
^location^http://
^quantity^reserve^minbid^duration^pri
vate

</EBAY_BULK_ITEM>
```

This is the word processing template you will use to create the individual eBay auction ads that you will email to eBay.

Now you might ask, What typeface do I use for this template? It doesn't matter because when you copy and paste, the text will be unformatted for plain text email.

The Merge

That word processing template sure looks complicated. But it's really a simple idea. Now you want to set up the mail-merge process so that your word processor will take the data from your database file (eBay Query subset of data) and fill up the template to create a series of eBay auction ads.

The Mail-Merge Document

First, open a blank document in Word 97. Next type in (or paste in) the word processing template (i.e., the combination of the eBay bulk upload template and the Chapter 13 template) but without the columns entered (see Figure 15.3). You will enter the columns as part of the Word 97 mail-merge setup procedure.

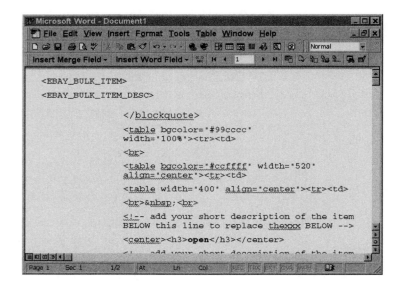

Figure 15.3   The word processing template without columns entered.

The next step is to import the data file into Word 97. Go *Tools, Mail Merge, Mail Merge Helper, Data Source, Get Data, Open Data Source* (see Figure 15.4).

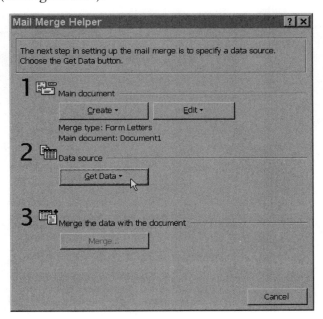

Figure 15.4   Import the data file into Word 97.

Now you are ready to enter the columns into the template.

Word 97 Mail-Merge Characters

The column names must be embedded in a Word 97 mail-merge document using the Word mail-merge process. The mail merge process shows the columns as mail-merge fields by putting arrowheads around them. An example follows:

«boilerplate»

You cannot duplicate the setup process just by putting the «...» characters around column names. Instead, you must go through the mail-merge setup process for the mail merge to work.

Place the cursor where you want to enter a column, and go *Insert Merge Field* to select the proper column (see Figure 15.5).

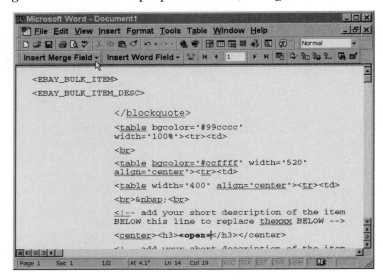

Figure 15.5   Selecting the column to enter into the template.

Finish entering all the columns (fields). Voila! You have a powerful mail-merge document.

The Mail Merge

Next you run the mail merge. To do so in Word 97, you simply click on the Merge to New Document button. Suppose you have 85 records (rows) in the data file. Word magically creates 85 different documents based on the word processing template (see Figure 15.6). Those 85 different documents are actually in one Word file.

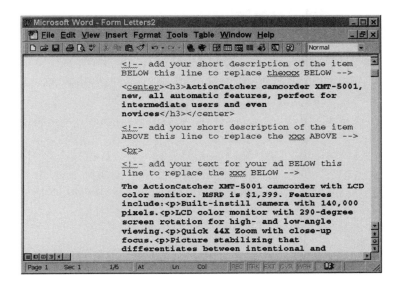

Figure 15.6 After the mail merge, Word 97 shows a portion of the first merged document.

So now the Word 97 file is a huge one. But you're not going to do anything with this Word 97 file. You simply extract all the text from it using copy and paste.

Email Submission

eBay requires you to submit the 85 documents via email. Consequently, the next step is to properly address a blank email message:

```
To: soho@ebay.com

Subject: [not necessary]
```

Now you're ready to send perhaps the longest email message you've ever sent. Make sure your email client is set for plain text.

Copy and Paste

Simply highlight all the text in the Word 97 file (all 85 documents). Copy it to the clipboard. Paste it into the blank email message. You have created a very long email message.

Not an Attachment

Note that you actually paste text directly into the email message. You do not attach a file to the email message. For some word processors, you may have to convert the document to plain text (ASCII text) before you can copy and paste effectively.

You must add two things to your email message before you send it. The first goes at the top of the message:

```
<EBAY_BULK>

<EBAY_BULK_EMAIL>seller@isp.com</
EBAY_BULK_EMAIL>

<EBAY_BULK_DELIM>^</EBAY_BULK_DELIM>
```

The first line tells eBay that the message is a bulk upload. The second line gives eBay your email address. The third line informs eBay of the delimiter you are using. eBay recommends ^ as a delimiter. At the end of the message, add the following:

```
</EBAY_BULK>
```

This tells eBay that it has reached the end of the upload. Now you have finished the email message. Send it.

Payment for Auctions

Before eBay will run your auctions, you must arrange payment. You can use a credit card, or you can send ahead a check. If payment has not been arranged, eBay will not run the auctions. Using a credit card makes managing your auction payments to eBay more convenient.

Benefits and Disadvantages

What are the benefits and disadvantages of the eBay Master Lister bulk upload system? It will take a commitment of time and energy to get set up to do bulk uploads. Is it worth it?

Benefits

A primary benefit is that you can save a lot of time if you run a lot of auctions. Entering the information for each auction manually is tedious if you run more than just a few auctions each week. A bulk upload is quick and relatively painless.

Another benefit is that you don't have to be a programmer to use the eBay bulk upload system. You can learn to do it yourself if you feel comfortable operating a personal computer. In addition, if you hire someone to set up your system, that person doesn't have to be a programmer or a database programmer. A webmaster or Web developer familiar with databases can easily make the eBay bulk upload system work. But using this book will save such a person a considerable amount of time and energy in setting up your system.

Step by Step

When you set up a database system for creating bulk uploads and for creating a catalog on an ecommerce website, write step-by-step procedural guides for each process that almost anyone comfortable with a PC can follow. Then you don't have to memorize the procedures, and you can have an employee complete the process from beginning to end. Keep in mind also that a part-time employee can do this sort of work on a PC at home.

Yet another benefit is that you can expand the number of your eBay auctions with the confidence that you can repeat your bulk upload week after week with little effort. This will enable you to start thinking about your eBay business with a larger vision for the future.

Disadvantages

One potential disadvantage is that all your auctions will start about the same time. If part of your auction strategy requires spacing your auctions apart in time, the bulk upload does not facilitate such a strategy without doing multiple mail merges.

Multiple Mail Merges

You can only bulk upload 100 auctions at a time. If you run 400 auctions a week, you will have to do at least four bulk uploads. That gives you an opportunity to stagger identical auctions so that they don't end close together. But, even if you run only 100 auctions a week, you don't have to upload them all at once. You can do several smaller bulk uploads so that you can stagger your identical auctions.

Another disadvantage is that this system could be much simpler if eBay accepted a delimited data file for upload instead of requiring that the information be sent in a template via email—a strange system indeed. Perhaps in the future eBay will switch to a delimited data file upload.

Another disadvantage to keep in mind is that this system requires a substantial amount of maintenance. Someone must maintain the data in the desktop database. If you run a lot of auctions, a database can save you a lot of time and energy (and money), but it doesn't reduce your work to zero. Someone has to maintain the data routinely for the bulk upload system to work. For instance, someone needs to add and delete inventory items, change prices, change specifications, etc.

If you have never used a desktop database manager, you will have to learn how to use one before this system will work for you. It's not difficult to learn, but you do have to learn how to build a table, enter data into it, and change the data in it. The alternative is to hire someone to do it for you.

Finally, you probably recognize that you can't do it all. To get set up to do bulk uploads, you may have to hire someone knowledgeable in databases rather than take the time to do it yourself. Moreover, many people reading this book are probably unlikely candidates to perform the tedious data-entry work that it takes to enter and maintain the data in a database. You need to hire someone who can type well and who is comfortable using a computer to do the routine data-entry and data-maintenance work.

Alternatives

What's the alternative to setting up a system as this chapter suggests? Use software made especially for managing an eBay business operation.

If you find the method this chapter outlines too burdensome, there is auction software you can use that will provide product management and eBay bulk upload functions for you. If you can get such software on a trial basis, try it, compare it to the system in this chapter, and decide which method is best for you. Since I wrote the first edition of this book, the software for setting up and maintaining an eBay business system seems to have improved. Take a look at Chapter 10 and also the following:

- Andale (*http://andale.com*)
- AuctionWatch (*http://auctionwatch.com*)
- AuctionWorks (*http://auctionworks.com*)

These websites offer a combination of software and services that will assist you with your eBay auction retail efforts.

Summary

Uploading auctions in bulk (Master Lister) is a special service eBay provides to retailers who sell a lot of merchandise on eBay each week. When you have many auctions to enter, entering them individually is tedious and time-consuming, even when you use templates and other aids. To do an effective and efficient job of bulk uploads, you need to manage your merchandise in a database. Once you have it in a database, you can do the bulk upload easily.

Because eBay requires the bulk upload to be submitted by email, you must transform your data into text form. The easiest and least expensive way to do so is to mail merge the data into a word processing document (template). The template you use for the mail merge is simply the one that eBay provides for the bulk upload. (You can also use an auction ad template within the eBay bulk upload template.) Once the mail merge is complete, you can highlight the entire content of the mail-merge–generated document and copy and paste it into an email message. Then send it to eBay. Once you get the step-by-step procedure well organized, it's a quick and efficient process that will enable you to expand your auction activities with a minimum of labor. It's also a system that someone working on a PC at home can handle well.

Although there are alternative programs or services, they too have a learning curve that you will have to master. Evaluate such programs and services carefully together with the procedures in this book, and pick a method that provides you with the easiest and most efficient and convenient means of getting the job done.

16

Taking Payment

Taking payment is so important to an eBay seller it deserves a chapter by itself. Why? Because payment is important to buyers. It's important to buyers for three reasons: capability, convenience, and safety. For instance, if a buyer doesn't have a credit card, he or she will not be able to pay if the only means of payment is via credit card. If the only means of payment is by money order and a buyer has to drive ten miles and stand in line to get a money order, the inconvenience will turn many potential bidders into passers (i.e., nonbidders). Of course, any means of payment deemed by a buyer to be unsafe will be likely to be avoided. However, safety is a personal perception that varies from buyer to buyer.

Consequently, for sellers to provide adequate customer service, a variety of payment methods must be acceptable. Perhaps you don't have to accept payments by all means possible, but you do need to give buyers some choices.

Payment Methods

The various payment methods follow. Accept payment as many ways as possible for maximum customer service.

Checks

Checks are the preferred way for Americans to pay. The vote is about 60 percent. Yet, the preferred way to pay online is clearly by credit card. What's going on?

I think the answer is that most buyers and sellers don't know that checks can now be used online as well as over the phone (since 1996). It works as follows:

1. The buyer gives the seller all the information from one of his or her checks via phone or email.

2. The buyer authorizes the seller to write a check for the purchase. The authorization is for a specific amount.

3. The seller inputs the buyer's information into a program such as TurboCheck (*http://www.turbocheck.com*). The seller uses TurboCheck to print buyer's check using check forms and a computer printer. The seller signs the check on behalf of the buyer and deposits it. (TurboCheck software is

inexpensive. The TurboCheck explainations of how online checking works serve as excellent resources to which you can refer or link your customers.)

4. The seller waits for the check to clear and then sends merchandise.

The biggest barrier to taking checks via the Web is that buyers have a difficult time understanding how the check-writing procedure works and why it's no more risky than sending a seller a check via snail mail. Therefore, they don't trust the method of payment, particularly if they don't have much reason to trust the seller.

The first two questions that come to mind are:

Seller: "How do I protect myself against a claim of fraud by the buyer?"

Buyer: "How do I protect myself against the seller using the information from my check in a fraudulent way?"

The next two sections of this chapter answer these questions, but it will be a few years before the public embraces the use of checks on the Web. In the meantime, see Billpoint later in this chapter for another workable means of accepting checks via the Web.

Protection against the Claim of Fraud by the Buyer

As the seller you can protect yourself against the claim of fraud by the buyer. Simply keep a record of the authorization. The authorization should include the check information plus a statement that the buyer authorizes the seller to write a check for a payment of a certain amount. If you take a check by telephone, you need to make a recording and archive it. If you take a check electronically, you need to archive the electronic text. Either way, should the buyer claim fraud, you can prove otherwise.

Protection against Fraud by the Seller

As a buyer, every time you write a check, you present the check for deposit. The seller takes possession. Any seller can use the information on the check to make additional checks and defraud you. Anyone at the drugstore, supermarket, video rental, telephone company, or elsewhere who sees your check has all the information necessary to make additional fraudulent checks. With that in mind, providing check information over the phone or electronically doesn't seem so ominous. Indeed, you have substantial protection against fraudulent checks because the bank will have to credit your account for any fraudulent checks or prove that you provided authorization for them.

What Does an Authorized Check Accomplish?

The most an authorized check accomplishes is reducing the duration of the transaction by the time it takes the check to get from the buyer to the seller via snail mail or FedEx. As the seller you must still wait for the check to clear before you can be sure of sufficient funds to cover it. There are electronic services that will inform you about a buyer's checking account (e.g., whether it has had problems), but they don't provide information about account balances, nor do they guarantee payment.

Try It

If you're a seller, try out this method. It could be productive for you. If you want to learn more about it, try the TurboCheck website, which has lots of information. This method has quite a bit of potential, but it will require you to educate buyers regarding how it works.

Miva Merchant Module

Miva Merchant (website transaction software) has an add-on module that facilitates checks via TurboCheck. At checkout, it's a choice along with credit cards and other methods. Read more about Merchant in Chapter 18.

Credit Cards

Most online transactions with a seller that accepts credit cards are credit card transactions. This is a very popular means of paying online. Thus, if you can obtain a merchant account that enables you to accept credit cards, you can expect to increase your eBay business significantly.

Merchant Accounts

In the past, merchant accounts were difficult to obtain, particularly for mail-order businesses and then for Web commerce. But times have changed. Normal merchant accounts with their relatively low cost (about 2 percent of a sale) still may be difficult to obtain, but there are many higher-priced alternatives. Research what's available at what price. Establish a track record, and work your way toward getting a normal merchant account.

What does it take to get a merchant account? A good credit rating and a banker who knows you and trusts you. But see PayPal and Billpoint later in this chapter for easy alternatives to using merchant accounts.

Money Orders and Cashier's Checks

Money orders and cashier's checks are reasonably safe payment methods. These are pretty secure for sellers to accept. However, they are easy to forge, and it's probably getting easier rather than more difficult to forge them. Fortunately, it's often easier to trace someone that's pulled a forgery scam online than it is offline. But that doesn't mean you won't get stuck. Be aware. Be careful. And to be safe, require a specific money order that you can recognize as not being a forgery (e.g., a postal money order).

Cash on Delivery

Cash on delivery (COD) is a time-honored means of collecting payment for mail-order merchandise (or Web merchandise). The risk to the seller is that the buyer doesn't pay, and the seller gets the merchandise back and gets stuck with high shipping costs too. Consequently, many sellers avoid this means of payment. Nonetheless, for certain markets, it may work well.

International Money Orders

How can you collect payment from abroad? It will take so long for the clearance of a foreign check that international money orders and credit card payments may work best. In addition, your bank may charge some absurdly high fee to clear foreign checks. Yet, this is a situation you need to research carefully. The potential of a global reach for your business is greater than you think. If you can work out a variety of payment methods to your satisfaction, you may get more business than you ever dreamed. Most retailers will ignore this market, leaving it wide open for the more enterprising.

Cash

Never take cash. Taking cash is the best way to get into a knock-down-drag-out fight with a buyer. Cash leaves no record or proof of payment for either party. Cash has a wonderful way of disappearing in transit. It's almost humorous that people resort to using cash when they should know better. Don't be the object of the humor. Just say no.

Special Payments for the Web

All the means of payment mentioned earlier are traditional. There are also many special means and schemes for making payments via the Web. Most are irrelevant because they are not widely used. Two stand out, though, because eBay patrons use them. PayPal has come to be widely used recently. People use Billpoint because eBay sponsors it.

What's the Score?

According to PayPal, as of September 20, 2000, PayPal was used in 2,572,423 auctions, and Billpoint was used in 495,897 auctions. These both became important payment methods in less than a year.

PayPal

PayPal (*http://www.x.com*) is independent of eBay but works well on eBay. It also works outside of eBay. It relies on credit cards. Buyers without credit cards cannot use it. It works as follows when initiated by the buyer:

1. Buyer (registered with PayPal) sends money to seller via an email to PayPal.

2. PayPal notifies seller by email.

3. Seller registers with PayPal. (If seller is already registered, skip this registration step.)

4. Seller ships.

It works as follows when initiated by seller:

1. Seller (registered with PayPal) sends a request for payment to buyer via an email to PayPal.

2. PayPal notifies buyer via email.

3. Buyer registers with PayPal. (If buyer is already registered, skip this registration step.)

4. Buyer sends money to seller via an email to PayPal.

5. PayPal notifies seller.

6. Seller ships.

The money comes from the buyer's credit card. Sellers do not have to have merchant credit card accounts to use PayPal. A seller can withdraw money from his or her account at any time. PayPal acts as the middleman but keeps all funds generated from the buyers' credit cards until the sellers withdraw the funds.

The seller never sees the buyer's credit card numbers, just the buyer's name and email address.

There is no registration fee. This service is free to buyers and casual sellers. PayPal makes money on the interest it gets on the funds it holds until sellers withdraw. For retail sellers (i.e., volume sellers), PayPal charges a $0.25 flat fee and 1.9 percent of the transaction amount per transaction. PayPal also provides additional useful services to retail sellers. For instance, it enables sellers to send automatic payment requests to buyers filled in with all the relevant auction information. It enables winning bidders to pay instantly with just a click on the auction page.

Referrals

PayPal has a referral system that pays $5 to anyone referring another person who becomes registered.

PayPal has become very popular with eBay patrons in a short time, and eBay now offers its own payment system called Billpoint, which works a little differently.

Billpoint

Billpoint is a procedure that enables sellers to take payment from winning bidders by credit card or electronic check without any special arrangements other than registering with Billpoint. In other words you don't need to have a credit card merchant account or special software to process electronic checks. eBay operates Billpoint, and it's the eBay official mechanism for easy payment.

It works for buyers too. Although buyers can pay via Billpoint without registering, registration makes such payment more convenient.

All processing is secure and handled by Wells Fargo Bank. As a seller, you can effectively use Billpoint not only as a means of offering convenient payment to winning bidders but also as a means of keeping track of your sales transactions. Billpoint keeps a history for you.

There is a lot of automation built into Billpoint. For instance, all the information for an auction is automatically entered into the seller's invoice prior to sending the invoice to the winning bidder. Go *Services, Buying and Selling Tools, Buyer Tools, eBay Online Payments by Billpoint* for detailed information and tutorials on how to register and use this handy service.

Registering is easy and quick whether you register a seller or as both a seller and buyer. Using the service, whether a buyer or seller, is also simple. The only limitation is a transaction amount ceiling placed on your account (up to $2,000 for credit cards and $200 for electronic checks). You cannot use this mechanism for large transactions such as buying a car (e.g., usually over $2,000).

How does it work? The seller sends a Billpoint invoice to the winnng bidder as soon as the auction concludes. The winnng bidder enters the requisite information for paying by credit card or electronic check. The seller never sees the information; that is, only Billpoint gets that part of the information. When the buyer pays, the order is complete. A confirmation automatically goes to the seller, and the seller ships. If the buyer has registered with Billpoint, the buyer's information is already in the system, and the buyer can make payment with one click instead of entering a lot of information. All in all, it's an easy-to-use, safe system of payment. If you are more than just a casual user of eBay, you will want to register as both a seller and buyer. The fees for using Billpoint, paid by the seller, are as follows:

Credit Cards

0–$15: Flat fee of $0.35

$15.01–$2,000: Flat fee of $0.35 plus 2.5 percent of the transaction amount

Electronic Checks

No fee

The buyer pays no fees. With Billpoint, the money goes from buyer to seller immediately and is not held by Billpoint.

However, in regard to checks, you will want to require a period to wait for electronic checks to clear before you ship. Clearance takes three days. Once you're notified via email that the electronic check has cleared, the check payment is guaranteed by Billpoint.

Instant Payment

You can offer instant payment to a buyer using the Billpoint "Instant Payment" device. An Instant Payment button goes in the auction page. For Instant Payment, you must specify:

- Shipping and handling
- Incremental shipping for Dutch auctions
- Sales tax
- Return policy

These costs must be fixed. Thus, when a buyer clicks on the Instant Payment button, the entire transaction is completed instantly because all the transaction information has already been provided by the seller. Naturally, if the shipping costs or other costs are not yet determined, a seller cannot offer Instant Payment.

Instant Payment Plus Fixed Price

Review the fixed-price "Buy It Now" alternative in Chapter 6, which enables a seller to sell under certain circumstances at a fixed price. You can combine the Instant Payment device with the Buy It Now device to create a powerful online selling system that will regularly, if not always, take the place of the full auctions. This is not a foolproof means of circumventing auctions, but you can make it work if you desire to sell at a fixed price.

Escrow

Expensive items should go in escrow. Escrow is not a type of payment. It is a method of ensuring that the merchandise is delivered and payment is made. It's not cheap. But it's safe for the buyer.

Everyone has their tolerance level. Mine is somewhere close to $1,000. Certainly, for anything over $1,000, I would want to set up the transaction in escrow, at least with an unfamiliar seller. Other buyers less affluent than I might have greater tolerances and other buyers more affluent than I may have lesser tolerances, although generally one would expect tolerance to increase with affluence. At some level or other, any buyer with brains is going to want the transaction to go in escrow. As a seller, you need to be ready to agree to requests for escrow transactions at some reasonable level of purchase price.

Summary

The name of the game for eBay sellers is to collect the winning bids via as many means as possible to provide maximum convenience to buyers. This is an important part of customer service. Fortunately, one of the easiest and most popular means of payment, credit cards, is now possible to offer to buyers through PayPal and Billpoint even by those sellers who do not have credit card merchant accounts.

VI

Advanced eBay for Sellers

17

Using eBay for Marketing

And you thought eBay was just for buying and selling things. On the contrary, eBay may be your best marketing tool. What better way for you to promote your business than to get your name out in front of people who are motivated to buy what you have to offer.

Compared to What?

If you run an ad in a newspaper, your target market (potential customers) may be 1/10 of 1 percent of the readers. You pay the same advertising rate as another business that has a target market of 5 percent of the readers. What if you could inexpensively appeal to a market where 100 percent of the "readers" were potential customers? That would give you a significant business advantage.

Suppose you sell authentic Japanese prints (reproductions) for an average price of $85 each. If you advertise in the newspaper in your community of 200,000, the ad will be expensive (and small too) and the potential customers few. You will have to entice them with an appealing ad. You'll be looking for those few out of 200,000 who are ready to buy Japanese prints today. Those people will then have to travel to your place of business to purchase the prints.

In contrast, on eBay the people come to you (come to your auction) because they are interested in buying Japanese prints and have found you through eBay's directory system or search engine. It is only a very small percentage of the people using eBay, but a small percentage of a couple of million people is still larger than a small percentage of 200,000 people. And the cost of the ad is much different.

The Plan

Now, let's say you have 120 prints in stock. If you put 50 or 100 in separate auctions at eBay, that's a *retail* sales plan that will be relatively expensive in regard to eBay fees (still inexpensive compared to newspaper advertising). If you put only one print up for auction, that can be a *marketing* plan.

How do you turn one auction into a marketing plan? Let's consider the retail plan first. If you put 100 prints on auction, that seems like a huge collection. In fact, art sells according to taste, and 100 choices are not very many, particularly if the prints are high-quality copies from several historical periods or artists (as is true with Japanese prints). Chances are most of the potential customers will choose to pass on the current collection. But they will be likely to return to see what you have to offer next time, and most will buy prints from you sooner or later. Nonetheless, this time most will pass. Therefore, sales may be disappointing.

If you auction one print, you'll probably attract the same people; but the time, trouble, and cost will be less. It's your job to leverage the visits to your one auction into multiple sales. You can do this with ingenuity if you realize that you're conducting a marketing plan instead of a retail sales plan. I'm not going to tell you how to conduct your marketing plan because there are many potential strategies. Invent some. Nonetheless, there are a few obvious ones that are worth mentioning.

Four Steps

First, you want people to see your entire collection, all 120 prints. You need to have an online gallery, a Web storefront. Your task then becomes enticing the potential bidders at your eBay auction to visit your website gallery. Second, you have to make it very easy for your potential bidders to leave eBay and go to your website. Third, you have to make it very easy for potential bidders to navigate your website and to buy something. Fourth, you have to make it easy for potential bidders to get back to eBay. Let's take these one at a time.

Entire Collection

People must be able to see your entire collection. That's the way to sell art. You need to have a website gallery. Setting up and operating a website is easier and less expensive than operating a real art gallery. It's also easier and perhaps less expensive than running 120 auctions four times a month on eBay. If you already have a website, I don't have to sell you on this idea.

How are you going to entice people to leave your auction and go to your website? I'll leave that up to you. One simple method is to ask them to.

Quick Link

Once you have talked them into going to your website, you have to make it easy for them. A link in your auction ad in the appropriate place accomplishes this nicely. But the link has to be highly visible, easy to use, and clearly explained.

Website

Your website needs to be attractive, up-to-date, and well operated with easy navigation. Chapter 18 covers what a basic commerce website looks like. You need to offer all means of payment and make it easy for people to complete a transaction.

Return Link

There should be multiple return links in your website to make it convenient for potential bidders to return to your auction on eBay. You will have to revise these links for each new auction (i.e., each week—each new auction has a different URL). If you do this, you have effectively made eBay part of your website. If you don't provide return links to eBay, you'll have fewer repeat visitors to your website in the future. People don't like to be left stranded.

In the Long Term

This is a long-term marketing plan. You want to make the appearance of your auction consistent so that people recognize it. You want to make the link to your website consistent so that people will learn to feel comfortable leaving eBay to visit your website. And you want to make the return trip consistent too.

Repeat Auction

You need to run the auction constantly; as soon as one auction is over, another should be in place. Naturally, you should change the print being auctioned each time to maintain interest in your auctions.

As a practical matter, if you're marketing on eBay, you may find it cost-effective to run multiple auctions in different categories as part of your marketing campaign. Usually, one auction at a time doesn't achieve the market penetration you can achieve by a more ambitious approach.

Serious Auction

Is this a serious auction you're running? From one point of view it's just a token auction to keep your business before the print-buying public as part of a marketing plan. Nevertheless, you have to take the auction itself seriously. A sale at each auction will definitely help your marketing plan. If potential bidders get the idea that it's a phony effort, they will resent it, and your marketing plan will not be as effective. If you find that you do not make a sale at most of your auctions, you may be conveying the impression that you're making a phony effort. In fact, your price may be too high. Sales are crucial to your marketing plan. Take your auctions seriously.

Other Businesses

Keep in mind that the Japanese print business is just one business. Each business has its own peculiarities. For instance, suppose you sell nine models of electric guitars ranging in price from $200 to $4,500. Rather than offer a different electric guitar at each auction (like the different Japanese print at each auction), you might offer the low-end guitar at each auction at an attractive price as a strategy to attract entry-level customers to your retail sales operation. Each business will have a different strategy, and even businesses selling the same things will have different strategies. A variety of strategies will work, and some won't. Experiment.

Marketing, Not Retail

The thing to remember is that a marketing effort on eBay is different from a retail sales effort. The objective of a marketing effort is to use eBay as a promotional or advertising vehicle. The sales are not necessarily made on eBay, and in many cases, sales will be made off eBay. The objective of a retail sales effort (not a marketing effort) is to sell merchandise on eBay. If you keep these two efforts separate in your mind and pay attention to details, you will be more effective in whichever strategy you choose to pursue. Confused planning regarding marketing and retail sales may yield disappointing results.

Retail and Marketing

Retail sales and a marketing effort on eBay can also be one and the same in some circumstances for some businesses. As long as you understand the difference between a retail sales effort and a marketing effort and decide to combine the two in a creative way, a combined effort might prove very successful for you. For instance, rather than sell 1 Japanese print, you might sell 15 each week on eBay but do it in such a way that it promotes marketing as well as retail sales volume. But a retail sales effort is not automatically a marketing effort, and a marketing effort can be something very different.

eBay User Agreement

When using eBay for marketing, be careful that you don't violate the eBay User Agreement. It requires that you do not sell an item on a website linked to an auction for a lower price than the reserve price (or minimum bid) for the same item being auctioned on eBay.

eBay seems to like the two-way-street approach. It allows links to your website (subject to the eBay User Agreement), but it likes to see links from your website to eBay in return. It seems to me that this is a sound marketing approach for both you and eBay.

Professional Services

Services are perhaps more difficult to sell on eBay than merchandise. Professional services are often intangible or loosely defined, and costs are often difficult for customers to estimate. But even if there is not a substantial opportunity for selling professional services on eBay, there is a solid marketing opportunity.

The Package

An attorney could offer divorce services at $120 per hour, real estate services at $145 per hour, estate planning services at $160 per hour, etc. That does not seem particularly appealing.

How about a marketing plan instead? Each week offer one package of well-defined legal services at a specific price. Do it simply as a promotion. Specificity attracts better than ambiguity. The package will attract potential bidders to your auction and then to your website if you have properly enticed them. What are the chances of selling the package? Perhaps remote. When it comes to legal services, they are usually performed on a custom basis to accommodate specific problems that clients have. However, the package gives people something specific to consider, and it may attract them to your website where you can provide them with as much information about your legal services and qualifications as they can digest.

A few people will want the package as presented. You need to be ready to perform the services specified for the price stated. Indeed, steady sales of the packages will help your marketing program, so an attractive package is important. However, many people who buy the package will eventually find that they really need custom legal services instead. So, the package will draw in new clients. Indeed, even those who do not bid on the package may be drawn to your website to see what similar or other legal services you offer. Thus, the package will draw in potential clients too.

Institutional Advertising

Normal advertising sells specific products. Institutional advertising sells companies. Because the scope and cost of *services* are often difficult to pin down in advance, specific advertising or promotion is difficult to devise. That's why institutional advertising is common for services. If you can sell someone on the idea of doing business with you or your law firm, you can negotiate the specific legal services and fees after a consultation session. What brings the client to you in the first place is institutional advertising, that is, the firm's name.

Unfortunately, institutional advertising doesn't seem to fit in on eBay where specific goods and services are auctioned. That's where the package of legal services fits in. It seems to be specific; but even after someone buys it, it may turn into something else due to most people's need for custom services. It's a hybrid idea. It's a package that interests people in doing business with you, but it's a package that most likely will turn into something else when the services are actually performed. It seems to me that selling packages of services on eBay is similar to institutional advertising.

Information Products

Most professionals provide information (e.g., advice) as a considerable portion of their normal services. Therein lies an eBay opportunity. Create information products and auction them on eBay. This makes a great marketing program and may even generate some significant extra income. Information products might be books, reports, surveys, or newsletters. Naturally, they will be specialized, reflecting the specialized expertise of the professionals creating them. People who are likely to be potential clients may buy such information products. And such information products help create knowledgeable clients who are more able to use your valuable advice. If you don't like the packaged services idea, try information products.

The Professions

Of course, professionals are a funny lot. Some professional organizations have rules about advertising and marketing that inhibit their members from doing the normal things to get business that other businesspeople do all the time. Consequently, if you are a professional, check your code of ethics carefully to determine what kind of a marketing plan you can ethically operate on eBay.

General Services

The general services category is much broader than professional services. Some services are, in fact, more like merchandise than services. For instance, an oil change and lubrication for your car are more like buying a bag of groceries than buying legal services, even though the actual oil and lubrication make up a modest portion of the purchase price. Yet the same service station that sells you the $25 oil and lube service acts like a lawyer when you bring your car in with a funny clunking noise. Sure, you get an estimate, but who knows what the scope of services and the final price will be. The point here is that general services can be anything from a merchandise-like package to a custom service. This makes general services quite appropriate to auction on eBay. You may even be able to auction general services in a retail program. You can certainly auction services as part of a marketing plan.

Services Included

It always seemed to me that manufacturers should give you the copy machine and charge you to service it. As it is, they charge you a modest price for the copy machine and a substantial monthly payment for the service. That's almost the same thing. Until eBay-local auctions, selling copy machines on eBay did not look very promising. Too large, too heavy, and who's going to service the copy machine when it goes to another city. But in a local market, a copy machine is easy to deliver and to service.

This is an example of a service that's attached to a product. If you want to sell your service, auction the product on eBay. There are probably better examples than the copy machine, but the idea is a powerful one. Because most services are performed locally, the proliferation of local eBays will provide fabulous new opportunities online for those who provide services attached to a tangible product. And if your service isn't attached to a tangible product, find one to attach it to. Then sell the product on eBay.

Summary

You can use eBay to support a marketing or advertising plan. So long as you keep the ideas of an eBay retail effort and an eBay marketing effort separate, you can do either successfully. You can even combine them creatively.

eBay provides you with a substantial marketing opportunity. Don't abuse the opportunity. Abide by the eBay User Agreement that puts certain restrictions on what you can do. Integrate your commerce website with your eBay auctions using links that run in both directions.

Marketing is one idea that can make eBay useful for professional and other services. Auction a package of services, an information product, or any product in order to promote your services via eBay. Find out that eBay is an inexpensive marketing medium with a great deal of potential.

18

Building a Website

This chapter starts where we left off in Chapter 14 regarding the use of databases to keep track of inventory. An inventory database is essential to a commerce website, assuming you sell a bountiful variety of inventory. A commerce website can be a profitable operation in conjunction with running multiple auctions on eBay. And an inventory control database is handy for keeping track of a retail operation on eBay too, even if you don't have a commerce website.

Hence, it makes good sense to use a database in your online retail operations.

A Commerce Website

What is a commerce website? Typically, it's a website that sells products. It has a catalog; a shopping basket for customers to accumulate products; a checkout procedure including automated shipping and sales tax calculations, credit card processing, and warehouse shipping notification; and order accounting. A short time ago, a system as just described was a major Web construction project and was expensive to create and operate. Today such capabilities are offered by dozens of Web commerce software packages for websites, and operating expenses can be quite low.

What does this mean to eBay retailers who run bulk auctions on eBay? It means that bulk auctions on eBay and a commerce website can work together to increase business. For instance, Dutch auctions are a good way to sell inventory in quantity on eBay. It's almost like selling inventory out of a catalog.

If you do conduct a retail operation on eBay, you might ask yourself, Why make buyers wait until the end of the auction? Have them come to your commerce website and buy immediately. As you will recall from Chapters 4 and 17, eBay does permit a link to your website from your auction ad. However, the eBay User Agreement states that you cannot sell the same products you are auctioning at eBay on your website at a lower price:

> Links in your auction ad may not link to any Web page where the same items are offered for sale at a lower price than your minimum bid or reserve amount or are concurrently listed for auction at a website other than eBay. (a paraphrase from the User Agreement)

A common practice among eBay retailers who have commerce websites is to auction their merchandise on eBay with reserves that are lower than the prices in their website catalogs. In many cases, the bidding has a natural tendency to increase the average high bids to an amount somewhere in the range of the prices in the website catalog.

It's clear to me that a commerce website and eBay are two very powerful online retailing tools. Why choose one over the other? Use both together in as many creative ways as you can invent to generate the highest possible volume of Web retail sales.

Links to eBay

You can link from your website to eBay three ways:

1. eBay home page

2. Your list of current auctions

3. A specific current auction

Linking to the eBay home page is a service to your website visitors and helps promote eBay. You have a vested interest in promoting eBay if you are running auctions there regularly. Someplace on your website—most likely your home page—you need to put this general link.

Linking to a list of your current auctions on eBay is not only a service to your website visitors but an arrangement that directly promotes your retail effort. You may want to use this link together with every item in your catalog that you auction on eBay either regularly or occasionally.

Linking to a specific auction is tough. The longest auction is ten days. That means that if you are linking to current auctions, you need to change your website every few days to keep up. This is a great way to operate, but it's only for the ambitious and diligent. If you have links on your website that don't work (stale links), it reflects negatively on your credibility.

URLs

To determine the URLs of the links you want to use, simply find the various Web pages on eBay. Then look in the Location (URL) window of your Web browser (see Figure 18.1).

Figure 18.1   URL window in a Netscape Web browser.

Highlight and copy (to the clipboard) the URL in the URL window (use right mouse button). Paste the URL into the appropriate hyperlink markup in the appropriate Web page on your website (use right mouse button).

eBay Buttons

If you want to use official eBay buttons for links instead of using text, eBay provides a way to do so. You can use eBay buttons with your eBay links, if you agree to the eBay Link License Agreement. You will find it on eBay under *Site Map*, *Buying and Selling*, *Promote your listings with link buttons* (see Figure 18.2).

One button is for a general link. The other button is for a link to specific items currently being auctioned. Your general link to the eBay home page will be as follows:

```
<a href="http://www.ebay.com">eBay
Home Page</a>
```

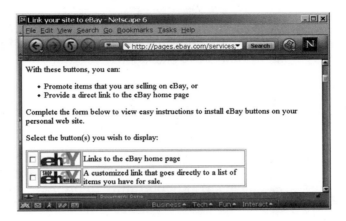

Figure 18.2   Link buttons provided by eBay.

Your link to a specific item being auctioned will be similar to the following:

```
<a href="http://cgi.ebay.com/aw-cgi/
eBayISAPI.dll?ViewItem&item=13682875"
>Blue Ridge Cup and Saucer Crabapple
Design</a>
```

Again, to get the address, go to the auction and look at the Location window in your browser. Highlight the URL in the Location window, and copy and paste.

Institutional Advertising

At your website, you can have a Web page dedicated to your business. For instance, put in a photograph of your retail store, warehouse, or office. Provide the history of your firm; if you've been in business for 20 years, toot your horn. Show photographs of your employees and yourself. You can do as much as you want to do. This is not an ad in the newspaper that costs $400 per inch.

Want people on eBay to know you're legitimate? Put a link in your eBay ad to this Web page. Let people know exactly where the link goes. Many potential bidders will pass on your invitation, but many others will take a look.

Information

Information can promote your business. The Web is an information medium. The amount of information you can put on a website is practically unlimited. Pull these three ideas together and you have a real opportunity to promote your selling effort. For instance, it's not unusual for professionals to give free seminars to attract potential customers. You can easily create a text tutorial on any topic on a website. Thus, a tutorial on estate planning will tend to bring potential clients to an estate planner's website. You can even add RealAudio to it.

Recently, while I looked for a camcorder to purchase, I ran across a commerce website (video retailer) that had a complete tutorial on shooting video with a consumer camcorder. It was quite valuable (and free), and I gave that particular website a more thorough visit than other video retail websites I visited. But, most interesting, I found that particular video retailer by searching (via AltaVista) to see what information was available on the Web about shooting video.

If you put information on your website as an attractor, it's one more thing you can link to from your eBay ad to establish your credibility and draw people to your website.

Note that I eventually bought the camcorder at an eBay auction.

Calculators

For what it's worth, Larry Chase, a Web marketing consultant, claims that calculators attract more website visitors than any other Web device. Figure out a calculator (or two or three) you can put on your website. Have a programmer program it in Java, Java-Script, or CGI scripts. People will use it if it does calculations that they need.

A leading example that everyone understands is a mortgage calculator at a real estate or mortgage brokerage website. You put in the amount you need to borrow, the interest rate, and the term of the loan, and the calculator calculates your monthly payment.

Once you've set up your calculators at your website, you can link to them from your eBay auction ad.

Catalog

It's not unusual for even small retailers to have hundreds or thousands of different items in inventory. It's probably not realistic to put all of your products up for auction each week, but you can put all of them in a Web commerce catalog like the one that Miva Merchant (*http://www.miva.com*) provides. I know one individual who has 7,000 items in the catalog for his one-person Web retail business using Merchant. The last part of the chapter will show how easy it is to maintain such a catalog with a desktop database.

Catalogs can include thumbnail photographs, full photographs, short descriptions, long descriptions, logos, prices, and shopping carts. You can choose to use any or all. I know one retailer who just names the products, gives the prices, and provides no photographs or other information. His reasoning is that his customers know the products (commodity-like products) well and don't need photographs or descriptions. They buy strictly on price, and he sells at attractive prices. Other types of retailers might be ill-advised to do the same. They need to feature photographs and voluminous specifications. Every retail business is different.

You can experiment with linking your Web catalog pages to your auction ads and vice versa. Again, just make sure you don't violate the eBay User Agreement.

Transaction Services

One of the most important elements of a good Web commerce program is the transaction services it provides. A customer goes to the checkout where the shopping basket shows up with the products that have been ordered. The prices of the products are totaled, sales tax (if applicable) is calculated and added to the total, shipping is calculated and added to the total, and a choice of payment methods is provided. Then the information for a particular payment method is received. All this information passes back and forth in a secure digital environment. This is all done by the Web commerce software. It provides an easy-to-use and convenient way for a website visitor to make purchases.

If it works for website visitors, why not for eBay bidders? If you have a commerce website, you can direct the high bidders at your eBay auctions to your website to make payments. It's convenient for the bidders, and it's convenient for you.

Incidentally, Merchant has a check-writing module that you can install, and Merchant will accept checks via the Web. This software is widely available, and Merchant is not the only Web commerce software program that does this. In fact, anyone can easily set himself or herself up to accept checks via the Web without fancy software, but by incorporating this payment method, Merchant offers even more convenience.

Online Processing

Once Merchant has accumulated all the information about the order and the requisite information for the particular payment method chosen by the buyer, what do you do with that information? There are two answers to this question. The first answer is that you do with the information what you would normally do if the information were collected at a retail store. For instance, if you have collected credit card information, you can call up via telephone and get approval (e.g., from Visa) for the transaction in the normal way. You also fill out a credit card charge slip and handle it as you normally would. The charge slip will not have the customer's signature, but you have electronic documentation (proof) that the customer charged the purchase.

The second answer is that you can also subscribe to an online service that will handle the credit card processing automatically for you online. Merchant will interact with a number of online credit card processing services should you choose to use one. This is a convenience to you, for which you pay, and has nothing to do with your customers. But you don't need this service to accept credit card payments from customers via Web commerce software; you can do it manually instead.

Merchant Account

You can't take credit cards unless you have a merchant account. So, without such an account, you will be unable to accept credit card payments through your Web commerce software and will therefore have no use for online credit card processing.

You get a merchant account through your bank. They are difficult to obtain without prior retail history and good credit. However, there are businesses online that will extend you merchant account privileges with certain restrictions. There are many different programs. Read and understand the details of the programs that fit your situation before you sign on the line. Some of the programs are quite costly.

Alternatives

See PayPal and Billpoint covered in Chapter 16 for alternatives to merchant accounts.

Accounting

Many Web commerce programs, including Merchant, provide a record of all the orders. If you do not have a separate accounting system to handle orders, this can be very handy. Even if you have a separate accounting system to handle orders, you can use the accounting capabilities of your Web commerce software for interim accounting. In the future, Web commerce accounting will plug nicely into a wide range of popular accounting software, and you will be able to handle orders seamlessly. For instance, Starbase-21 (*http://miva.starbase21.com*) sells a module for Merchant that enables it to pass order information to QuickBooks (*http://www.quicken.com*).

Cost

The cost of Web commerce software varies widely. Miva Merchant software costs $500 the first year and $99 per year thereafter. You must use it at an ISP that has a Miva server; there are over 100 of them. The nice thing about Merchant is that you can often use it for no additional fee over and above your normal ISP Web host service (e.g., $30 per month). Other Web commerce software packages use other business models. Typical is a cost of $500–$15,000 for the Web commerce software and $40–$400 per month for the

ISP service to run it on. Virtually all Web commerce software requires a special server in addition to a Web server to operate. Some Web commerce software is even provided for at no additional cost by some ISPs, but you need to investigate what such free software offers. The features of Merchant provide a good standard against which to measure competing software products because Merchant is robust.

Customer Service

Buy all the software you can afford in order to provide customer service at your commerce website. Merchant or another good Web commerce software program is a good start. There may be other software that does other things too. But when all is said and done, it's up to you to invent some new things. We're in the first inning of the ball game, and there is still a lot to be determined in regard to how customer services will be played out on the Web.

Merchant Modules

Starbase-21 sells many Merchant modules that extend the features of Merchant, including many that enrich customer service. Other modules are available for sale or free. Although this doesn't relieve you of inventing your own customer service, it does give you additional building blocks. Check out other commerce software for customer service features.

Who?

Who is going to take care of your commerce website? The nice thing about Merchant and some of the other Web commerce software is that you don't have to be a programmer to use them. For instance, once you get Merchant up and running properly at your

website, you can keep it going with minimal technical maintenance (e.g., perhaps a few hours a month). The maintenance of
your Merchant catalog via a database, which routinely takes time,
is actually a time-saver over other methods of accomplishing the
same things and can be done at the desktop.

A webmaster or Web developer can handle Merchant. A webmaster doesn't have to be a database expert to design and use a simple
database such as the one offered by this book, but he or she does
have to learn how to use a database program. This may be a task
that your bookkeeper or another skilled employee can learn to
handle. Database managers such as Paradox, FileMaker, and
Access are easy to use.

eBay and Merchant

Apparently eBay, with all its database expertise, decided not to
reinvent the wheel. eBay has been using Miva Merchant for its
eBay Store catalog. Go *Community, eBay Store* to see the catalog, which constitutes the eBay Store.

Commerce Website Database

In order to stock your commerce website catalog efficiently, keep
your inventory in a desktop database such as Access. Make your
daily inventory adjustments; change your prices; delete sold
inventory; and do it all offline with an interface that's easy, quick,
and convenient to use. (Online interfaces for Web commerce software are notoriously slow to use.) Then in one quick gesture,
upload the data you need to your website commerce catalog. The
result is an entire new catalog with up-to-date information, that is,
up-to-date inventory and prices. Some corporate commerce websites have catalogs connected directly to database servers, but you

have to have tens of thousands of unique items in your inventory before you need such a system.

Website Catalog Database

What are the fields (columns) that a website catalog needs? To illustrate, this chapter continues to feature Miva Merchant. The columns Merchant requires follow:

Column	Description
name	Inventory item
price	Sales price
web	One-character indicator
catcode	Category code
prodcode	Product code
description	Item description
wt	Item shipping weight
tax	Tax code
thumb	URL of digital thumbnail photo
image	URL of digital photo

Now we have to review the database from Chapter 14 to see which of the preceding columns already exist and which we need to add. The database columns follow:

Column	Column Name
Product	product
Manufacturer	manufacturer
Wholesale cost	cost

Shipping weight	shipwt
Number received	received
Number sold	sold
Number in stock	instock
One-line title	title
Category	ebaycat
Bold type	bold
Category featured	featurecat
Featured	feature
Location	location
Quantity	quantity
Reserve	reserve
Minimum bid	minbid
Duration	duration
Private	private
Opening line	open
Ad body	ad
Shipping cost	shipcost
Terms	boilerplate
Website URL	weburl
Image URL	imageurl

Comparing the two sets of columns, the following are the same:

    product = name

shipwt = wt

ad = description

imageurl = image

That means that to the database from Chapter 14, we'll have to add the following columns:

Column

price

web

catcode

prodcode

tax

thumb

Now the database is as follows:

Column	Column Name
Product	product
Manufacturer	manufacturer
Wholesale cost	cost
Shipping weight	shipwt
Number received	received
Number sold	sold
Number in stock	instock
One-line title	title
Category	ebaycat
Bold type	bold

Category featured	featurecat
Featured	feature
Location	location
Quantity	quantity
Reserve	reserve
Minimum bid	minbid
Duration	duration
Private	private
Opening line	open
Ad body	ad
Shipping cost	shipcost
Terms	boilerplate
Website URL	weburl
Image URL	imageurl
Sales price	price
Indicator	web
Category code	catcode
Product code	prodcode
Tax code	tax
Thumbnail image URL	thumb

Now we have a table that holds data for inventory control (Chapter 14), eBay auctions (Chapters 14 and 15), and Miva Merchant (this chapter). To get the Merchant data out of this table, we need to create a query (Merchant Query) that pulls out only what's needed for Merchant and no more:

Table		Merchant Query
product	—>	product (name)
manufacturer		
cost		
shipwt	—>	shipwt (wt)
received		
sold		
instock		
title		
ebaycat		
bold		
featurecat		
feature		
location		
quantity		
reserve		
minbid		
duration		
private		
open		
ad	—>	ad (description)
shipcost		
boilerplate		

weburl

imageurl   —>   imageurl (image)

price   —>   price

web   [not needed for query]

catcode   —>   catcode

prodcode   —>   prodcode

tax   —>   tax

thumb   —>   thumb

Thus, the Merchant Query pulls out the data from the following columns. However, the columns must be in the proper order for Merchant, so the Merchant Query also arranges the columns in the proper order:

Column

product (name)

price

catcode

prodcode

ad (description)

shipwt (wt)

tax

thumb

imageurl (image)

There you have it! All the columns you need are in one convenient table, and the Merchant Query extracts just the columns you need for the Miva Merchant online catalog. (Note that the Web column is needed to administer the Merchant database on the desktop but is not needed for the Merchant Query.)

Now, exactly what do you do with the Merchant Query? You export the data in a delimited format (e.g., comma delimited) to generate a delimited database file. Then you upload that file to Miva Merchant on your website. Merchant uses the data to fill the catalog. If data already exists in the Merchant catalog, Merchant replaces all the existing data with the new data to generate an entire new catalog. The new catalog has up-to-date inventory and prices.

This is easy to do. It is much more convenient than attempting to maintain Merchant via the Web by manually entering and deleting data from the Merchant database. The fact that you can maintain one table of data to serve three purposes provides real convenience and cost savings.

Review

If this database stuff still seems complicated to you, let's review it. Here are the steps:

1. Use a desktop database manager such as Paradox, File-Maker, or Access.

2. Put all the data you need for everything into one database table by creating as many columns as you need for your inventory control data, your eBay auction data, and your Merchant data.

3. Maintain the data at the desktop in the database manager.

4. Extract and export via query only the data set you need for your eBay auctions.

5. Use the data as outlined in Chapter 15 for bulk auction

uploads.

6. Extract and export via another query only the data set you need for your Merchant database.

7. Use the data as outlined in this chapter for putting products into your Merchant catalog.

It's pretty straightforward. Of course, I've intentionally kept the examples as simple as possible for the purposes of explaining them in the book. As you can see from reading Chapters 14, 15, and this chapter, however, your database for inventory control will undoubtedly need more columns than the sample provided. The inventory control database example was provided for inspiration, not for actual use.

A Less Serious Website

Do you need to have a full-fledged commercial website? It seems to me that if you go to the trouble to create your own website, making it a commercial website does not entail much extra operating effort, although the initial setup work will probably be greater. However, you can create a Web page or a series of Web pages at some hosting services without going to the extra effort of creating an entire website. There are even free Web hosting services:

- Angelfire (*http://www.angelfire.com*)
- Crosswinds(*http://www.crosswinds.net*)
- FortuneCity (*http://www2.fortunecity.com*)
- Geocities (*http://geocities.yahoo.com/home*)
- Homestead (*http://www.homestead.com*)
- Tripod (*http://www.tripod.com*)

Certainly, you can do many things at a Web hosting service, short of creating a commerce website, that can help your retail efforts on eBay.

If you want to take this idea a little further, you can opt for a hosting service that specializes in providing commercial (storefront) websites. Some of those are free too. Try:

- Bigstep (*http://www.bigstep.com*)
- eCongo (*http://www.econgo.com*)
- FreeMerchant (*http://www.freemerchant.com*)

Marketing

Your commerce website will not sell anything without an aggressive Web marketing campaign. People have to know about you, be motivated to visit you, and find you. Marketing is just as difficult and expensive on the Web as it is in real life. The difference is that offline, virtually everything costs money. *Time* magazine is not going to do a tradeout with you (e.g., a half-page ad for sweeping out the Chicago bureau for three months). On the Web, however, you can substitute time for money. You can carry out an aggressive Web marketing campaign if you want to spend the time to learn to do it and then the time to do it. Marketing on the Web is beyond the scope of this book, but it's clear that without a serious marketing effort no one will come to your commerce website.

eBay can be part of that serious marketing effort. eBay will sell inventory. eBay will bring potential bidders to your website via links. eBay will keep your name in front of the people in your market. And, eBay is inexpensive. In addition, you can potentially create some synergy by integrating your eBay auctions into your commerce website as much as is practical. But for most businesses, that will not be enough. You will have to develop other marketing campaigns.

Summary

Can you have a retail business that exists only on eBay? I suppose, but there are a lot of benefits to establishing a commerce website too. One is that you can offer better customer service generally, and you can offer better service to your eBay customers too.

A commerce website is a considerable project to get off the ground. It requires routine maintenance to keep it going. But through the magic of database technology, the entire project can be integrated into your inventory, business, and auction accounting system for maximum efficiency and minimum labor. And it can be done without a programmer. It's another powerful way to sell at retail on the Web. Operating a commerce website together with auctions, you can build some retail synergy.

You can't build a Web commerce site without intensive marketing, however, and that's where eBay helps again. Part of your marketing plan can include marketing and sales on eBay.

In short, if you're successful selling at retail on eBay, establishing a Web commerce site takes you to the next level.

19

What's behind eBay Businesses?

What's the business behind the eBay businesses? It's inventory! Where are you going to get some inventory to sell, inventory at a low price that you can sell at a higher price? This chapter surveys a few ideas. But it only makes a ripple in the surface of the endless sea of available inventory.

The Basics

Before getting into the ideas for acquiring inventory, you need to consider and keep in mind some retailing basics.

Sales Tax License

You are not a retailer until you have a sales tax license. Once you have one, a lot of doors will open for you; it's also a lot of ongoing paperwork.

Drop Shipping

Unless you have the money to purchase inventory and the warehouse space to store it, your best bet is to think *drop shipping*. Drop shipping doesn't come cheap, but when you're starting out, it makes a lot of sense. You inventory nothing. When you make a sale, the wholesaler (drop shipper) ships directly to your customer. You never have possession of the merchandise. Slick.

A Variety of Ideas

An assortment of ideas follows. It's my hope that these ideas will get you thinking. But the best ideas for you will be your own, not mine.

Wholesale

Talk a wholesaler into selling you inventory, perhaps even extending you a little credit. Sell the merchandise on eBay for a profit. This is a proven method of retailing that hardly needs much explanation. Some wholesalers will sell to anyone who knocks on the door. Others are superselective. There are a hundred positions in between.

As simple as this seems, it's not a no-brainer. Some wholesalers sell at prices as high as, or even higher than, discount stores. You have to know your market very well and make sure you have a healthy spread between your wholesale prices and your eBay auction prices. Needless to say, eBay bidders are not looking to pay full retail prices.

Special Mail-Order Wholesale

There are special wholesalers that sell merchandise to amateur retailers operating in special markets such as mail order. Are such retail sales profitable? Probably for some people. Probably not for most people. Don't enter a contract with one of these wholesalers with your eyes closed. Evaluate the opportunity carefully, and do a little test marketing (test auctioning) before you commit yourself to this scheme. One advantage that these wholesalers usually offer is drop shipping.

Government Surplus

Army-Navy-Air Force surplus. Now there's an interesting business. But I don't think it's one I'd like to be in. Still, military surpluses are not the only surpluses that the government has. The governments (federal, state, county, and municipal) all have surpluses, and they all sell off used and even new merchandise and supplies from time to time. They do it at special sales and auctions, seldom without public notice. Be there, and buy some inventory cheap. Make sure it's something you can resell easily for a profit on eBay.

Closeouts

Closeouts are excess inventory that someone wants to unload quickly for whatever reason. The seller might be a manufacturer, a wholesaler, a retailer, or even a high-volume user (e.g., the government). The price is often well under wholesale. Ten to twenty cents on the dollar is not uncommon. You must usually buy in high quantities to participate.

There is an entire closeout industry with closeout shows and periodicals. Get plugged in, raise some money for inventory, buy for ten cents on the dollar, auction for 35 cents on the dollar on eBay, and make your fellow eBay denizens happy. A profitable deal all around. One closeout retailer that uses eBay extensively is eValueville (*http://evalueville.com*). Visit the website to see what's happening.

The following are some potential sources of useful information about closeouts or closeout inventory:

- CloseOutNow (*http://www.closeoutnow.com*)

- Closeout Sources Directory (*http://www.halcyon.com/rlucas/Closeout.Sources.html*)

- Discount Warehouse (*http://www.closeouts.digiscape.net*)

- iSolve (*http://www.isolve.com*)

- Lee Howard's Business Inventory Closeout Sources Directory (*http://www.chambec.com/closeout.html*)

- Liquidation (*http://www.liquidation.com*)

- Maverick Enterprises (*http://amaverickent.com*)

- MUSA (*http://www.merchandiseusa.com*)

- Rebound (*http://rebound.com*)

- redtagbiz (*http://www.redtagbiz.com*)

- RetailExchange (*http://retailexchange.com*)

- RO-EL On-Line (*http://www.ro-el.com*)

- Rothman Closeouts (*http://www.rothmancloseouts.com*)

- Sav-On-Closeouts (*http://www.sav-on-closeouts.com*)

- TDW Closeouts (*http://www.tdwcloseouts.com*)

- Tradeout (*http://www.tradeout.com*)

- uBid (*http://www.ubid.com*)

Not That Easy

Closeouts sound like an easy business. However, dealing in closeouts is competitive, like any other business, which means you have to work hard to find closeouts on which you can make a reasonable profit. Remember, too, that closeouts usually include merchandise that a manufacturer or retailer could not sell in the normal course of business.

Auctions

Local auctions are known for their bargain prices. Ironically, as most of us know from experience, this isn't necessarily true. Sometimes things sell for more at auctions than they do elsewhere. Nonetheless, local auctions do remain a potential source of bargains. If you can buy low at an auction and sell higher on eBay, you have yourself a business. This works well with individual items such as antiques. But it also works for bulk inventory. Frequent your local auctions, and buy stuff you know you can resell on eBay for a profit.

Special Products

There are some special products around that have a lot of appeal but aren't generally available. You know. You see them advertised for $19.95 on obscure TV channels, like the superpotion that shines your car and makes your coffee taste better too. Find out how you can buy them at wholesale. Auction them on eBay.

Find an inventor who has manufactured some clever product, has 500 in his garage, but doesn't know what to do with them. These guys are all over the place. I knew a guy who invented a clever rack that holds a supermarket plastic bag open for the purposes of garbage disposal. The rack goes on the back of the door under the kitchen sink. It's quite handy and eliminates the need for plastic garbage bags that you have to buy. He never was able to market it effectively and probably still has 300 in his garage nicely packaged. Perhaps you can auction a product like that on eBay at wholesale prices to dealers in lots of four dozen. Or perhaps you can auction such products individually at retail prices.

Manufacturers

You don't always have to go through a wholesaler. Many manufacturers will deal with you directly and sell you inventory at wholesale prices. It makes sense to ask.

Special Manufacturing

Have something made for you to sell. Gee, you could invent something. But you don't have to go quite that far. How about lining up a beer mug manufacturer to reserve some time for your production run two weeks before the Super Bowl. You license the logos from the National Football League (NFL) prior to your production run. As soon as you know which teams will play each other, you plug the team logos into your Super Bowl beer mug design and start your production run.

You immediately start your Dutch auctions on eBay. In fact, you can do preliminary Dutch auctions at early-bird prices even before you or the bidders know which teams are going to play. Some people will buy the mugs even if their favorite team doesn't make it.

By the time the first auctions are finished, you should have inventory to ship. Better yet, have the mug manufacturer drop ship. You'll do most of your business in two weeks, but there will be some late sales, too, perhaps even a second run for mugs proclaiming the winner.

Special manufacturing doesn't have to be for a special event. It can be any mass-produced product that is customized for your retail sales.

Remanufacturing

Defective items plague manufacturers. They are returned (under warranty) new, or almost new, with some small thing out of whack that can be easily fixed or replaced at the factory. Once fixed and tested, the unit goes back on the market as refurbished merchandise. For all practical purposes, it's as good as new.

Laws in some states may prohibit such practices, and returned items must be disassembled for parts. The parts then go to a special assembly line where they are reassembled into refurbished merchandise. Quality is high.

Normal dealers often do not want to carry refurbished merchandise. This creates an opportunity for special retailers who will market the refurbished items at prices below market for new goods. There are a lot of people successfully selling refurbished merchandise on eBay.

Small-Time Manufacturing

Small local manufacturers often have trouble marketing their products for lack of high-horsepower marketing departments. And some small manufacturers make some pretty unusual things that will draw a lot of attention in a large marketplace like eBay. Look around your locale. You may find a manufacturer with some attractive products, not widely available, that you can sell on eBay.

Art and Handicrafts

Artists and craftsmen are small local manufacturers. Some have unique products that have significant market potential. Others have bread-and-butter products that always sell. Many do not have any marketing skills, or even if they do, they still do not like to market their products. This common situation creates opportunities for you to buy low and auction appropriate products on eBay for a profit. With intelligent choices, you can realize a higher profit with these sales because many of the products have no standard prices and will not be compared to discounted goods.

Estate Sales

People buy so much stuff. Some of it they wear out, and it isn't worth much. Some of it they hardly ever use and perhaps never even take out of the box. Then they croak. The relatives just want to get rid of the stuff. Voila, the estate sale. If you're a buyer at an estate sale or auction, you can buy low and sell higher on eBay. If you're the auctioneer for the estate, perhaps you can auction for higher prices on eBay than you can at a local auction and make more money for less work.

Make the Rounds

One way to pick up general inventory is to make the rounds of the places in your community where you can routinely purchase goods well below their market value. These include:

- Garage sales
- Thrift stores
- Flea markets
- Swaps, exchanges, and trade shows

In addition, you can occasionally pick up wholesale inventory locally from:

- Going-out-of-business sales
- Retailers' excess inventory

For instance, a retailer that has to put 200 towels on sale for 60 percent off list price might be willing to sell them to you for 70 percent off list price, if you take them all and pay cash.

Packages

I have written a book about audio-video production, digitization, and publication on the Web. To introduce readers to sound recording systems that they can use for professional-quality audio (voice for education and training), I propose three recording systems in three price ranges in the book. The equipment in the highest two price ranges is offered more to spur intelligent decision making than to recommend unique equipment. However, the equipment in the bottom price range is unique. It's all Radio Shack equipment; it's quite inexpensive, and it works pretty well (for voice).

An ambitious retailer could take the specified Radio Shack recorder, microphone, and mixer together with my book and a copy of RealProducer (software) and package them as a professional kit for putting streaming sound on the Web. This kit would cost about one-fourth as much as a kit for higher price range equipment and would be almost as good for many purposes (e.g., for voice). The packaging together of these items would provide a real service to those who wanted to get off to a quick start with high-quality streaming sound at a low price.

This is actually a poor example because you can't get the Radio Shack inventory at wholesale unless you're a Radio Shack dealer. But you get the idea. Put together a package that people need, and auction it.

The Web Department

You have the product knowledge and know some HTML, but you don't have the money for inventory. A local retailer has the inventory but doesn't understand the Web or eBay and doesn't have time to start or operate a website or a multiple auction effort on eBay. Make the following proposal:

You will:

1. Auction the inventory on eBay.

2. Manage the eBay fulfillment operation.

3. Eventually build a commerce website.

4. Operate the commerce website in conjunction with continued auctions on eBay.

The retailer will:

1. Supply the wholesale inventory.

2. Provide merchant credit card services.

3. Split the profits with you.

You become, in effect, the retailer's "Web Department" but on a partnership basis. This arrangement has a lot of flexibility. It can start out informal. Then, if successful, it can evolve into a department of the retailer's operation or into a separate business by itself.

The point here is to work for a share of the profits, not for a salary. Insist on a share of the ownership. That makes you an entrepreneur, not an employee. It may be lean pickings for a while, but if the business is successful, you will make more money over the long haul.

Wheeler-Dealer

Wheeler-dealers will do well on eBay. In my estimation, *wheeler-dealer* is not a negative term. It's simply a term that indicates that someone is aggressive and clever in making deals (transactions, sales) that work for both buyer and seller. Most of the best wheeler-dealers I know give excellent customer service. If you can wheel and deal in a specific industry, you may find that eBay can add a whole new dimension to your business activities.

Good Deals

None of the foregoing opportunities are necessarily good deals. Yet they're all potentially good deals. It just depends on how you work them.

You can read advertisements that will say you can get rich overnight selling government surplus if you just subscribe to a certain publication. That you can get rich may be true, but if you do, it will not be overnight. It will not come to pass without a lot of effort on your part. If you attend all the government sales and auctions you can find out about, know your markets well, and have a well-organized eBay auction operation, you can probably make some money this year and more next year selling government surplus on eBay. But you're probably not going to get rich from the inventory you buy at the first government sale you attend. In fact, you might attend a dozen government auctions before you find something that you want to buy for resale and then get outbid. Bummer.

However, we don't want to end this chapter on a bad note. The opportunities for making money on eBay with minimal capital are fabulous, even if they're not get-rich-quick schemes. If you are reading this book in 2002, you can still get in on the ground floor. This is a dynamic new international marketplace still in its infancy, and it's not going to go away.

Summary

There are plenty of places to get inventory. When you start looking, you will find many more than I have covered in this chapter. eBay is a new international 24-hour-per-day marketplace with millions of consumers that scream for more inventory. If you can find the right inventory at the right price, you can sell it on eBay.

VII

Useful Aids to Selling on eBay

20

Using Web Authoring Software

An authoring software program is one that takes media and arranges them into a presentation. You can think of a word processor as a text authoring program. For the purpose of this book, we are interested in Web authoring programs. Because the Web is a multimedia medium, Web authoring programs are multimedia-authoring programs, which means they handle a variety of media.

Multimedia and the Web

The media generally used on the Web are text, color graphics, animation, streaming sound, streaming video, MIDI music, and embedded programs (e.g., Java applets). Of the greatest interest for running auctions on eBay are text and color graphics (digital photographs). Anything more may interfere with the efficient functioning of your auction ads.

Implied in digital multimedia is interactivity. The primary interactive device is the link. The link enables you to have choices: The simplest is stay where I am or click a link and go somewhere else. Links can be important for eBay auctions. With these simple ideas in mind, you can learn to author your own eBay ads, and even Web pages, using a Web authoring program.

Netscape offers Composer as its Web authoring program, and it comes free with the browser. Microsoft offers FrontPage Express as its authoring program, and it comes free with the browser.

FrontPage

FrontPage is Microsoft's website building program that comes with a price. Don't confuse it with FrontPage Express, which is more like a word processor and is free.

These two Web authoring programs are not only easy to use but quite similar to each other. In fact, they were both designed as Web word processors, albeit word processors for Web text. But remember, the Web is a multimedia medium. Both of these Web authoring programs handle other media competently too.

You will find using these programs about the easiest way you can do Web work without knowing HTML. Nonetheless, it always pays to know HTML. You never know when you might have to fix some little thing that the Web authoring programs can't seem to get quite right.

I do not encourage you to use both of these programs on the same Web pages. You're just asking for trouble. Chose one or the other and stick with it. Because the two are so much alike, this chapter covers only one, Composer. If you can understand Composer, you won't have any trouble using FrontPage Express.

You will also find that using these authoring programs is incompatible with hand coding and editing. If you can code HTML, you can work more efficiently using an editor or authoring program, such as Allaire's HomeSite, that does not change your HTML. Composer and FrontPage Express, however, do their own thing, and that makes subsequent editing both tedious and inefficient. Do not use either of these if you want to do your own HTML coding. You will be disappointed.

Basic Assumption

This chapter assumes that you will be using Composer or FrontPage Express to create an eBay auction ad. This is a basic assumption about a special purpose, and some of the things this chapter covers may not apply to general Web development work.

Composer

Open Composer and start typing. It doesn't get any easier. It's just like using a word processor (see Figure 20.1). Read my book *Web Pages the Smart Way* (AMACOM, 2001) for more extensive coverage of Web page authoring.

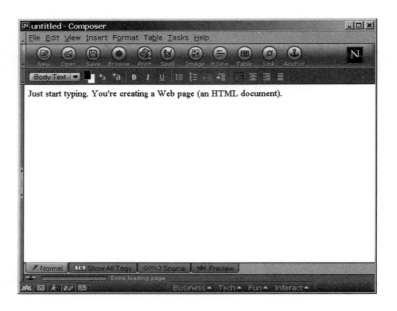

Figure 20.1   Open Composer and start typing.

Want to add some headings? Do it. It's just as easy as using a word processor and virtually identical (see Figure 20.2).

Unless you know something about HTML, however, you may not fully understand how to format your headings and other typographical devices. For instance, <h1> is the largest heading, <h2> the second largest, <h3> the third largest, and <h4> the fourth largest. Few Web developers use <h5> or <h6> because you never quite know what you will get. Just understanding this HTML heading scheme will enable you to use Composer better, even if you never do any HTML coding. When you use Composer with templates too, it helps to know a little HTML.

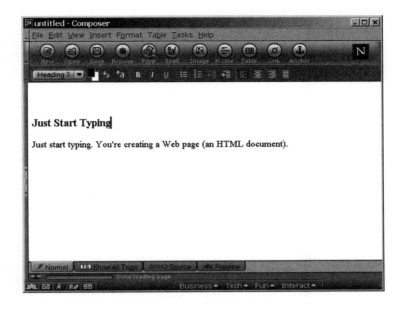

Figure 20.2   Add a heading.

Text

Don't do funny things with text. Keep it simple, readable, and well organized. Unless you have something unique (e.g., a work of art), potential bidders just want to read quickly and move on. If you have what they want at a reasonable price, they will be likely to bid. If you don't, they won't. No amount of jazzing up your eBay auction ad is going to change that. Help potential bidders to quickly get the facts and information that they need from your auction ad.

Typesetting

Typesetting is pretty straightforward for an eBay auction ad. Browsers have Times New Roman or Times (serif fonts) for their standard font; they have Arial or Helvetica for their sanserif font; and they have Courier for their monospaced font. Beyond those, you're kidding yourself; only a few people will see anything else you use because the rest don't have the requisite fonts installed on their computers. If you want to do some fancy typesetting on your website, read my book *Typography on the Web* (AP Professional, 1998). If you want to do some fancy typesetting for your eBay auction ad, forget it. It's not worth the trouble because few will see it as you see it, and you lose control over the typesetting process when you don't use the standard three fonts.

Chapter 13 discusses readability. Typesetting is about readability. Good typesetting is easy to read. Lousy typesetting is hard to read. And guess what? If a potential bidder cannot read your ad easily and quickly, he or she is apt to move on without finishing it. Better pay attention to your typesetting. Chapter 13 provides some brief readability and typesetting guidelines. Review them before you do the typesetting for your eBay auction ad.

Graphics

You can easily place color graphics (e.g., digital photographs) in your eBay auction ad. Just place the cursor where you want the photograph to go, and click on the graphics button (see Figure 20.3).

The image markup is *<img src="[URL]">*. You will need to enter the URL of the photograph as you learned to do in Chapter 12, and it will magically appear.

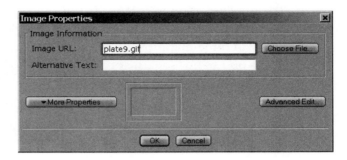

Figure 20.3   Inserting a photograph.

Unfortunately, it will not appear on your computer screen. You will have to test your eBay ad on the Web (but not necessarily at eBay). Upload the ad to any website and test it with your browser. You can see your Web page text at any time in your browser on your own computer, but the photographs and other media will not show if you are using the correct URLs for display in the auction ad.

Links

You place a link (correctly called a hyperlink) just as you do a photograph. Click on the link button (see Figure 20.4).

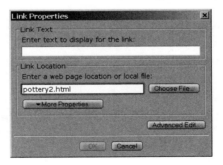

Figure 20.4   Inserting a link.

In this case, however, the link has a beginning markup *<a href="[URL]">* and an ending markup *</a>*. Whatever is between these markups is the hot spot of the link. When someone clicks on the hot spot, he or she goes to the URL specified in the link markup.

You need to enter the URL for the link. Notice in your Web browser that the text that is in the hot spot of the link is a different color. That's how people find links.

Background Color

Changing the background color can prove attractive, but only if you are careful. Review Chapter 13, which covers browser-safe colors. Any colors you use that are not browser-safe may become different colors in someone else's browser. Colors are not consistent unless they're browser-safe.

Also remember from Chapter 13 that the background color should not impair readability. That means light background colors with black type, or dark background colors with light-colored type. The background color and type color must contrast too. A medium background color with medium type color that does not contrast is essentially unreadable.

Keep in mind that you do not want to set the background color with the *<body>* markup for the entire Web page for your eBay auction ad. It will interfere with eBay's color scheme. That's practically suicidal. Use a table, and set the color background for the table. The Chapter 13 template shows how to limit your color changes to your portion of the entire Web page.

Tables

To avoid changing the color of the entire Web page and to keep your text in a column that will fit in every browser, including WebTV, you can create a table. The background color of the table becomes the background color of only your portion of the eBay auction ad (Web page), and a column will confine text to within the column boundaries. Click on the table button to start a table (see Figure 20.5).

Make your table one column and one row. Then make the column exactly 500 pixels, align the table to the center, set the table border to 0, and set cell padding at 20. Although the table is outlined in your Composer window with dashes, the dashes don't show in a browser window.

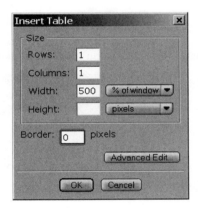

Figure 20.5   Installing a table.

Now within the column, do all your authoring (see Figure 20.6). The result will be an attractive and readable column of text with an appropriate margin on each side (see Figure 20.7).

You can have tables within tables. With different background colors, tables can provide a polished appearance to a Web page (see Figure 20.8).

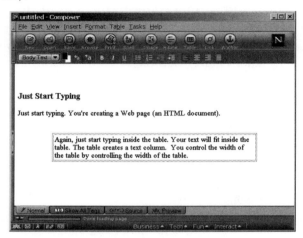

Figure 20.6   Filling in the table in Composer.

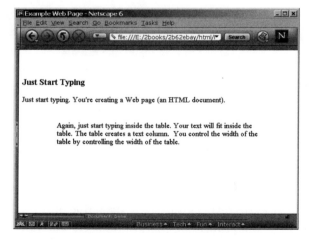

Figure 20.7   Table in Web browser.

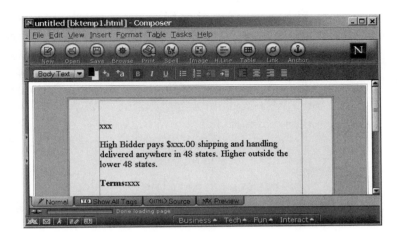

Figure 20.8   Two tables—one inside the other—with different background colors in the template. A third table contains the text.

Browser

You can check your work at any time with your Web browser. Just open the auction ad HTML file in the browser. Before checking your work, *first*, save the HTML file in Composer, and *second*, reload the Web page in your browser. You will see your latest up-to-the-minute work.

Chop It Off

When you're done with your authoring, you have to chop off the head of the document. Composer makes Web pages. You need only a portion of a Web page. Therefore, you need to chop off the head of the Web page before you can submit it to eBay as the body of your auction ad.

This is your last act of Web page developing. Don't do this before you're ready to submit your work to eBay. Save your Web page file and close Composer. Open Windows Notebook or any other plain text editor. Load your Web page. Highlight the *<body>* markup and everything above it. Then delete it. Next go to the bottom of the Web page and highlight the *</body>* markup and everything below it, and delete it. Now you've got something you can copy and paste into the eBay auction input (*Sell Your Item, Description*) in the Sell section on the eBay website.

eBay passes on to you some formatting for your portion of the Web page by using the *<blockquote>* markup. This puts a thin margin on the left and right of the Web page. You can ignore this, and all your Web development will take place inside the margins. Or, you can nullify the markup by starting your portion of the Web page with the *</blockquote>* markup. If you will notice, the Chapter 13 template starts with this markup. If you do this, end your portion of the Web page with the *<blockquote>* markup.

Summary

Web page authoring programs are easy to use. Use one to make a Web page. Chop off the top and bottom and enter it via copy and paste as you would any description of a product to be auctioned. The result can be a nicely formatted presentation that can be better and *easier to read* than the presentation resulting from the normal entry of text in the *Description* input in the *Sell Your Item* form.

21

Using Image Software

Why have a graphics software tutorial in an eBay book? Hey! It's fun to touch up your digital photographs for your eBay auction ads. And you will find a few other techniques useful too. Graphics programs range from Adobe PhotoShop at well over $700 to freeware or shareware programs you can download from the Web. Some are quite easy to use. Some are incomprehensible. But we will attempt only a few simple things and leave the more incomprehensible programs to those who want to learn a lot more.

In fact, many graphics programs make easy-to-use darkrooms. Before you use a graphics program, however, you first have to digitize your photographs.

Digitizing Photographs

Chapter 12 covered digitizing photographs. If you have questions, review Chapter 12. This chapter will assume that you have the photographs on your hard disk or on a Kodak Picture CD. However, know something about those darn photographs? They're never quite as they should be.

The more photographs you take, the more you start to emulate a professional photographer. Where we might take one roll of film, a professional will take six or eight rolls. No wonder professionals get better pictures. But taking all those photographs takes time and even money (for film). All we really need are a few simple photographs to use for our eBay auction ads, and we only have the time and money to take a few shots. It's not easy to always do our best photographic work with such time and money restrictions. That's where the graphics editing program comes in; it's a digital darkroom.

The Digital Darkroom

You can do amazing things with graphics editors. Using color graphics is highly complex technology that's impossible to understand without a lot of study. The top programs have extensive and robust capabilities. Using Adobe PhotoShop proficiently, for instance, entails applying it to specific graphics activities. You can spend months, or even years, learning how to use it with photographs. Then, if you want to use it to create digital watercolor paintings instead of photographs, the learning begins all over again.

In contrast, this chapter will simply cover four things you can do quickly and easily to improve your digitized photographs. The program is the freeware IrfanView, version 3 (*http://members.home.com/rsimmons/irfanview/*).

IrfanView

This program was picked because it is a freeware program that you can download from the website mentioned. It's a capable program, but there are commercial programs that offer additional functionality and convenience. If you do a lot of image preparation work, you might consider buying a program like PaintShop Pro (*http://www.jasc.com/psp.html*) for about $100.

Some versions of Microsoft Office 97 and 2000 come with image editing programs. Microsoft has had so many different image editors over the years, however, that I won't attempt to give you a current name.

Today a computer or a video card (powers your monitor) usually comes bundled with an image editor. If you know you have one, try it on some digital photographs. If you don't know whether you have one, look around your hard disk for an unfamiliar program. You just may find an image editor. Image editors usually have the word *photo*, *picture*, or *paint* somewhere in their name.

Contrast

When shades of black and gray are similar and when colors are similar, a photograph tends to have a flat, dull look. When you digitally increase the clash of the blacks, grays, and whites, particularly around the edges of objects, and when you digitally increase the clash of the colors, a photograph comes to life. This is contrast. You have to be careful, however, that you don't introduce too much contrast, or the photograph will look unnatural. But increasing the contrast just the right amount in a photograph will often make it look sharper. For IrfanView, go *Image, Contrast.*

How do you know what the right amount is? You can see it. As you apply the contrast, you will see the photograph change before your eyes (see Figure 21.1). Not all graphics programs will do this, but you want to use one that does.

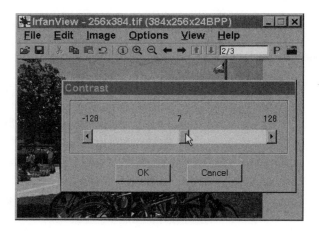

Figure 21.1   Applying contrast in IrfanView.

You can move the Contrast control panel off the program window in actual use, enabling you to see the photograph. It's hard to find a photograph that doesn't seem to improve with added contrast. You will probably find yourself adding contrast to all your eBay product photographs.

Brightness

Increasing brightness is less straightforward than adding contrast. Sometimes it works, and sometimes it doesn't. If you have a particularly dark photograph, you may want to increase the brightness. However, as you increase the brightness, the colors start to look increasingly bleached out. It's more likely that you will want to decrease the brightness a little. The colors will often become richer and more saturated. For IrfanView, go *Image, Brightness* (see Figure 21.2).

Unfortunately, as you decrease the brightness, a photograph takes on an ominous darkness. In combination with increased contrast, however, a photograph can take on a rich look that's full of life. Consequently, you will probably find, as I have, that you must use both of these controls to improve the look of photographs. More times than not, I reduce the brightness a little and boost the contrast to get a substantially improved photograph. Indeed, it's amazing how much you can improve the look of a dull photograph by changing only contrast and brightness.

Figure 21.2   Using the brightness control.

Gamma

Gamma is the light intensity of the monitor. It is another way to adjust the brightness and works a little differently than the brightness control. It wouldn't be mentioned here except that in some graphics editors the contrast and brightness controls, which are sometimes displayed together, are displayed along with the gamma control. If the control for gamma is not displayed with contrast and brightness controls, you can find it elsewhere in a graphics program. For IrfanView, go *Image*, *Gamma Correction*.

How Do You Do It?

Again, as you adjust the brightness, contrast, and gamma controls, the photograph will change before your eyes. Play with the controls (systematically). Have some fun. When you get a look that you like, it's time to save the photograph. (Click on *OK*.) The photograph is now the image that you adjusted it to be.

What if you want to go back to the original? That's OK. You haven't altered the original photograph until you save your work. That brings up an important point. You might want to keep all your original photographs somewhere special on your hard disk. When you decide to adjust one, make a copy first. Adjust the copy and save it. That way you'll always have the original.

Sharpen

Some image editors have a hybrid control called *sharpen*. Use this instead of using contrast, brightness, and gamma. It's quicker and easier, and it works well. For IrfanView, go *Image, Sharpen*.

If it doesn't work as well as you want, you can fall back on contrast and brightness controls.

Cropping

If you have the software to crop a digital photograph, you don't have to frame as carefully in your viewfinder when you take photographs. In fact, most inexpensive digital cameras take a 640 × 480 image, which is too large for an eBay ad. Anything larger that **400 × 300** will take too long to download, might be too large for your HTML work, and is more than you need. That means that you have to shrink your digital photographs to 400 × 300 (or smaller), or crop them to 400 × 300 (or smaller). Virtually every graphics editor has a cropper.

IrfanView has a resizer wherein you enter the numbers (the dimensions) you want. For IrfanView, go *Edit*, *Resize* (see Figure 21.3).

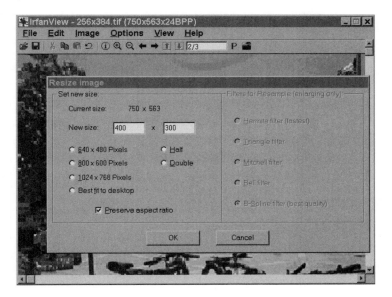

Figure 21.3   Cropping by the numbers.

IrfanView also has a visual cropper, go *Edit*, *Crop* (see Figure 21.4).

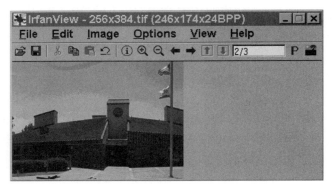

Figure 21.4   The cropped image.

File Formats

There are many graphics file formats. Whatever you start with, you must eventually convert your photograph to a GIF (.gif) or JPEG (.jpg) format. You can also use PNG (.png) format, but it doesn't work in early Web browsers. Most graphics editors will convert photographs from one file format to another. Simply save in the file format you want (see Figure 21.5).

Figure 21.5   Saving a TIF photograph to the GIF format in IrfanView.

GIF

GIF files are compressed as much as 2:1 without loss of quality. However, they are only 8-bit files, that is, 256 colors. You need at least 256 colors to make a photograph look real, so GIFs work OK.

JPEG

JPEG files can be compressed a little or a lot. JPEG compression is "lossy," which means that quality diminishes during the compression process. The greater the compression, the smaller the file and the greater the loss of quality. But JPEGs are 24-bit files, that is, 16 million colors. Consequently, JPEG files can look good, particularly when they're not compressed much. JPEGs work better than GIFs for photographs because they have more colors.

PNG

PNG is a new graphics file format just starting to come into use on the Web. It's an advanced file format that can carry with it extra information regarding the photograph. However, using its advanced capabilities is well beyond the scope of this book.

There's More

Graphics editors offer a lot more than this chapter covers. Some offer much more than others. You can spend as much time and energy as you want processing photographs. You have two steep learning curves to climb. The first is technical. Color is highly technical as is the digital technology that makes color possible on a computer. The second is artistic. To make good graphics, whether photographs or anything else, you have to have some artistic skills.

Using this technology is great fun. At the same time, our objective is a simple one: just post some photographs with our eBay auction ads. It's not much fun to get bogged down in digital color technology just to accomplish something seemingly simple. Therefore, a good strategy is to stick with the simple approach of this book.

Summary

The procedure this book recommends for processing your photographs is simple:

1. Take a photograph.

2. Digitize it. (If already in digital form, transfer it to your hard drive.)

3. Crop it to a suitable size.

4. Adjust it (i.e., brightness, contrast, and perhaps gamma). This step is optional.

5. Upload it to your storage place on the Web for your eBay photographs.

6. Put an image markup in your eBay auction ad to pull it in.

This is a simple strategy and an easy one that will accomplish your goal of posting photographs to get more bids and, therefore, higher bids on your eBay auction items.

VIII

Specialty Auctions

22

Local Auctions

If a nationwide auction makes sense, what about local auctions? After all, many items don't trade well at long distances but do trade well inside metro areas. Then there's language and proximity considerations. eBay is international, but not everyone speaks English or lives in the US. What about local auctions based on language or geography?

eBay has answered these questions by creating local auctions in the US and national and local auctions in foreign countries.

US Local Auctions

Local eBay auctions provide a convenience for bidders and extra exposure for sellers. They are designed to handle large or heavy inexpensive items or other items not appropriate for long-distance commerce. For instance, a desk worth $100 that costs $150 to ship almost anywhere will be difficult to sell nationally on eBay. But in a local auction, a buyer will drive across town in a borrowed pickup to take delivery.

Office equipment, industrial equipment, hardware, garden supplies, livestock, and the like are all good candidates for local eBay auctions. If it's large or heavy, when eBay comes to your area, sell it at a local eBay auction.

For Bidders

You will find local eBay auctions in 63 regional areas in the US named for their biggest metro area (as the book went to press). You can access these local auctions on eBay's home page (Figure 22.1).

Figure 22.1   Selecting a local auction.

Each local auction has its own home page where you can find custom information and a unique starting directory. The local auctions themselves, however, are just a subset of the general eBay auctions. In other words, eBay creates the local auctions by filter. Everything is filtered out except auctions originating from within the local area. Consequently, this is a convenience for potential bidders rather than a truly separate auction.

You will see in Figure 22.2 that the local auctions do not have directories as robust as the full eBay auctions.

Figure 22.2   Local auction home page for San Francisco.

eBay designed the local auctions this way to avoid blank lists for thinly traded items. Nonetheless, you can use the eBay search for specific local items productively if you find the directories unproductive.

eBay local auctions have great potential. In a few years as eBay expands its general membership, it will be able to engineer more custom features into each of its local auctions. They will not remain mere digital filters. They will take on their own character and serve local populations more agilely. Until then, however, they do help you navigate more easily when looking for items that only make sense for purchasing locally.

For Sellers

The local auctions give an extra boost in marketing power for your items, particularly the items that do not make sense to sell nationally. When you auction an item, you do not have to elect a local area, but you lose nothing by doing so. You gain having your item appear in a local auction as well as the national auction. There is no additional cost for local auctions.

The question comes up, What if potential buyers want to see the item? You need to handle this just like you would if you put an ad in the local newspaper; that is, if you don't want someone to come to your home, you may have to arrange to have the item inspected somewhere else. (See Chapter 23 on auctioning vehicles for more discussion on local inspections.) Keep in mind, too, that you can normally get more information on an eBay bidder than you can on someone who answers your newspaper ad by phone.

Street Address

eBay has stated that it will not give out your street address to anyone.

Use common sense and be clear in your auction ad what your policy is regarding inspection and shipping. For items appropriate for local auctions but inappropriate for shipping, you might want to indicate "For pickup only."

Real Estate

Real estate, which does not work well for national auctions, seems a little iffy for local auctions too. Real estate auctions may be inhibited by real estate laws. The laws vary from state to state. It will be interesting to see how this ultimately works out. In addition, the complexity of real estate transactions does not seem to conveniently fit into the normal eBay procedures. Real estate auctions are permitted on eBay, but they are the only auctions that are *not* binding on buyers and sellers and have a different eBay fee structure.

In the future, more real estate may be brought into the eBay fold. Now, however, real estate does not play a major role on eBay.

Strictly Local

Some other goods and services are strictly local, that is, it doesn't make as much sense to auction them on national eBay. Chapter 17 uses an attorney for an example of marketing services on eBay. Yet, most attorneys provide services only locally. Such a marketing plan will make much more sense on a local eBay than on national eBay.

A restaurant provides another prime example. It doesn't make much sense to auction off a dinner for two nationally, unless the restaurant happens to be in one of the top-ten tourist destinations. But on a local eBay, auctioning dinners might prove to be an effective means of increasing business.

As this book goes to press, there are over 4,000 categories of goods and services being auctioned on eBay. There are probably 16,000 ways to effectively sell these goods and services on eBay. Most of them haven't been invented yet. The local eBays will add more goods and services and more ways to effectively auction goods and services. Most of those ways haven't been invented yet either.

If you think you've missed getting in on the ground floor of eBay, you haven't. The local eBays will be the next ground floors. The local eBay auctions will develop different dynamics and new opportunities.

Foreign Auctions

There has been a huge volume in international transactions on eBay, mostly people from other countries buying items in the US. That will continue. In the meantime, eBay has established itself in several other countries:

Australia

Austria (in German)

Canada

France (in French)

Germany (in German)

Italy (in Italian)

Japan (in Japanese kanji)

United Kingdom

These are not filtered auctions like the local auctions in the US. They are separate auctions using local currencies and the local language. These auctions also follow local customs so as to make them more acceptable to users. Therefore, don't compare them to local auctions in the US. Each is different (see eBay Germany Figure 22.3).

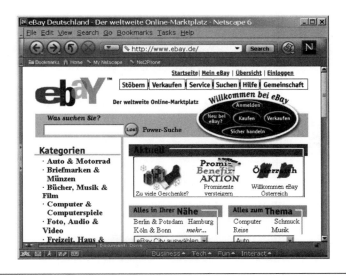

Figure 22.3   eBay website for Germany.

For Faraway Buyers

You might be able to find some interesting, even exotic, merchandise on these foreign auctions. They present a unique opportunity to shop abroad without ever leaving your home. You have five serious considerations, however, that might make foreign shopping difficult.

Language

First, you must be able to search and find items. Then you must be able to pick out items in which you are interested. Finally, you must be able to read the auction ad. If you can't speak German, this is going to be impossible to do on eBay's auction in Germany.

Communication

Once you want to bid, or are a winning bidder, you will have to communicate with the seller. Unlike most foreign buyers who buy on eBay US, you cannot count on the foreign sellers speaking English. You will most often have to speak the local language.

Currency

The eBay auctions in other countries use the local currency. You will have to make arrangements to pay for the items you purchase in the currency of the auction. Some sellers may agree to take payment in US dollars, but it's not something you can count on. Some sellers may accept US credit cards.

Shipping

Shipping becomes a problem for purchasing in many foreign countries because distances are so long. You have to make a financial judgment as to whether the shipping costs preclude purchasing the specific item you want to purchase abroad.

Taxes

You need to learn about taxation in the country in which you want to make a purchase. US citizens are used to considering the sales tax (paid to states). Similar taxation in foreign countries may seem abusive and financially unacceptable. Indeed, the local taxation may be complex or have multiple layers compared to the simple sales tax collected in the US.

Then there is the import tax (tariff). When you import something to the US, you may have to pay an import duty. There are certain exemptions, but the law is not simple, and you might get surprised.

What to Do?

If you are serious about buying in foreign countries on eBay, it will require some research on your part to be successful. Nonetheless, eBay will permit you to bid on its auctions abroad without obtaining special memberships, and foreign buying on eBay opens opportunities not easily available by other means.

For Faraway Sellers

One reason sellers on eBay have been able to sell so well to people in other countries is that certain US merchandise is popular but unavailable or much more expensive in other countries.

General Considerations

Your job is to find out what merchandise sells well abroad. It is a small percentage of all US merchandise. What it happens to be depends on local tastes, taxation, commercial customs, competing goods, and a variety of other considerations.

Books about Computers and Software

Computer books sell in Europe for about three times the cost in the US. Why? That's a tough question to answer, but they do. That presents an opportunity for someone like me to sell computer books in Europe at a profit but also at a price considerably below the local market. Many high-tech personnel in Europe can read English, making the computer book market in Europe an attractive opportunity for US authors and publishers.

Don't forget, however, that it's one thing to sell to people abroad via the eBay US auction. It's another to actually offer merchandise for sale on eBay auctions in foreign countries. You will have the same problems as buyers, so read the earlier section For Faraway Buyers. You will have to consider language, communication, currency, shipping, and taxes in addition to discovering merchandise that will sell well. Keep in mind that foreign countries have cultural differences far greater than the differences between the states in the US. Generally, what sells well in Nebraska can be expected to sell well in North Carolina. What sells well in France may not sell at all in Germany.

Specific Opportunities

For occasional buying and selling on eBay's foreign auctions, the effort is more trouble than it's worth. The real opportunity is becoming a specialist in one country and making it a business.

With a little determination, you can learn to speak, read, and write a foreign language. That's perhaps the toughest part. Learning the commercial byways and the taxation aspects is almost certainly easier. Finding products that make sense to import or export is a matter of endless experimentation.

There is a huge amount of merchandise sold abroad that is not available in the US but that will sell well in the US. In buying such merchandise abroad for resale in the US, eBay gives you a cost-effective business opportunity unimagined before the Web. Go for it!

Likewise, certain US merchandise is popular abroad. If you can sell it on a foreign eBay auction profitably but at a lower cost than it is available locally, you have a cost-effective business opportunity not imagined before the Web. Go for it!

Get a Partner

Want to short-circuit the learning curve? Instead of learning the foreign language and byways, find a US resident (immigrant from the target country) who knows them already. Form a partnership and start an import/export business using eBay.

Perhaps a long shot but a relationship that might work is to find someone in the target country to be your partner, that is, find him or her via the Internet. It's difficult enough to form workable partnerships with direct personal contact. It's clearly a long shot to arrange a partnership with someone you don't know via the Internet. But it's been done successfully.

The important thing to remember here is that most people will not do what is suggested here. The effort is simply too much. The entry to the import/export business is said to have a high *threshold* that will keep most people out. After all, how many people will learn French in order to sell merchandise in France? If you're willing to cross that threshold, you may find it profitable.

The Threshold Is Lower

The threshold to enter the import/export business remains high because of language barriers. But due to the Web, the capital requirements have dropped. Formerly, to enter the import-export business took significant capital for travel and communication as well as the personal effort to master the language learning curve. Today, due to Web (specifically eBay) and Internet communications, the capital required to start an import/export business is potentially much lower even though the learning curve remains as high.

Who's the Competition?

If capital requirements are lower today, where is your competition? If you are an immigrant to the US who speaks English and already knows the language and byways of the target country, you're going to be a potentially formidable competitor. If you're not an immigrant but want to start an import/export business via eBay as suggested, your best competition may come from immigrants in the US from the target country. By learning English and living in the US, immigrants potentially understand the two cultures well enough to make the import/export business work on eBay.

If you are not an immigrant, you need to be cautious about what you import or export. There are certain highly competitive import/export businesses that almost certainly will not be good opportunities for you. But these are usually major industries that do not represent the niche opportunities in which you are more likely to be interested.

Summary

The genius of eBay is that it creates a huge national market for goods and even services. But some goods and services do not sell well in the national market. As the eBay local auctions develop, eBay will come to encompass a greater variety of goods and services and provide new markets locally. This evolution provides new opportunities for eBay members.

eBay's foreign auctions deliver the eBay magic to new markets in the countries where they locate. Such auctions also open opportunities for all eBay members as eBay takes on more of an international character. Although part of the eBay market has always been international, the new foreign auctions will also rapidly expand (between nations) the type of people-to-people and retail-to-consumer trade that eBay auctions support.

23

eBay Motors

Does it make sense to buy a used car in Boston when you live in San Francisco? It might. It depends on what you're looking for. The local market even in large cities tends to be thin when you're looking for something specific. There are so many brands and models.

Now, if you're looking for a used, midsize sedan, 1997–1999 model, in top-notch condition in San Francisco, you won't have any trouble finding one. However, if instead you're looking for a used Mercury Sable LS sedan, 1997 model, with leather seats, in great condition, you might have some trouble finding one in San Francisco. Considering that the Sable is a popular car and San Francisco is a huge market, the lean pickings for your choice seem a little surprising. So, even for cars, eBay with its national marketplace can work magic for you (see Figure 23.1).

Figure 23.1   eBay Motors home page.

In fact, eBay makes a perfectly logical place to buy or sell cars. If you buy a car and live within 1,000 miles of the seller, you can hop on an airplane for less than $200 and drive the car home in a weekend. If you live 3,000 miles away, you can have the car shipped for under $900. If your prospective purchase is a good deal even after factoring in the cost of delivery from a distant city, why not buy the car?

Dream Vehicle

In 1998 I saw a ten-year-old Chevy Suburban for auction on

eBay with reasonable mileage about 3,000 miles away—in Florida. The seller had an excellent reputation on eBay after several hundred transactions. He represented that the vehicle was in excellent condition and that he could provide all the service records. His eBay auction ad provided a wealth of information about the vehicle. Because I backpack, climb mountains, and explore canyons in Utah and Colorado and leave vehicles at remote trailheads for ten days at a time, this vehicle had special appeal for me. Chances of finding a similar vehicle in similar condition in the Bay Area classified ads were not great.

The question was, Would I fly to Florida to buy this vehicle? It was a moot point because I already had a similar vehicle that got me where I needed to go. But if I had not had such a vehicle, I would have seriously considered flying to Florida to buy that Suburban. It appeared to be a well-maintained vehicle in great condition with plenty of miles left. The flight would have cost several hundred dollars, and the drive back several hundred more, but the extra money may have been worth it for a vehicle in good condition that's not so easy to find.

As a seller, you can potentially generate more interest in a vehicle in the national market. eBay provides a cost-effective means of reaching that market.

But Even If

Even if you don't like the idea of a national market being a good place to buy or sell a used vehicle, don't forget eBay reaches local and regional markets as well.

Buying a Car Nationally

Being a national market, eBay often offers more choices, particularly when you want something specific or unusual. A possible drawback to an eBay purchase is your inability to inspect the vehicle before traveling to the seller's faraway city. But that might not be such a disadvantage with the proper safeguards.

My Buying Experience

As mentioned, I need a 4×4 vehicle to drive the dirt roads and jeep trails to reach the trailheads. My 1987 Isuzu Trooper 4×4 had 198,000 miles on it in the summer of 2000 and was still running well, but I knew that if anything major went wrong with the vehicle, it would not be worth repairing.

It didn't seem prudent to me to buy a new Trooper because the thought of leaving a new $30,000 vehicle at a trailhead 70 miles from the nearest pavement for ten days at a time seemed a little too risky for me. Therefore, I wanted to buy a 1992–1997 Trooper in top condition with low mileage, for which I expected to pay $7,000-$14,000.

The San Francisco Bay Area where I live has about seven million people. Even in this huge market, I had few good choices in Troopers. But on eBay I occasionally found Troopers I would buy (before I was ready to buy), and the winning bids were often at or below blue book wholesale. An unusual number of these acceptable Troopers auctioned on eBay were in Texas 2,000 miles away. I figured I could pick up a vehicle in Texas myself for $600 in travel expenses or have it shipped for about the same cost. With a purchase at or below wholesale, the cost of delivery made sense, and I would get exactly what I wanted. Therefore, eBay offered a solid marketplace in which to seriously seek a vehicle.

Why so fussy? Why not another 4×4? I am very partial to Troopers and was not willing to settle for anything else. Had I been willing to purchase any comparable 4×4, it would have been much easier to find a vehicle at home.

Local Action

Starting in August, I regularly checked a local car mart (weekend auto sales in a municipal parking lot), local auto sales publications, metro classifieds, and Web classified listings. In addition, I had a local used car dealer looking for a Trooper at the regional auto auctions for me.

I had checked Trooper auctions on eBay every couple of weeks starting in March just to observe. In preparation for a potential immediate purchase, I started checking Trooper auctions on eBay three or four times a week in early August. Which would it be, an eBay purchase or a local purchase? (To be continued.)

Determining Value

Determining value is essential to intelligent negotiation. Vehicle values fall within certain ranges. If you know what those ranges are, you can do your best to purchase wisely. Otherwise, you're operating in the dark.

The Blue Books

The best way to determine the value of any car is to consult a publication containing the value data on a wide range of brands and models. These are generically referred to as "blue books" and are published by several publishers. I have found Edmunds to be the most widely available (sold in bookstores), and now Edmunds has the leading website (*http://edmunds.com*) where you can look up the value of cars and trucks going back ten years (see Figure 23.2).

Edmunds provides a retail value and trade-in value on every vehicle. The retail value is what a vehicle in top condition generally sells for. The trade-in value is what a dealer will pay you for your old vehicle (in top condition) when you buy a new one. In other words, the trade-in value is the *wholesale* value.

Figure 23.2   Edmunds website.

Kelly (the original Blue Book—*http://www.kbb.com*), also on the Web, is one of Edmunds' competitors. I have found that Kelly generally shows a wider range of values for each vehicle than Edmunds. Thus, for a 1996 Trooper (basic model), Edmunds showed a range of $10,495 (wholesale) to $12,800 (retail); Kelly showed a range of $9,095 (wholesale) to $13,350 (retail). The National Automobile Dealers Association (NADA—*http://www.nada.com*), a blue book service used by many lenders and dealers and also now online, showed a range of $12,200 (wholesale) to $14,625 (retail) for the Trooper. However, NADA seems to calculate its yearly vehicle mileage allowance differently than Edmunds or Kelly. I have found over the years Edmunds to be an accurate predictor of value.

Adjust the Value

When using Edmunds (or Kelly or NADA) to determine value, remember that you need to adjust the general published values for the following: mileage, condition of vehicle, and optional equipment. The published values are for a vehicle in top condition with about 13,000 miles per year and with standard equipment for that model (NADA apparently uses a lower mileage-per-year factor).

Unfortunately, you never know without asking which blue book the other party (the seller) or your lender uses.

The Spread

What does the spread between wholesale and retail value mean? It's simply the markup a dealer seeks. A dealer acquires a vehicle at its trade-in value when a buyer buys a new vehicle and trades in the old one. Dealers also acquire used vehicles at auction at wholesale prices. The dealer sells the vehicle traded in (or purchased at auction) for a markup to cover expenses and make a profit. A dealer's expenses include the following:

- Preparation of the vehicle for sale
- Financing to carry inventory
- Dealership overhead
- Advertising
- Salesperson's commission

A private sale is not exactly the same. Typically, the seller in a private sale has lower expenses than a dealer. That's a primary reason that private sales tend to have a purchase price between wholesale value and retail value, usually closer to wholesale.

Bidding

Purchase negotiations need to be realistic to be successful. As a buyer, your first step in negotiating a transaction is to determine the blue book values for a particular vehicle. My experience over the years shows the following for the final purchase price (based on Edmunds):

Above retail: a con.

At retail: presumably an average purchase.

Between retail and wholesale: good buy.

At wholesale: great buy.

Below wholesale: a steal.

In regard to eBay, you can shift the spread down a little:

Above retail: much too much.

At retail: too much.

Between retail and wholesale: average purchase.

At wholesale: good buy.

Below wholesale: great buy.

Why are vehicles less valuable on eBay? There are two reasons. First, the sales effort is potentially less trouble and less expensive for the seller; therefore he or she can accept a lower price. Second, a buyer takes more risk buying a car in a faraway place than he or she does locally. Therefore, buyers are not willing to pay quite as much for vehicles on eBay as they would locally. Buyers also have the expense of getting the vehicle home.

How should you bid? You need to determine the top price you're willing to spend for a particular vehicle and then bid up to it. In other words, bid it just like any other auction using blue book values to guide you.

My Experience

My experience buying and selling cars for myself and relatives goes back about 35 years and is limited. I have no dealer experience. Therefore, based on your experience, you may want to disagree with some of the conclusions I have reached regarding the values at which purchases are made.

The best deal I ever made was buying a three-year-old vehicle in top condition with very low mileage for about $2,000 under blue book wholesale, from a dealer. This recent deal (offline) took three hours of verbal wrestling, but it was worth it.

How to Protect Yourself

How do you protect yourself against purchasing a defective vehicle? Well, how you do it for a local purchase shows how you might do it on eBay.

Local Purchase

The standard buying procedure is to visually inspect a vehicle. You can judge the exterior and interior condition reasonably accurately. But it's the engine that requires some expertise. I always take the vehicle to a mechanic who does inspections for car purchases. These inspections cost $50–$100.

If you deal with a seller who will not let you take the vehicle for an inspection by a mechanic, you should pass and find another vehicle to buy. Otherwise you take the risk that the engine (or something else major) is defective.

Between your visual inspection and a mechanic's inspection, you will get a pretty good idea of the true condition of the vehicle. This procedure is not foolproof, but it's much better than sticking your head in the sand.

eBay Purchase

Alas, when you buy a vehicle on eBay in a faraway city, what can you do? First, you need to deal with eBay sellers who have good reputations (solid positive feedback). Second, you need to get full information on the vehicle. Third, you need to see plenty of photographs, one from every angle, to do a preliminary visual inspection. Fourth, if these are not included in the seller's auction ad, you need to request them. If the seller won't provide them, forget the vehicle and move on to another.

With honest information and a reputable seller, you can make a reasonably safe decision. It's not a risk-free decision, but it's workable. Remember, if the vehicle turns out to be as represented, you're stuck buying it. Better test drive one exactly like it before you commit yourself to some heavy bidding.

Seller-Arranged Inspections

eBay has attempted to get off the ground a system of seller-arranged vehicle inspections (through Saturn dealers). The idea is that the seller takes the vehicle to a third-party mechanic for inspection (at seller's expense) and then uses the results of the inspection to help sell the car by providing the buyer with useful and presumably accurate information. If this program can be expanded so that it's available to all sellers nationally, it will help alleviate a serious concern of buyers.

If you arrive in the faraway city to find the vehicle is not as represented, you have reasonable grounds to back out of the deal, and you should do so. For that reason, you should, if possible, travel to the faraway city to inspect the vehicle immediately after the auction before the seller requires you to put down a deposit. Otherwise, in a dispute, you may lose your deposit.

Test Drive and Engine Inspection

It's up to the seller whether to allow you a test drive or an engine inspection before completing the transaction. These inspections are your best protection against getting a lemon, and it seems silly to travel all the way to the seller's city to pick up the vehicle if the seller won't let you (an out-of-towner) do what most sellers will allow buyers in their locale to do. The honest seller takes little risk in allowing these inspections. After all, it's the buyer who travels at his or her own expense to make these inspections. It takes a serious buyer to do so. Consequently, if these inspections aren't allowed, take a pass and go on to another vehicle.

Before the Auction

Some sellers allow an inspection and test drive before the end of the auction but not after. This is not workable for out-of-town buyers.

Victor Owens of Brooks Automotive, the chief mechanic who has taken good care of my family's cars for many years, recommends the following:

- Ask for a pre-purchase check similar to one normally done during an oil change and lubrication, except more thorough.

Check to see that everything on the vehicle both inside and outside works.

- Ask for a smog check (required upon transfer in some states). A successful smog check generally indicates that a vehicle operates properly, but it is not conclusive.

- If a vehicle has over 80,000 miles, have each engine cylinder's compression checked manually. A compression check done on a scope saves time and sometimes costs a little less but is not as accurate as a manual check.

- Always have a vehicle checked in daylight, not at night.

- Have the mechanic do a test drive. In a test drive, a mechanic can uncover problems that others would miss.

For older vehicles, perhaps the most important test is for cylinder compression. If the engine passes the cylinder compression test, it will probably not require major repair work soon.

Inspections don't necessarily take a long time, but scheduling is often a problem. Nonetheless, many service stations will do a pre-purchase check without an appointment because they are likely to lose the business otherwise.

A pre-purchase check costs $50–$100. A compression check is often extra and costs $50–$100. An emisions check is also extra, and the price is set by the state and varies from state to state.

Any Purchase

For any purchase, whether local or on eBay, you can collect paper-work to protect yourself. Don't miss this opportunity to make your prospective transaction as safe as possible. Get a Carfax Vehicle History Report (*http://www.carfax.com*), formerly known as the

Lemon Check, to determine the history of the vehicle (see Figure 23.3).

Figure 23.3   Carfax website.

Carfax reports the following in its Vehicle History Report:

- Salvage history

- Odometer fraud

- Multiple owners

- Flood damage

- Major accident damage

- Fire damage

Review the reports to make sure they meet your satisfaction. If the seller provides the reports, make sure that they have a recent date.

The Lemon Check Speaks

The first time I did a Lemon Check on a Trooper that I was seriously considering buying, it showed a salvage title. This means that title to the vehicle had been taken by an insurance company that considered the vehicle totaled. The vehicle was then sold at a salvage auction to the seller. The seller repaired the vehicle and tried to sell it to me without disclosing the prior damage. (The Trooper looked great and ran well.) The question is: How well was the vehicle repaired? I passed. Someone else can take the time to answer that question. Unlimited Lemon Checks for two months cost $20, a wise investment.

Also ask the seller to provide copies of maintenance receipts if available. You can get a picture of how well the seller cared for the vehicle.

Buying a warranty for the vehicle you purchase is always a good idea. You can purchase your own warranty, at the time you purchase the vehicle, from a firm such as 1Source (*http://1sourceautowarranty.com*).

State of residence

Warranties cost from $300 to $1,800 depending on the vehicle, what you want covered, and for how many miles or years you want coverage.

Consummating the Transaction

To complete the transaction, go with the seller to the Department of Motor Vehicles (DMV) or whatever it's called in that state to complete the transfer of ownership and collect all the paperwork. Make sure all the seller's liens are removed from the title and that the title is free and clear. You pay sales tax and vehicle registration fees in your home state. If you are buying out of state, you will pay only nominal transaction fees, nominal temporary registration fees, and no sales tax. Going through the transfer process at the DMV with the seller is your only assurance that everything is done correctly.

Always make sure you check the VIN (Vehicle Identification Number) of the vehicle against the VIN on the title. Otherwise you may find yourself very embarrassed at some point in the future.

Don't forget to have your car insurance in place prior to the transfer of ownership. You are liable for your newly purchased vehicle.

Escrow

You may need to set up the transaction in escrow if:

> You cannot be present in the faraway city when the transfer of ownership takes place; or

> There is a lender lien on the title (the seller owes on the vehicle); or

> You are borrowing from a lender to make the purchase.

This is extra paperwork that is sometimes tedious to arrange, but it may be necessary.

Escrow.com

For a 1 percent fee, Escrow.com (*http://www.escrow.com*) will provide an escrow transaction. It will verify payment for the seller, and it will withhold payment from the seller until the buyer has inspected the vehicle and is satisfied. Although the fee seems reasonable, as the book went to press, this service was inadequate for many situations. It did not handle loan payoffs.

Bank Escrow

An escrow agreement is particularly valuable when the seller still owes funds to a lender on the vehicle, and he or she will use your purchase money to pay off the loan. The escrow is your only assurance that the seller's loan gets paid off.

Perhaps the best place to arrange the escrow in the case of a loan payoff is the seller's lender. The seller's bank can adroitly handle the transaction because it can pay off the seller's loan instantly with the buyer's purchase payment.

Informal Escrow

Many lenders will do informal escrow arrangements. Rather than using a formal escrow agreement, for instance, a buyer's lender might accept an executed bill of sale and title from the seller. In return, the lender will give the seller a letter stating that the seller will receive a check for the purchase price as soon as the paperwork for the buyer's loan transaction is complete. When two lenders (seller's and buyer's) are involved, you can expect them to work out the details of completing the transaction, often without a formal escrow agreement.

Let the escrow agent worry about the transfer details. But don't overlook the problem of taking responsibility for the vehicle immediately after the transaction is complete. The escrow agent isn't going to put your vehicle in his or her garage until you get to town if you happen to be buying from afar.

TitleTransfers.com

Try this dot com company to handle the transfer documents. It might make your transaction easier and more smooth, particularly when there is not a lender involved on either the buyer or seller side. However, understand that this is not necessarily an escrow arrangement and does not provide all the protections of an escrow arrangement.

Escrow Fee

An escrow arrangement is so germane to an eBay vehicle transaction, which involves a seller's loan payoff, that the escrow fee should be split. Indeed, this is true for most eBay vehicle transactions except where the seller can provide clear title and the buyer and seller can go to the DMV together to complete the transaction. eBay is not going to dictate the terms of agreement for a transaction, but as a practical matter and as a matter of fairness, the buyer and seller should split the escrow fee. Ask the seller to do so prior to the conclusion of the auction.

Dealer

Dealers do vehicle transactions every day as part of their business role. If the seller is a dealer, leave the details of the transaction to the dealer-seller and don't worry about an escrow arrangement.

Dishonest Dealers

When I say you can rely on dealers to take care of the details of the transaction, I am referring to most licensed car dealers. They can be expected to take care of the paperwork properly. But there are always a few dishonest ones around, so proceed with caution. Make sure you are dealing with a reputable dealer.

Verification

To bid more than $15,000 on eBay, you have to either put your credit card on file or go through the ID Verify process (see Chapter 4). This is something to note because many vehicles will cost more than $15,000. This assures eBay and the seller that the bidder is a known person, not someone fraudulently hiding behind an alias and playing bidding games.

Life is a two-way street, however, and you might consider requiring that the seller register with eBay to bid over $15,000 as if he or she were a buyer. It's you who incurs the financial risk of an incomplete transaction. Suppose you travel from San Francisco to Boston to pick up the vehicle only to find that the seller doesn't really own it. He's selling it for a friend and has represented himself as being his friend. And suddenly his friend changes his mind about doing the deal. You've just made a trip to Boston for naught. Hence, if a seller refuses to get ID Verify, you might consider passing and moving on to another vehicle.

ID Verify

In my opinion, ID Verify should be a basic requirement for participation in eBay as either a buyer or seller for transactions that exceed a reasonable amount (e.g., $500). Due to the dollar size of a vehicle sale and the financial risk that a buyer takes in traveling to pick up the vehicle, ID Verify should be mandatory for both buyers and sellers participating in eBay Motors. eBay is remiss in not requiring ID Verify of both.

Agency

In some cases you will find that the seller doesn't really own the vehicle. He or she is selling it for someone else. Before you take a plane ride from San Francisco to Boston as the winning bidder to pick up the vehicle, you need to make sure that the auction is binding on the seller. The only way to do so is to get a copy of the agency agreement between the true owner of the vehicle and the person or company that auctioned it on eBay.

Don't Take the Risk

For the only Trooper on which I bid via eBay, this very problem came up. It is common for vehicles to be auctioned on eBay by people who are not the owners. Most of these formal or informal agencies will not be a problem. You don't want to take the risk, however, of traveling to a faraway city to find that the true owner doesn't want to sell for the winning bid and is not legally bound because a valid agency agreement doesn't exist. Or, you don't want to find that the vehicle has been sold by the true owner to someone else. So, ask for a copy of the agency agreement before you venture to the faraway city.

Mediation

Insist that the seller agree to mediation in regard to disputes that may arise from an auction transaction. SquareTrade, the eBay recommended service (see Chapter 8), is a great way to do this inexpensively and effectively. Vehicles make financially large transactions. It's well worth it to have the most complete protection possible; mediation through an organization like SquareTrade can provide you with insurance that you will get treated fairly. In fact, SquareTrade thinks of itself as a type of insurance.

Sight Unseen

Some buyers seem willing to take more risks than others. They will buy a vehicle, not inspect it, and have it shipped to them from afar. This seems kind of crazy. But it might not be as crazy as it seems. Assuming that the vehicle has not been fraudulently misrepresented by the seller, what's the worst case for the buyer?

The buyer should not buy the vehicle in the first place if the shipping cost plus the purchase price exceeds the retail value. Therefore, at worst, the buyer will have a vehicle that he or she doesn't want but nonetheless one that was purchased at retail value or below. The buyer should be able to sell the unwanted vehicle in his or her local market. Thus, the entire process can often be a small loss or even a wash financially. Unfortunately, the sales tax is an ever present burden but usually not a disaster.

I don't advocate that you make a purchase this way, but in certain circumstances it may be worth the risk. The more difficult it is to find the vehicle you want, the more likely you will be to take risks as a buyer when you do find your dream vehicle.

eBay Local Purchase?

Can you do a local purchase on eBay? Certainly. If a seller in your city sells your dream vehicle on eBay, it makes things simple for you. Treat such a purchase like any local purchase. You can insist on the proper protections covered in this chapter, and you're present to act in an expeditious manner to complete the transaction. Indeed, many eBay vehicle transactions are local transactions.

Seller "Maltactics"

Some sellers state that they reserve the right to cancel their auction at any time. That means they will sell the vehicle on eBay unless they get a reasonable offer locally in the meantime. This is unfair. Pass on such sellers (which are usually used car dealers).

eBay rules, however, state that sellers cannot cancel auctions unless they cancel all the bids first. To explain themselves, sellers need to give a creditable reason for the cancellation, which subjects them to potentially negative feedback. If a seller cancels, give negative feedback.

Impulse Buying

Americans love cars and trucks. It's easy to get carried away when buying one. And impulse buying for cars and trucks, unlike for other merchandise, tends to linger for days instead of hours or minutes. Don't let impulse buying affect your rational approach to buying a vehicle on eBay. Don't take shortcuts. They usually lead to unnecessary risks. Do what you have to do to protect yourself. If you don't make a deal on one vehicle, you will find another good deal on eBay sooner or later.

My Buying Experience (conclusion)

What was the conclusion of my quest for a Trooper? I continued watching Trooper auctions on eBay through the second week of October and continued to look for a Trooper locally. I found AutoTrader and cars.com (more on these later) to be very useful in finding vehicle classifieds for my locale. I found the metro newspapers and other print publications almost useless.

From the beginning of August until the first week of October, there was only one Trooper (near Chicago) on eBay on which I bid. I was outbid by a little bit in the preliminary bidding a day before the auction ended, but I might have been competitive in the last few minutes of the auction. Unfortunately I had an important four-hour meeting that prevented me from participating. (I don't recommend absentee—proxy—bidding on expensive items such as vehicles.)

During this period, there was a paucity of Troopers on eBay. For one day there were none. For one week there were only two. It was very discouraging.

I got so desperate that I even drove to Napa, not too far away, to see a six-year-old Trooper listed in AutoTrader without a price by a dealer. It turned out to be in good condition but with high mileage and a price that was *twice* blue book retail. I didn't even bother to make inquiries.

Through AutoTrader I found a Trooper in San Francisco. I drove into the city to see it early on a Saturday evening and got caught in a traffic jam, which added two hours to my one-way trip. Consequently, it was dark when I inspected it. Four days later I tried to make an offer on it. In the phone conversation it came out that the Trooper had no backseat. In the dark I had assumed that the backseat was folded down; instead, it wasn't there at all. Scratch another possibility.

Suddenly a 1994 Trooper in Dallas appeared on eBay (minimum bid about $1,500 under blue book wholesale with no reserve). It was a little fancier than I wanted and it had normal mileage for its age. It was offered by a used car dealer. About the same time I also found a local Trooper on AutoTrader at a good price with low mileage. I wanted to see the local Trooper before bidding on the Dallas Trooper. By the time I had inspected and test driven the local Trooper, the dealer pulled the Dallas Trooper off eBay. No one had yet bid on it. There were only nine hours left until the end of the auction when I logged on to make my bid, but the Dallas Trooper was gone. This was a disappointment, and it's the sort of disappointment that works to diminish the vitality of eBay Motors.

Dealers' Practices

It appears to me that used car dealers commonly withdraw vehicles from eBay auctions presumably because they have sold the vehicles off their lots. Although it is permissible to withdraw where no one has bid or to cancel all the bids at the time of the withdrawal, it's a practice that certainly tends to give eBay Motors a bad name and should not be allowed.

For many people, a vehicle is a big-ticket item and not something to bid on casually. No one wants to bid until they have arranged specific financing and developed a plan to complete the transaction in a faraway city. That often takes time and energy. To have an auction withdrawn after going through the preparation to bid sours a lot of potential bidders, I'm sure. When appropriate under eBay rules, you should consider giving such dealer behavior negative feedback.

Likewise, when you're the seller, keep your vehicle on eBay until the end of the auction, or you may receive negative feedback that will hurt future sales.

So, I missed making my bid on the Dallas Trooper and ended up making a deal on the local Trooper (found through AutoTrader) instead. The seller and I had an appointment to take the vehicle in for a pre-purchase inspection by a mechanic in his neighborhood (at my expense), a condition of the purchase deal. The day before the inspection, the seller, who had not asked for a deposit, called to say that he had sold the vehicle to someone else who had put down a $500 deposit on the vehicle. Scratch another deal. Ironically, this Trooper had been on AutoTrader for five weeks without anyone showing any interest.

As for the local used car dealer who attempted to find me a Trooper at the regional auto auctions, he finally found one and bought it for me at a good price. Unfortunately, although I almost never see a Trooper I don't like, I didn't like this one. It had a moon roof that my wife loved but that I didn't want for safety and maintenance reasons. And it had an odor, which was unidentifiable. The odor seemed quite unpleasant to me, although no one else would admit to being able to smell it. The odor did it. This Trooper was not meant for me. Fortunately, the dealer never buys a vehicle he can't sell off his lot at a profit. Consequently, he was amenable to letting me off the hook in regard to our informal purchase agreement, and I didn't buy it.

Smelling Is Believing

The Trooper I rejected was a very nice vehicle. But it illustrates an important point. Even though vehicles are much the same, they are different too. In this case, I could have lived with the moon roof (and made my wife happy), but I couldn't live with the odor. If you obligate yourself to a purchase before an inspection, you want to have an out.

Soon thereafter I found another local Trooper in AutoTrader that I purchased from a private party. It was a fancier model than I wanted but was in top condition with low mileage, and I bought it for $800 over blue book wholesale. Thus ended my ten-week search.

Later when I put my old Trooper up for auction on eBay, I found several nice Troopers that I might have purchased that seemed to be lower priced than the one I bought. This proves that had I been more patient, I may have made a better purchase. The ten-week period that I searched for Troopers on eBay turned out to be something of an unusual Trooper drought.

The Last Word on Buying

If you need a vehicle immediately and you insist on getting what you want, you will probably spend several thousand more dollars for the same vehicle than you will if you can shop for a vehicle casually. In my case, I had all the time in the world and actually looked seriously for ten weeks until I found what I wanted at a reasonable price. Had I been in a hurry, I'm sure I would have spent more for the same thing.

Selling a Car Nationally

Selling a vehicle nationally potentially brings in more buyers than a local effort. More buyers mean a higher price, a quicker sale, or both. This is particularly true for unusual cars, antique cars, or classic cars, but it's also true for ordinary vehicles.

The best place to start finding out how to sell a vehicle on eBay is to read the section for buyers earlier in this chapter. That will give you some ideas about the plight of the faraway buyer. If you can accommodate buyers, you're more likely to sell your vehicle for the highest price possible on eBay.

Determining a Car's Value

Read the earlier section in this chapter on determining value. If you realistically want to sell your vehicle on eBay, you will need to sell it at a price that appeals to eBay buyers. It's not likely that you will sell it at full retail value for the following three reasons:

1. In the local market you will have a difficult time selling a vehicle at full retail. A typical private sale (not a dealer sale) in my experience is closer to wholesale than to retail value.

2. A normal eBay buyer has to spend $200–$900 to pick up the vehicle or have it delivered. That has to come out of the price, or what's the point of buying on eBay?

3. A buyer runs the risk of traveling to pick up the vehicle in a distant city, being dissatisfied with the misrepresented condition of the vehicle, and returning home empty-handed. That could cost as much as $500 or more, a substantial risk. It's

not smart to take that risk and pay full retail too.

As a seller you might ask, What's the point of trying to sell a vehicle on eBay if sales prices are likely to be lower than full retail? There are several answers to that question:

1. A local sale is likely to be lower than full retail too.

2. A $200–$900 downward price adjustment looks less significant as the price of the vehicle increases.

3. Some vehicles will take a long time to sell in the local market, perhaps many months. It may be quicker to find a buyer on eBay.

4. For many vehicles, there are more potential buyers on eBay than locally. That means more possibilities and a greater likelihood of a successful transaction.

5. If you sell only via eBay, you are not likely to have a lot of people coming to your home to take a look at the vehicle.

6. Selling on eBay is easier than selling locally in many cases.

7. There are always potential eBay buyers who live in your city. Thus, an eBay auction has local possibilities.

Perhaps a more relevant question is, What can you do to maximize the purchase price that an eBay buyer is willing to pay?

Winning Bid

To inspire the maximum winning bid, you need to lower the buyer's risk and make it easy for a buyer to purchase the vehicle from you. That's why reading the early part of the chapter is so important. If you see things from the buyer's point of view, you can make a purchase more appealing at little or no cost to yourself.

Do the following to entice potential buyers:

- Provide complete information on the vehicle.

- Permit a test drive and engine inspection after the auction and prior to making the sale final (for out-of-town buyers only).

The less risk the buyer has, the more the buyer will be willing to bid.

My Selling Experience

My 1987 Trooper ran well, and almost everything worked; but by November it had 200,000 miles and a body that looked drab. The blue book value gave it a range of about $1,000–$3,500. I thought that I might sell it for $1,800. So, I started with a minimum bid of $1,400 and no reserve. It seemed that the only interest I would generate in such a vehicle would be local. Few people will travel to a faraway city to buy an old vehicle like this regardless of the price. In the case of my Trooper, something under $2,000 seemed about the right price.

Would I be able to sell this vehicle via an eBay auction? (To be continued.)

Protecting Yourself

A seller generally takes less risk in a vehicle sale than a buyer. But there's still risk.

Local Buyer

A local buyer will want to inspect and test drive the vehicle. Meet the prospective buyer in a public place, not at your home. Dealing with strangers at your home may not be advisable.

eBay Buyer

Some eBay bidders make a winning bid just for the fun of it, with no intention of completing a purchase transaction. As a seller, it's tough to protect yourself against such people who abuse the system. Treat them like bidders in any other eBay auction. Give them negative feedback.

These miscreant bidders pose an unfortunate threat to vehicle sellers. Many people who sell a vehicle have already purchased their replacement vehicle. They own two vehicles at once with double loan payments and double insurance payments. They don't want to waste time selling their old vehicle. Winning bidders who don't perform can cost sellers money in this situation.

As a seller, however, you shouldn't go overboard to protect yourself against phony bidders. Simply require a payment (e.g., $1,000) within a short time (e.g., three days) to flush out the phonies. Make the remainder of your purchase process buyer-friendly. Someone who makes a good-faith payment and then travels to your city to inspect the vehicle is not likely to be a phony.

Test Drive and Inspection

Locally, you will have trouble selling a vehicle to an intelligent buyer without allowing a test drive and an engine inspection. Ideally, you will take someone with you to meet the prospective buyer in a public place (e.g., Burger King) to allow the inspection.

Test Drive

Before allowing a test drive, politely require that the prospective buyer produce a driver's license. Note the name and driver's license number. As a seller, I always go on the test drive. If you go on the test drive, agree with the prospective buyer where you will go and what time you will be back. Leave the person who came with you at the public place (together with the prospective buyer's driver's license number).

Some people may not want to go on the test drive with a stranger. Don't go if you don't feel comfortable. Let the prospective buyer go alone.

Many prospective buyers will show up for the test drive with their spouse or a friend. Some may show up with several friends. You may feel threatened by the extra people. If so, decline the test drive and leave.

Engine Inspection

If the test drive is successful, many buyers will want to take the vehicle for an engine inspection. Many service stations will give priority to such inspections, and you can get one done in a short time. As a seller, you need to know of several such places nearby so you can make a recommendation to the prospective buyer. Get an understanding that the inspection is at the prospective buyer's expense.

Treat the engine inspection like the test drive. You can go along or let the prospective buyer go alone. If you go, determine beforehand where the vehicle will be inspected and let someone know where you're going.

One way to avoid the engine inspection is to have the vehicle fully inspected yourself before offering it for sale. Don't take it to your local favorite mechanic. Take it to a service center (with a corporate name) that issues a detailed computer-generated report. For high-mileage vehicles, make sure the report includes manual compression tests on each engine cylinder or a comparable test. Make xerox copies of the report to send to prospective buyers. The report must be recent to have credibility. This will satisfy many prospective buyers, but not all.

eBay Buyers

Allow an eBay winning bidder the same inspections you would allow a local prospective buyer. Why wouldn't you? Follow the same procedures. Your personal risk is lower because a stranger from out of town is probably less likely to be a threat.

Keep in mind that a prospective eBay buyer who can inspect and test drive the vehicle and have the engine inspected after the auction will take less risk in the purchase and will be willing to buy for a higher purchase price.

Verification

I believe ID Verify is essential to both buyers and sellers in vehicle transactions. The ID Verify costs you about $5 (one time only) and verifies to eBay and the world that you are who you say you are. The ID Verify is easy and convenient to obtain (see Chapter 4).

Buyer

eBay requires that a buyer who bids over $15,000 have ID Verify. This requirement is not good enough for vehicle transactions. You should require that *any* winning bidder, regardless of the purchase price, have ID Verify.

Eliminate the Phonies

Requiring ID Verify for winning bidders will eliminate a lot of phony bidders who have no intention of completing a purchase. Until ID Verify becomes more widely accepted, however, you may reduce the number of legitimate bidders, too, by making such a requirement.

Seller

Although not required of vehicle sellers at the time this book went to press (a serious oversight on eBay's part), you need to get your own ID Verify. Why would a buyer travel to your city to buy your vehicle without knowing for sure that you are who you say you are and that you are the owner of the vehicle? I wouldn't.

Don't Assume

Don't assume that because the buyer has paid for the vehicle that he or she will carry through on the paperwork, such as getting a new title. Buyers have many reasons why they don't get around to registering the transaction and officially take title. One of the primary reasons is that they must pay sales tax when they officially take title to the vehicle.

Suppose a buyer sits on the paperwork and does nothing. As the seller, you still have your name on the title. If anything happens with that vehicle (e.g., an accident), you may be liable.

Therefore, walk buyers through the closing transaction at the DMV and make sure they have title to the vehicle before you bow out of the picture. Otherwise you might find yourself faced with a legal claim based on the fact that you're still the owner of record for the vehicle.

Mail-In Forms

Some states, such as California, have a mail-in transfer report that the seller can send to the DMV after the transfer to report the transfer. As the seller, make sure you mail this to the DMV after the transfer, if you didn't do the transfer at the DMV.

SquareTrade Mediation

Although SquareTrade mediation provides insurance for buyers against unfair treatment by sellers, fairness is a two-way street. An unhappy and wrathful buyer can make your eBay life as a seller miserable. Thus, mediation is also insurance for sellers that they won't get treated unfairly by buyers.

Using Escrow

Escrow transactions are always appropriate for big-ticket items on eBay. Vehicle sales are not exceptions. Offering to handle the sale transaction in escrow will inspire buyer confidence, ultimately resulting in a higher sale price.

Information Sells

This book continually stresses that information, not hype, sells merchandise on eBay. This is particularly important for big-ticket items such as vehicles. Provide prospective buyers with complete information on the vehicle that you auction. Include:

- Year, brand, and specific model

- Optional equipment

- Color

- Mileage

- VIN

- Detailed description of vehicle, including its condition and history

- Manufacturer's specifications (available from Edmunds)

- Good photographs from various angles

- Engine inspection report (to be provided upon request)

- Maintenance records (to be provided upon request)

- Carfax Vehicle History Report (to be provided upon request)

- Edmunds appraisal (to be provided upon request)

If you provide anything less, you will lose potential bidders for each item you delete. The ultimate result will be a lower winning bid.

Don't Waste Your Time

If you can't provide most of the information above, don't waste your time auctioning on eBay. You will be unlikely to have a successful auction. Attempt to sell your vehicle another way.

Appraisal

You can generate a presentable Edmunds (or Kelly or NADA) appraisal report free by going to the website and looking up the vehicle. You must have complete and accurate information on the vehicle to generate an accurate appraisal. As an alternative, suggest that prospective buyers go to the Edmunds (or Kelly or NADA) website and do the appraisal themselves. But you have to provide them with complete information to enable them to generate accurate reports.

Photographs

I believe it's practically impossible to sell a normal vehicle on eBay without providing at least one good photograph. The more, the better. Look at dealer auctions on eBay. They always include at least a few good photographs, and they're the expert sellers.

Take a photograph from every angle: front, back, right side, and left side. Shoot the inside through the driver's side door, from the rear (van or SUV), and at the dashboard. The photographs should be clear and sharp. Also photograph every noticeable blemish.

Seeing photographs is the primary way a potential buyer has of making a purchase decision. If you ignore this fact, you eliminate most potential buyers and make yourself look like an eBay rookie.

My Selling Experience (conclusion)

After several family distractions (sick mother, Thanksgiving, and Christmas), I finally got around to preparing my Trooper in January for auction. My eBay auction ad read as follows.

1987 Isuzu Trooper II S

4Dr – 4WD

Maroon

201,000 miles

VIN: JAACH14L7H6412895

2.3 4-cylinder engine, 5-speed manual transmission, power steering, power brakes, air conditioning, AM-FM cassette, almost new Firestone P235 75 R15 105S M/S Wilderness AT tires (replacements for the recalled Firestone Wilderness ATs), up-to-date maintenance.

Vehicle runs well. Everything works except:

- Left front parking light (white)
- Interior overhead light (works erratically)
- Backup lights (switch on transmission not working)
- Oil pressure gauge
- Light for LCD panel in AM-FM cassette player (clock)

Vehicle has a bent engine hood, which detracts from the appearance. The hood works OK. The front seats, while functional, are well worn.

Air conditioner runs well but not at its maximum as it has not been charged in over 6 years.

The engine burns oil. How much is difficult to tell because oil is apparently also leaking through a gasket. Oil loss is about 1 quart per 600 miles in normal driving, less on long highway trips.

Troopers are great off-road vehicles and fun and comfortable to drive otherwise too. Seller just purchased a 1995 Trooper.

This vehicle is ideal for someone in the San Francisco Bay Area or nearby who has a need for an old SUV that runs well.

Seller will split escrow fees with out-of-Area winning bidder. Carfax.com Lemon Report (http://www.carfax.com) will show clean title. Seller will also provide an emmissons report at sale as required by California law. You can do an appraisal at Kelly Blue Books (http://www.kbb.com).

Terms: Cashiers checks (or PayPal – Billpoint).

$200 deposit within 3 days. Remainder due on transfer of title within 10 days.

Bidders from Bay Area call to inspect before end of auction. Out-of-Area winning bidder can inspect after bidding is final.

Thanks for your interest.

I may have been able to get the Trooper to the eBay auction prior to January, except that I couldn't find the time to clean, polish, and photograph it. When I finally got around to doing the work, it took a whole day. Thus, I was able to include 11 photographs in my auction ad. The auction resulted in one bid of $1,400. The buyer (430 miles away) was scheduled to pick up the Trooper on Friday the next week. I recieved a check for $1,400 that cleared. On the Thursday night before the buyer picked up the Trooper, I found out I had a problem with the title. It was lost. For a duplicate title, I had to get a release on a loan that was paid off eight years before. It would take a little time to get the release.

The buyer showed up to claim the Trooper. He was a pleasant middle-aged man who had driven into town with his elderly father in a late-model Lincoln. Before he inspected the Trooper, I explained the title problem to him. He said, "Fine." He asked no questions and signed the transfer papers. He got into the Trooper and drove away without even looking it over. The entire transaction took less than five minutes.

I'm bullish about eBay Motors. It will evolve into a dynamic vehicle marketplace over the next few years and gain a significant market share at the expense of local classifieds. It's doing well already.

Online Alternatives

eBay doesn't have a corner on the online market for used vehicles sales as it does for general consumer-to-consumer sales via its normal auctions. Plenty of competitors share the market. Most fall into the category of electronic "classified ad" listings. Included (not an exhaustive list) are:

autobytel.com (*http://autobytel.com*)
AutoTrader (*http://autotrader.com*)
Autoweb (*http://autoweb.com*)
Best Offer (*http://www.bestoffer.com*)
CarDay (*http://carday.com*)
cars.com (*http://www.cars.com*)

iMotors.com (*http://imotors.com*)
MSN CarPoint (*http://carpoint.msn.com*)
StoneAge (*http://www.stoneage.com*)

Most of these websites seem limited in usefulness, in either buying or selling a used vehicle, with two exceptions: AutoTrader and cars.com. Interestingly, eBay has an investment in AutoTrader and an agreement to feature an AutoTrader link on eBay Motors (see AutoTrader in Figure 23.4).

Figure 23.4   AutoTrader website.

AutoTrader electronic classifieds are useful. Just as useful are the classifieds at the cars.com website. You will find both AutoTrader and cars.com easy to use, although the Java applet that lists the classifieds at cars.com is a little temperamental (see Figure 23.5).

The remaining websites on the list generally do not seem as useful. But you can almost certainly find what you're looking for with eBay Motors, AutoTrader, and cars.com, and you can also use all three to sell.

The one unique website is iMotors. Although it has only a few vehicles for sale, it will find a vehicle for you within a short time—guaranteed. It does an inspection to determine the condition of any vehicle it finds and discloses the results. And it has actual *physical* locations around the country where you can consummate the transaction and pick up your newly purchased used vehicle. This is the online version of the local used car dealer who goes to the auto auctions looking for a vehicle to buy for you, except that iMotors actually has multiple buyers at multiple regional auto auctions trying to find a vehicle for you.

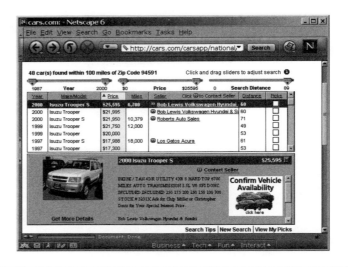

Figure 23.5   Website Java applet at cars.com.

Fees

The fees for selling vehicles on eBay are different than for other things. Currently you pay $25 for a insertion fee and an additional $25 for a final value fee if the vehicle sells.

Kruse International

Although eBay Motors includes the auction of collector cars, eBay owns 30-year-old Kruse International (*http://www.kruseinternational.com*), which offers live collector car auctions (events) in about 40 places during the year. Think of Kruse as a collector car auction both on the Web and off the Web. The auctions on the Web take place on eBay Motors. Kruse features the results of its off-Web auction on its website. This is a good place to find sales comparables to use for the appraisal of collector cars.

Summary

It works! Yes, it makes sense to buy and sell vehicles in the national vehicle market that eBay enables. It's not perfect. Like any other means of buying or selling, it has its problems and its expenses, but it can work for you. This chapter explains how it can work for you, whether buyer or seller, safely and with minimum financial risk.

If you don't believe in the national market for vehicles, eBay reaches the local vehicle market too. With over 20 million eBay members, about 7 percent of the people in your locale will find your vehicle on eBay if they happen to be looking for one to purchase.

This relatively new addition to eBay is not finished. eBay Motors will continue to evolve until it becomes a more convenient vehicle emporium for both buyers and sellers. But it works well already. Try it.

24

Businesses

Auctions on eBay can work for businesses as well as individuals. This chapter provides some ideas for businesses.

Errata

Just as the book was going to press, the eBay Business Exchange disappeared and was replaced by Services for Business (eLance), a specialty auction area for businesses (with work to be done) and freelance services to come together. This chapter was immediately rewritten and placed in the book at the very last minute. However, it was too late to change the book cover or the Index. Consequently, this chapter may seems out of place, but it is actually up-to-date.

Therefore, you need to ignore all references to the Business Exchange on the cover and elsewhere in the book. There may also be some enteries in the Index that refer to text in this chapter that no longer exists or is on a different page than indicated. The first section of this chapter Business Considerations remains the same. The second section of this chapter Services for Businesses is new.

The book could have been more easily published as it was originaly written, but keeping readers up to date and providing information on eBay's newest specialty auction eLance was given priority. Nonetheless, the eBay Business Exchange doesn't appear to have completely disappeared, and its remanents can now be found under the eBay Theme entitled Business, Office & Industrial.

eBay is to be commended for experimentation. It is not self-evident what will work well as a specialty auction and what will not. Good luck to eBay with Services for Business and future endeavors, if any, in business-to-business auctions.

This chapter is not about retail businesses selling merchandise on eBay to consumers. It is about all businesses buying goods and equipment for their own use and selling (auctioning) goods and equipment no that they longer need. Businesses, like individuals, can auction or bid on eBay. Whether it makes sense to do so depends on judgements that may routinely differ from those of most individuals, yet made on similar considerations.

The remainder of this chapter is about freelance professional services, which are important to many businesses. Individuals who provide such services to businesses now have a special place on eBay in a specialty auction named Services to Business, or eLance.

Business Considerations

eBay auctions work much the same for businesses as they do for individuals. eBay provides no special considerations or special mechanisms for conducting auctions for businesses. Thus, you need to examine the normal eBay auction buying-selling procedures to see how your business can make best use of eBay.

Review

Review the Risk and the Transaction Overhead sections of Chapters 2 and 3 to get a better feeling for how costs (buyer's or seller's overhead) may affect a transaction.

Opportunities for Buyers

Businesses, as buyers, need single items (e.g., equipment), and the Business Exchange is a good place to buy goods and equipment on which a business can realize a meaningful savings. Additionally, a business can buy the bulk merchandise it needs to fuel its everyday operations. That requires that the availability of such goods on eBay be dependable and that shipping not be a prohibitive expense.

Time Factor for Businesses

The time commitment for businesses to buy something is not favorable. An eBay transaction can be a long process from a buyer's point of view. Whether it makes sense for a business to have an employee go through the procedure will depend on the size of the transaction and the potential for savings compared to other means of purchasing similar items.

Supply for Businesses

The supply for buying at auctions has yet to be proven for businesses, although there is certainly plenty of goods and equipment available on eBay. As eBay figures out how to make its local auctions more useful, it will develop much more potential to create a healthy supply of the type of goods and equipment that businesses buy.

Individual Buyers

See Chapter 2 for similar considerations for individuals. But what works for individuals does not necessarily work for businesses.

Opportunities for Sellers

Businesses need to sell goods and equipment. Suppose you manage a small radio station that has four Sony TCM5000EV portable audiocassette recorders (expensive field recorders for news reporters) in good condition. You are installing an all-digital studio system, and you can no longer use analog recorders even for field use. Where do you sell four TCM5000EVs? Another radio station perhaps, but beyond that, it might be tough. eBay provides a ready, willing, and capable market in which you can sell such equipment.

Businesses always have something to sell, such as old office machines, old office furniture, and excess office supplies. eBay provides an appropriate place to sell such goods and equipment.

Everyone needs office things. The primary drawback here is the shipping cost.

If you sell an old heavy-duty copy machine for $2,000, the $150 for shipping isn't going to kill the deal. But if you sell a run-of-the-mill office desk for $100, the $150 for shipping will kill the deal.

This points out one of the weaknesses of the eBay market: Large or heavy items that aren't worth much don't make good items to sell on eBay. The shipping costs will kill the deal. However, this also points out a hidden strength of eBay: A portion of the eBay market will always be local to a seller. It's not a stretch to think that you can find a local buyer via eBay who will buy your heavy office furniture and come across town in a pickup truck to take delivery.

The Time Factor for Businesses

The tough consideration for businesses is: How much time does it take to sell something on eBay? An employee will have to do it. Will it ultimately be less expensive to haul the equipment to the city dump than to attempt to sell it on eBay?

Auctions don't require much time. You need to create the advertising copy and create the eBay auction. Because the auction is a silent auction, no further action is required except to answer buyers' questions, if any. When the auction is over, you have to communicate with the buyer to arrange for payment and shipping. The process seems manageable without a great deal of employee time. If buyers renege or other problems appear, the time expenditures by employees will increase. If multiple (identical) items are sold one at a time to different buyers, the time commitment can also be burdensome.

The Market for Businesses

The market for businesses will always be substantial. There are always new business start-ups looking for usable assets at reasonable prices. Many businesses need more office equipment or specialized industrial equipment each year. Even individuals need equipment for home offices and businesses.

When businesses need to get rid of something, it's often not just one item. It might be ten cartons of $8\frac{1}{2} \times 11$ inch paper (100 reams) or 40 cases of 10W40 motor oil (480 quarts). eBay is a good place to auction such surplus supplies to another business.

New Goods and Equipment

Just as in the normal eBay auctions, there are businesses selling new goods and equipment to other businesses. This can make a good business for an entrepreneur who has enough capital to deal in high quantities, high-priced goods, or surplus goods.

Individual Sellers

See Chapter 3 for comparable considerations for individuals. Again, what works for individuals, however, does not necessarily work for businesses.

Government Entities

If eBay auctions work for businesses, they can work for government entities too. The only difference is that certain government entities have to follow regulatory procedures for buying and selling goods and equipment. Auctions on eBay may not satisfy such procedures. Nonetheless, government entities come in all sizes and shapes, and there's no reason they can't use eBay the same way businesses and individuals do, regulations permitting.

Services for Business

eBay now features a specialty auction named Services for Business wherein freelance service providers (e.g., attorneys, Web developers, and writers) bid to provide services for your business project. The other name for this specialty auction is eLance (i.e., *e* for electronic and *lance* for freelance).

The goal of this service is to have those with business projects needing outside expert workers offer the projects for bidding on eLance. Individuals who have the requisite qualifications to do the work then bid a price to do the project. Businesses can also find qualified people via eLance and request that they bid on the projects (see Figure 24.1).

There are no shortages of dot com services on the Web that purport to match those having projects (work to be done) to people who can do the work. For eLance, the difference is the auction process. Any registered eLance member (a person representing a business) can offer a project to be bid. Any registered eLance member (a freelancer) can bid on a project. The auction is the means by which they get together. The feedback system, which differs from the normal eBay feedback system, keeps freelancers honest.

The eLance system generally provides more information on members than does eBay, and it can be a lenghty endeavor for bidders (freelancers) to register. Additionally, the eLance feedback system provides more information on member transactions than does the normal eBay feedback system.

Figure 24.1   Services for Business also know as eLance.

To get a better idea of what eLance is doing, look at the eLance home page where a menu of services is offered. You will see several categories.

Categories

At the time this book went to press the following categories were offered at eLance:

Administrative Support

Business Strategy

Graphic Design

Software & Technology

Web Design & Development

Writing & Translation

Each category had subcategories. For instance, Administrative Services was divided into several subcategories:

Data Entry

Other - Administrative Support

Printing

Event Planning

Presentations

Transcription

Word Processing

Thus, eLance already covers a lot of territory. Long before the popularity of outsourcing, freelance services were already very valuable to many businesses. Today many more businesses depend on freelancers. eBay presents a great way to match freelancers (service providers) with projects at a reasonable bid price. Note that the categories require specialized, skilled workers or professionals who are ready to perform as freelancers.

Freelancing

Just because you're a skilled worker or professional doesn't mean you're a freelancer. A freelancer is someone who's ready to work, has a place of his own or her own to work, is set up to deal with clients, and spends time marketing his or her skilled or professional services.

Registration

If you do a good job of it, registering as a services provider on eLance can be a lot of work. You need to provide a complete resume covering the following areas of your background:

Education

Employment

Professional Certificates

Professional Licenses

References

In addition, for a fee, you can have eLance verify some or all of the various representations in your resume such as your college degree. All information verified shows a check mark by it. Businesses with projects will want to know that you can do the work, and verified background information is more valuable than unverified information.

Businesses that have projects must also register. However, only people can register. Thus, if you are a business that desires to offer projects to be bid, you or another person from your company will have to register and provide a credit card number (for verification). The information required for registering as the person (business) who provides projects is minimal.

Fees

It does not cost anything to register, offer projects, or make bids. But eLance gets 10 percent of all fees paid to service providers for their work on projects. Thus, eLance is primarily a marketing system for freelancers.

Select

As this book went to press, a new program was scheduled to go into effect on eLance. Those service providers who pay for substantial verifications and pay a monthly fee can be in a special category named Select service providers. Presumably, more lucreative projects (based on minimum project fees) will become available to those service providers who take the trouble and pay the fees to qualify. Such projects will not be available to other eLance service providers who have not bothered to qualify or who cannot qualify due to the lack of verifications or expertise.

For businesses, the Select service providers mean more dependable quality, presumably, due to the varifications required of the service providers.

Auctions

The projects (with minimal information) are put out for bid by businesses. Individual service providers then bid a price to do the work. A business chooses a service providers based on whatever criteria it wants to use. A business is not obligated to choose the lowest bidder. Indeed, it has no obligation to even choose a service provider found on eLance.

Brief Review

A brief review of the activity for technical writers showed hundreds of technical writers registered and one project up for bid.

A review of past auctions regarding technical writers shows a modest number of low-dollar projects many of which were not awarded to an eLance service provider.

This does not bode well for the success of eLance. eBay will somehow have to bring businesses and freelancers into better balance in an effort to make eLance work effectively. Without more projects to be bid, eLance will quickly lose the attention of freelancers.

Feedback

If you're a freelancer (service provider), you'll have to be on your best behavior and provide first-rate services because you get rated on a scale of 1 to 5 stars. You can't afford to make your project manager unhappy because everyone will know, as the following legend shows:

5 Stars: Greatly exceeded expectations

4 Stars: Exceeded expectations

3 Stars: Met expectations

2 Stars: Did not meet expectations

1 Star: Was far below expectations

Unfortunately, businesses are not rated, making the rating system one-sided.

Summary

Businesses and government entities can use eBay to their advantage buying and selling just as individuals do. Whether it makes sense to do so requires an evaluation of the time and effort necessary to administer the auction process.

The eBay Services for Business specialty auction eLance attempts to bring freelance service providers together with businesses that need outside services. It does so via a bidding process on projects put out for bid.

25

eBay Premier

eBay bought the old San Francisco auction house of Butterfields to acquire the expertise to auction valuable fine art and artifacts online. eBay Premier is the result. Any reputable auction house or dealer can use it to auction, and it has the look and feel of an elegant auction house. More importantly, it provides the necessary framework for effectively auctioning valuable items that fall into specific categories:

Asian Art

Books & Manuscripts

Decorative Arts

Dolls & Toys

Fine Arts

Jewelry & Timepieces

Memorabilia

Miscellaneous

Native & Tribal Art

Butterfields, of course, is one of the most active auction houses on eBay Premier. See the eBay Premier website in Figure 25.1.

Figure 25.1   eBay Premier website.

You will find few items with minimum bids under $200. Consequently, it's not quite the same as auctioning collectibles on eBay. It's different in other ways too.

Buyers

With eBay Premier buyers get the protection of expertise. Sellers must meet a certain standard (set by eBay Premier).

> The sellers on eBay Premier are leaders in their fields, with world-class reputations. In order to offer items on eBay Premier, each seller is required to guarantee the authenticity of the items it is offering.

Thus, not just anyone can sell. That means you are more likely to be buying from a knowledgeable seller on eBay Premier. As a buyer, this gives you more protection than in the normal eBay auctions. No cryptic information. Should the seller breach the guarantee of authenticity, eBay Premier will refund up to $50,000 for an item. Go *Help, Buyer Guide* on eBay Premier to see the guarantee details for buyers.

No Registration

No registration is required for bidders beyond the normal registration for eBay. Thus, any eBay bidder can bid in this high-class auction.

All the eBay SafeHarbor and feedback protections apply on this special auction in addition to the special guarantee.

To get off to a good start looking for fine art and artifacts, go *Browse* on the navigation icons. Browsing is great fun if you like fine art. Otherwise, use the search mechanism or select a category (see Figure 25.2). These are similar to but work separately from the normal eBay auctions.

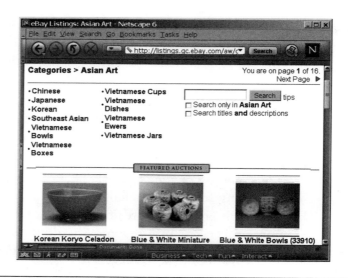

Figure 25.2   Asian Art category on eBay Premier.

Sellers

Many of the sellers are established auction houses worldwide such as follow:

> Alibris (rare books)
>
> Antiquorum (timepieces–Switzerland)
>
> Bloomsbury (rare books–England)
>
> Butterfields (variety–owned by eBay)
>
> Dorotheum-Net (variety–Austria)
>
> Great Gatsbys (variety)
>
> Lawsons (variety–Australia)
>
> Lempertz (variety–Germany)

However, you don't have to be an auction house to be a seller. You can be a dealer . A small sampling of dealers includes:

Adin French Antique Jewelry

Bess Cutler Gallery, Ltd.

Blue Dolphin Antiques

I. Brewster & Co.

China Avante-Garde, Inc.

David Kenny Oriental Art

Fraser's Autographs

Galerie Zygos

Gallery Cristiani

Golden Gate Gems

LatinArte

Martha Hopkins Struever LLC

Marsh & Marsh

Persian Merchantile Co., Inc.

Romero de Martinez Gallery

Sellbay, Inc.

William Holland Fine Arts

To register as a dealer for eBay Premier, you must apply via an online form on the eBay Premier website. eBay will grant dealership status only to well-qualified dealers who can prove their professional status. Dealers are also required to give certain guarantees to buyers.

Can you sell something if you're not a dealer? Yes, you can sell on consignment. You can contact one of the dealers listed on eBay Premier to arrange a consignment sale. For example, Butterfields (owned by eBay) is developing a special program for consignment sales.

Keep in mind that selling something on eBay Premier is not the same as eBay. First, the item has to fit into one of the categories encompassed by eBay Premier. Second, it must have more than a trivial value. Third, you must supply comprehensive and reliable information on the item. And fourth you must certify (guarantee) that the item is authentic.

Live

It was bound to happen sooner or later on eBay, a live auction via the Web. And eBay PremiereBay Premier makes a great place to experiment with live auctions. Fine art auctions handle the expensive items that make it worthwhile to go to the expense of broadcasting such auctions live on the Web. You can hear the auction via RealMedia (audio) and participate in the bidding via a form in the Web page. Although live auctions are not necessarily meant to be experimental, you should certainly view them that way. Jump in and experiment. Live auctions via the Web will have their place.

Consult the Live Auctions section of eBay Premier for specific instructions on participating and bidding. You must sign up ahead of time to bid in live auctions, and of course you must be an eBay registered user. This provides you with an opportunity to participate in something a little different on eBay even if you don't bid.

Summary

eBay Premier provides a great opportunity for serious collectors and fine art aficionados to consider a larger selection of items than they normally would in their own city or region. eBay Premier is national and international in scope. Currently nascent, it promises to grow into a huge showcase of high-class items sold in high-class auctions by high-class dealers.

26

Half.com

Wow! I discovered Half.com while writing this second edition. It's a powerful and easy-to-use website that enables you to purchase goods at a fixed price. Eight million items were listed in December 2000. The idea is that the goods are used and sell for less than half price. But the goods can be new, too, or sell for much less than half price. No wonder eBay bought Half.com. It nicely supplements the eBay consumer-to-consumer auction transactions with fixed-price transactions.

More Than Half

Half.com allows merchandise to be sold for more than half list price, too, but doesn't recommend it.

This eBay strategy, to provide a fixed-price alternative to the auction system, works well for mass-manufactured entertainment products that don't physically depreciate, and it works well for consumers and sellers alike. The auction mechanism does not handle the commerce for these types of items adeptly. It will be interesting to see what additional items eBay will include for sale, if any, in Half.com in the future (see Figure 26.1).

Figure 26.1   Half.com website.

Buyers' Benefits

Now, we're not talking about selling everything as eBay does. Half.com limits its offerings to books (printed), music (CDs), movies (VHS, DVDs), and games (electronic). These are called intellectual property. The nice thing about some intellectual property is that once you've used it, you usually don't want to use it again (e.g., once you've read the book or seen the movie, you don't want to do it a second time). Yet the benefits are the same for the next person who uses it (e.g., the next person who reads the book or sees the movie). For digital intellectual property (e.g., CDs and games), the experience is just as high quality for the second user as the first. Half.com provides a mechanism that enables anyone to sell such goods at low fixed prices in an efficient and smoothly operating national and international market.

Books

Think of Half.com as a used bookstore online, one that offers hundreds of thousands of titles.

Buying Books

Here's what I bought on my first try (see Table 26.1). I've been meaning to buy and read these books for a while.

The savings provided me with an incentive to buy. My savings was $42.82, that is, 64 percent off list. A shipping and handling charge of $6.85 was added to my order. Keep in mind, these are not impulse purchases that I happened to see on a table as I walked to the checkout counter of a bookstore and will never read. I will actually read these books just as soon as I can break my indentured servitude to my publisher.

Table 26.1   Books and Savings

Title	Purchase Price	List Price
Passage to Juneau: A Sea and Its Meaning (Raban)	$6.37	$26.50
Passionate Sage: The Character and Legacy of John Adams (Ellis)	$6.47	$15.95
The Power Broker: Robert Moses and the Fall of New York (Caro)	$10.79	$24.00

And in Addition

In addition to the books, I got two 1-year magazine subscriptions (from an offering of 100) free: *PC Magazine* and *Conde Nast Traveler*. This is another story and may not be a permanent feature of Half.com, but it was an interesting bonus.

Alas, I could not find the eighth and final volume of Page Smith's *People's History of the United States*. But Half.com has over 8 million items for sale, and it turned up later.

Since my initial purchase, I have purchased an additional six or eight books. Now, before I buy books I need immediately, I always check with Half.com first.

And if It's Not in Stock

If you need a book immediately and it's out of stock, Half.com will display several online bookstores, where you can purchase the book new, and show the prices. This enables you to go to the online bookstore with the lowest price and purchase the book new for immediate delivery.

Out of Stock

For Half.com, "out of stock" means that no seller has submitted the book for sale. The catalog database for Half.com is huge, but Half.com cannot possibly have all titles in the catalog. Half.com depends on its sellers to provide the inventory. As soon as a seller provides a book, it is in stock and available for purchase. Half.com has millions of books in stock.

Music

Not much here for me. I tried finding Bach, Handel, and Mozart, but it was lean pickings. However, there's plenty of popular music. My daughter found the Backstreet Boys easily enough. The Boys' list had 20 albums, all *in stock* (on CD). This is a great source of music CDs.

Movies

I found the Kenneth Branagh version of *Hamlet*, a favorite of mine listed, but it was not in stock. I did buy *Chariots of Fire,* about the 1924 Olympics, a wonderful movie. This is undoubtedly a larger selection of movies than you will find locally.

Games

Because I don't play computer games, I don't have much to report here. Keep in mind, however, that the digital game industry is larger than Hollywood in dollar sales. We're talking big money. Any website that can save a kid a few bucks, or parents a few hundred, is a welcome relief to purchasing full retail.

Searches

You must make your searches on Half.com very carefully. For instance, the author C. S. Forester must be placed in the search window precisely as "C. S. Forester" or "C. Forester" to work properly. The following entries will *not* return a list of books by this author:

1. C.S. Forester (no space between the C. and S.)

2. CS Forester

3. C S Forester

4. C Forester

5. Forester

I have not been able to find certain books by searching on an author that I have found searching with the ISBN number. It's evident the books are all there in the catalog at Half.com if you can find them. In other words, this search engine doesn't work as well as it should, something that eBay (Half.com) needs to correct.

When all else fails, go to Amazon.com and search. Come back to Half.com with the ISBN or UPC numbers.

Numbers

The ISBN (International Standard Book Number) and the UPC (Universal Product Code) are standard industry inventory numbers, often expressed as bar codes, found on products in the Half.com catalog.

The Half.com database is independent of inventory. Therefore, you will find books that are "out of stock." This makes a very complete database possible, enabling you to order books that are not in stock. As soon as someone offers such books for sale, your purchase will automatically take place, and you will get the book. Or, rather than purchase automatically, you can elect to be notified when a book you want comes into Half.com's inventory. (Searches work similarly for other items.)

Reputation

The rating (feedback) system works a little differently on Half.com. Only sellers get rated. After all, the buyer buys for a fixed price immediately with a credit card. Why rate buyers? However, sellers are rated by buyers. Consult the Half.com rating guide to learn how to rate sellers.

The ratings are from 1 to 5 and are based on how quickly the seller confirms the order, how quickly the seller ships, how well the seller classifies the condition of merchandise, and how well the item is packaged for shipping. The following explains the ratings:

1. Poor

2. Fair

3. Good

4. Very good

5. Excellent

As a buyer, be honest, and be fair. But contribute to making the reputations on which buyers depend. Rate the seller.

As a buyer, you will want to check sellers' reputations. Unlike an eBay auction, you do not necessarily have any contact with sellers. You just wait for the item to arrive and hope you don't have to wait too long. If a seller has a cumulative rating of 4.1, you won't worry about customer service. You will probably want to avoid a seller, however, with a cumulative rating of 1.7.

Selling on the Half

As a seller, you have to be on your toes to remain successful. Just as in eBay auctions, good customer service is a must.

When you are just a casual seller, you may not worry too much about your reputation. Nonetheless, the system requires that you give good customer service. In the spirit of eBay and Half.com, you need to make an effort to take care of details and ship promptly. Most merchandise is shipped by the US Postal Service special book rate, which is slow. Any delays you add to the inherently slow shipping will be agonizing to many customers.

For a Half.com retailer, keep in mind these are low-cost, high-volume items that require a well-organized fulfillment operation. If you can't get the sold items out the door and in transit in a hurry, you will have a lot of disappointed customers. That may mean low ratings and a lackluster reputation.

Selling Procedures

It's easy to offer an item for sale. You just enter the ISBN number (for books) or the UPC number (for other items), the price, the condition, and comments. You can also offer shipping by Priority Mail (faster than Special Rate). Your item goes into the vast Half.com catalog; that is, the item appears in stock.

It's your responsibility to ship the item adequately packaged. When someone buys your item, you are notified via email by Half.com and must confirm within 48 hours that you have the item and will ship it. You must then ship within 24 hours after confirmation. If you do not follow this procedure, the order may be canceled, subjecting you to a low rating. If you're slow, you may not get a top rating.

Generally, you need to set your prices realistically. Half.com recommends the following price structure (percentage of lowest online retail price new):

Like new 50%

Very good 45%

Good 40%

Acceptable 35%

Remainders, which are new books that did not sell in the bookstores, might be sold for more than 50 percent. In practice, however, remainders sell for lower percentages. Many books sell for below the suggested percentages. For each item, Half.com does list a selection of retail prices at certain online retailers (e.g., Amazon.com) that are generated automatically.

Shipping

Unless you offer Priority Mail and the buyer elects it, you can ship the item any way you want. The special rate for books is the least expensive and is what will be expected by buyers. Half.com will reimburse you for shipping according to Table 26.2. The reimbursement is the same regardless of what the actual shipping costs are.

You need to send the bottom half of your order confirmation with the merchandise. You can also send a receipt. You are not permitted to send anything else (e.g., promotional materials) with the merchandise without Half.com's permission.

Table 26.2   Reimbursement for Shipping

	Special Rate	Priority
Hardcover		
First item	$2.03	$3.75
Subsequent items	$0.83	$1.50
All Other Items		
First item	$1.58	$3.75
Subsequent items	$0.58	$1.00

Fee

Half.com takes a 15 percent fee on sales. Half.com provides the Web catalog, completes the sales transaction, and collects the purchase price on all sales (via credit card). Sellers merely list the merchandise and ship it. Seems like a reasonable arrangement. You get paid by Half.com at least once a month and in the case of sufficient volume twice a month. Half.com takes no listing fee; listing is free.

Business?

Can you make a business out of selling on Half.com? Sure. In the publishing industry, books that don't sell in the bookstores are said to be *remainders*. Since books are sold on consignment (a practice started during the Great Depression), the bookstores return unsold books to distributors, which in turn return them to publishers. You may be able to get remainders from bookstores, distributors, or publishers at very low prices. Sell them on Half.com.

Likewise, you can find sources of excess inventory for music CDs, movie VHS tapes and DVDs, and electronic games. Find some sources of inventory that can be purchased at a low price, and sell the inventory profitably on Half.com.

Summary

It's not an auction, but it complements eBay nicely with fixed-price inventory for a few types of merchandise. If you like books, music, movies, or digital games, give it a try.

Appendix I Top 10 Tips

The top 10 tips for success on eBay for both buyers and sellers follow, not necessarily in order of priority:

1. Play by the Rules. The eBay rules were set to make sure that people deal with each other fairly. If you don't play by the rules, you may be unfair to others and undermine eBay. You may even break laws or incur legal liability.

2. Take eBay Seriously. eBay is not a game. It's a new international marketplace where valuable business is transacted.

3. Protect Yourself. Don't be paranoid, but don't be foolish either. Follow standard protective practices that make sense, just as you do offline.

4. Give Feedback. The core of eBay is trust. Feedback determines an eBay member's reputation. You want to make sure that the eBay members with whom you deal get the reputations they deserve so that eBay patrons will know who to trust.

5. Pay Attention to Detail. This means know eBay rules and procedures and follow them carefully. Provide plenty of detail on the items that you auction and on your sale requirements. For items on which you bid, review carefully the seller's auction and sales requirements. Whether seller or winning bidder, follow through diligently after the auction.

6. Research Market Value. Whether you're a buyer or seller, your best technique is to know the value of the item auctioned. With an accurate value, you can make smart decisions.

7. Keep a Cheerful Attitude. Buying and selling can be fun. No one likes to do business with a sourpuss, whether it's at a retail store or on eBay. Being pleasant can go a long way toward solving a lot of difficult problems.

8. Treat eBay as a Lifelong Asset. It's only a few years old, but it will be around for a long time. You will be able to use it profitably for longer than you think. Some pundits have said it's only a passing fad. Don't believe them.

9. Contribute to the eBay Community. A dynamic and successful marketplace is always a community. Sooner or later you will have opportunities to make a contribution to eBay or to other eBay members. Answer those opportunities.

10. Develop Your Own Approach. Only experience will lead you to auction practices with which you will be comfortable and successful. A book can be helpful, but what works for an author may not work for you. Invent a new eBay technique.

———

This top 10 list is not loaded with specific details that will make you an eBay wizard immediately. Nonetheless, it points out some things for you to consider in developing successful eBay practices.

Although the top 10 list does not provide the *details* you need for success on eBay, this book does. Read it through once. When you have a question later, use the book as a reference. Most authors, including me, write books they would like to use as references. When I buy and sell on eBay, I use this book as a reference for details that I have forgotten.

Appendix II Top 8 Tips

The top 8 tips for successfully auctioning items on eBay follow, not necessarily in order of priority:

1. Research the Market Value. This is the first and most important step in listing something for sale. If you set your minimum bid or reserve too high, no one will bid. If you set it too low, you will shortchange yourself.

2. Pile It On. Put as much information about the item as you can gather in your auction ad—information, not hype. The Web is an informational medium, and there is no practical space limitation. Lack of adequate information is almost certain to bring lower winning bids and in many cases no bids at all.

3. Always Include a Photograph. Pictures sell. There are a very small percentage of items that don't need a photograph. The rest do. Provide multiple photographs for expensive items (e.g., at least five or six sharp photographs for a vehicle).

4. State Your Requirements. Clearly state your requirements for sales to inform bidders of what to expect. Be sure to include everything that will cost winning bidders money.

Tell Them Before

If you intend not to sell to bidders with undesirable feedback, state that in your sales requirements. Then check the feedback on the leading bidders. If one is undesirable, email him or her before the auction ends to state that you will not accept the bid and ask him or her to retract it.

5. Remember the Search. Craft your auction *title* to include keywords for buyer searches and also to be readable.

6. Answer Inquiries Immediately. Always answer bidder email inquiries immediately. If you wait, you may lose a bidder. A robust auction ad will help reduce bidder inquiries.

7. Follow Through. Most winning bidders will expect you to take the initiative to complete the transaction after the auction ends. Contact winning bidders by email within a half-day (a half-hour is better) after the auction ends and restate the details of your sales requirements. Keep a record of all documents, including the auction ad and all emails, for reference. Provide the buyer with a receipt. After the transaction is complete, don't forget to submit feedback on the winning bidder.

eBay Retailers

If you sell regularly on eBay, you will need to develop a system for handling auctions that will keep you well organized and responsive to buyers. It doesn't take more than two or three auctions at the same time to completely confuse you if you aren't organized to handle the action.

8. Provide Good Customer Service. You are the seller, and the winning bidder is your customer. The customer is always right. Put customer service first. Keep a cheerful attitude. It's your responsibility to set a cheerful tone for the follow-through process. On eBay, customer service is the name of the game.

This top 8 list will help you focus on what's important for success in auctioning your items on eBay. Always keep in mind that excellent customer service has come to be expected online, and eBay is no exception.

Appendix III Top 9 Tips

The top 9 tips for successful bidding on eBay follow, not necessarily in order of priority:

1. Research the Market Value. There will always be alternative places to acquire at market value any item on which you bid. By researching market value, you know when you are getting a bargain and can move aggressively. You also know when there is no bargain to be had, and you can look elsewhere to obtain the item.

Knowing the market value of the item is the single most important technique for successful bidding on eBay.

2. Save Your Insanity for Unique Items. Don't get carried away bidding on a Sony camcorder. There will be dozens more exactly like it available on eBay soon. However, when you bid on a unique item (e.g., an antique eight-color painted steel sign advertising the Monongahela Bakery), the market value of the item may be of less concern to you than the amount you are willing to spend to get the item.

3. Check the Seller's Feedback. Once you check the seller's feedback, you will either develop confidence in dealing with the seller, or you'll avoid the auction.

4. Consider the Details. Review carefully the auction offering and the seller's requirements. Also consider the bidder overhead expenses (e.g., shipping costs). Factor these into your bid.

5. Contact the Seller. Email the seller to get any additional necessary details you don't have to make a well-informed decision regarding whether to bid and what maximum amount to bid.

6. Develop a Repertoire of Bidding Techniques. No one bidding technique works best for all auctions. Learn and experiment with a variety of techniques and use them when appropriate.

7. Put Defeat in Perspective. Being outbid almost always means that someone else was willing to bid more than you. It doesn't necessarily mean that your bidding skills are deficient. You will rebound to bid again another day.

8. Follow Through. Follow through in a timely manner after the auction. If the seller doesn't contact you within a reasonable time, take the initiative to contact him or her. Keep a record of all the auction documents; save the auction ad and all emails for reference. After the transaction is complete, don't forget to submit feed-back on the seller.

9. Don't Default. If you're the winning bidder, follow through to purchase the item. Failure to make the purchase will subject you to negative feedback and legal liability.

———

This top 9 list does not guarantee success in every auction, but it will help you develop an intelligent and successful approach to bidding on eBay.

Appendix IV eBay Magazine

eBay Magazine (*http://www.ebaymag.com*), an independent publication, is not for everyone. But if you are a regular on eBay, you will probably find it worth the subscription price ($19.99 per year). It has information for both consumers and eBay retailers, information you will probably have a difficult time finding conveniently elsewhere.

Cover Story The feature articles cover topics of consumer interest but also cover ecommerce.

543

eCommerce There are always several profiles on PowerSellers, people who are successful eBay retailers. In addition, other articles cover various general ecommerce topics as well as those related specifically to eBay auctions.

Technology With general digital technology to cover as well as advances in eBay and ecommerce technology, this section covers a broad scope of topics.

Internet Life Articles on eBay experiences and activities round out this section.

Trends This section provides vignettes on various eBay activities and retail trends.

Buzz It keeps you up to date on what's happening in the digital world.

Bids & Pieces This section covers auction news.

The Edge This section written by experts includes columns by both regular and guest columnists.

If you're a little confused about how this magazine is organized, I don't blame you. So am I. In addition, it changes from issue to issue. Nonetheless, it contains a wealth of information if you want to take the time to dig through the trivial to find what's important to you.

Perhaps the most useful portion of the magazine for eBay businesses is in the back under the label eBay Insider. This includes:

Trend Trackers Different people have been assigned to keep track of various eBay auctioning activities (e.g., stamps, autographs). You can keep up to date on your specific activity.

eBay Site Barometer A monthly matrix chart shows *growth*, *demand*, *cooling*, and *hot* for certain categories. Take a look. It's revealing. It's followed by a list of the eBay categories and where they fit into the matrix chart. (The chart itself isn't big enough to include all the numerous eBay categories.)

Top Categories This shows the heaviest auction action for the past 30 days, that is, the top categories of items and their volumes.

Sidebar Commentaries Throw in a couple of sidebars commenting on the Barometer, and you have information that may be valuable to your eBay business.

Were this just a consumer magazine, it probably wouldn't justify comment other than a passing mention. But it contains enough valuable information for eBay businesses that it's worth your attention if you're an eBay retailer. Even the ads might inform you of something you can use (buy) to improve your auction business.

It's difficult to applaude or criticize this magazine because it seems to have no competition with which to compare it. So, take it for what it is: perhaps the most convenient source of current information on eBay activities and commerce.

Appendix V Illicit Practices

This is a listing of practices not permitted by eBay that may result in your suspension from eBay should you intentionally or unintentionally use any of them. Additionally, many of these may be prohibited by the laws of your state and subject you to civil or criminal liability. Most are commonsense, but there a few that may not have crossed your mind as being illicit.

Again, this is my version of these rules and prohibitions, and you need to read the eBay SafeHarbor Policy for more complete and up-to-date coverage.

Don't stand for others abusing you, abusing other eBay members, or abusing eBay itself. It's your marketplace. Report illicit activities or even suspected illicit activities to *safeharbor@ebay.com*. eBay is not a game or recreational activity. It's a serious and valuable mechanism for online commerce.

General Offenses

Shill Bidding Using a second alias or other eBay members to artificially raise the level of bidding.

Extortion Threatening to leave unjustified negative feedback if another member doesn't meet your demand. Even if negative feedback is deserved, the best policy is to never make a direct threat. Always be subtle. Those deserving the negative feedback will get the point. The best way to avoid making an inadvertent threat is to stay cool and never deal with the other party when your anger is out of control.

Criminal Acting in violation of criminal statutes. Doing so on eBay does not somehow exempt you from such statutes. Cyberspace is real, as the judge will be sure to tell you. Remember, it's easier to trace offenders online than it is offline.

Suspension Accumulating feedback (the total of your positive and negative ratings) to reach a negative 4 results in your automatic suspension. .

Feedback Offenses

Defensive Shill Feedback Using a second alias or other eBay members to artificially increase your positive feedback or to artificially increase someone else's negative feedback.

Solicitation Offering to sell, trade, or buy feedback.

Bidding Offenses

Bid Siphoning Offering via email the same merchandise for a lower price to the bidders in a current auction.

Auction Interference Communicating with other bidders during an auction in such a way as to reduce the number of bidders in order to keep the bidding low.

Bid Manipulation Manipulating the bids to discover the current high bid (e.g., using a bid retraction). Another offense is manipulating the bidding using a second alias or other eBay members to raise the number of bids above 30 in order to put the item in the HOT category

Non-Payment Not paying when you are the winning bidder. You are not allowed to be a deadbeat on eBay and still retain your eBay membership.

Persistent Bidding Bidding after a seller tells you your bids are not welcome. A seller has a right to reject bidders.

Bid Shielding Using a second alias or other eBay members to raise the level of bidding to protect a low bid (e.g., the high bid is later retracted, enabling the low bid to win).

Selling Offenses

Auction Interception Misrepresenting yourself to be the seller in order to collect payment from a winning bidder.

Fee Avoidance Manipulating the eBay system to avoid paying fees.

Non-Performance Not delivering the auction item to the winning bidder.

Identity Offenses

Misrepresentation Misrepresenting who you are or giving false contact information is an unjustifiable abuse. It undermines eBay and the integrity of the eBay marketplace and is strictly forbidden by eBay. In many states it may be considered fraudulent conduct. People who think they can get away with this type of behavior are mistaken. Criminal activity is easier to trace online than offline. eBay also prohibits passing yourself off as an eBay employee.

Invalid Email Address Using an invalid or defunct email address.

Participating Under Age Only those 18 or over are permitted to participate in eBay. If you are under 18, get an adult (e.g., a parent) to buy and sell for you. eBay certainly recognizes that there are responsible people younger than 18 who would make wonderful eBay citizens. Unfortunately, state laws regarding financial responsibility make it legally impossible for eBay to accommodate those under 18.

Miscellaneous

Interference Interfering with eBay online operations. Always follow eBay guidelines for using eBay. For instance, you could probably load enough text in your auction ad to be the equivalent of a small book without hearing from eBay. But if you maliciously loaded in the equivalent of 50 books with the thought of slowing down eBay operations, you would certainly jeopardize your membership.

Spamming Sending unsolicited email to other eBay members. Sure, you can easily get their email addresses, but use other members' email addresses only for conducting business in regard to a specific auction, not to build a mailing list and not to contact all the bidders on a specific auction.

Threatening Threatening bodily harm to another eBay member or otherwise threatening via email.

Contact Information Making public another member's personal data such as his or her email address. This means not providing such data in feedback as well as in other eBay public places.

Vulgar Language Using racist, hateful, sexual, or obscene language in an eBay public area

Index